160

Western Electric
Chicago, Ill.

4,00

THE PRIVATE SECRETARY

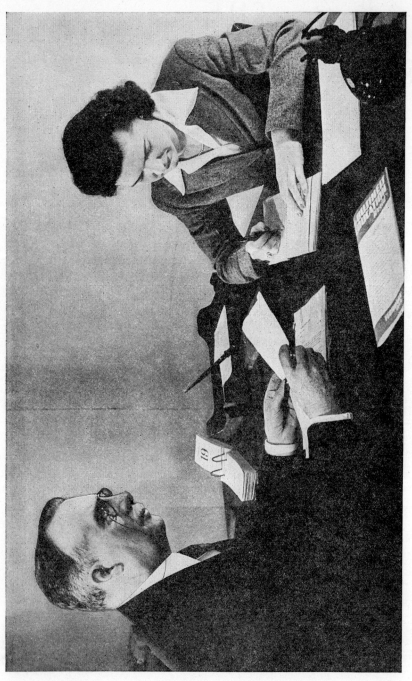

A SECRETARY TAKING DICTATION

Note secretary is facing dictator and writing with a pen. The cap is off, lying on desk by pad. The letters already answered lie face down at left of secretary. A pile of unanswered letters is in front of the dictator. Note desk calendar pad and in-box at his left. The

THE
PRIVATE SECRETARY

A College Text

JOHN ROBERT GREGG, S.C.D.

THE GREGG PUBLISHING COMPANY

NEW YORK　CHICAGO　BOSTON　SAN FRANCISCO　TORONTO　LONDON

Printed in the United States of America

PREFACE

The Private Secretary is one of a series of Gregg texts that have held the leadership in secretarial training since the introduction of this finishing course over thirty years ago.

The first of the series, *Office Training for Stenographers*, by Rupert P. SoRelle, appeared in 1911. It was the first text to give teachers the instructional materials and the teaching plan they needed in order to train their students as efficient office workers.

This pioneer contribution by Mr. SoRelle was succeeded by revisions and enriched offerings, always with the one objective uppermost: that of giving the teacher—

1. The most practical and up-to-date presentation of those business customs and procedures with which a private secretary should be familiar.
2. A well-balanced series of assignments by which the student could test the business knowledges and skills thus far acquired, and in so doing be broken in for the first job.

The second book in the series appeared in 1922 under the title *Secretarial Studies*, by SoRelle and Gregg. A revised edition appeared in 1927. This book was followed in 1934 by the first edition of *Applied Secretarial Practice*, and in 1941, by the second edition, by John R. Gregg.

The Private Secretary, the latest in the Gregg series, has been written to meet a growing demand by colleges for instructional materials that are different from those used in secondary schools. Factual information, of course, cannot be changed; and much of the content of a secretarial text is factual. The organization of the material, however, and the assignments can be changed; and in this regard *The Private Secretary* is entirely different from *Applied Secretarial Practice*.

The organization of the text matter and the assignments for *The Private Secretary* are based on the assumption that the student is employed by a mythical business firm. Through several transfers from department to department during his training period, the student is thoroughly "broken in" as a private secretary, capable of filling that position in the average business office.

To make the course as businesslike as possible, this text should be considered as a secretarial handbook for constant study and reference in connection with the daily assignments. In so doing, both the instructor and the student will maintain the proper relationship between the text matter and the assignments. The assignments must be done as nearly under actual office conditions as possible, and each finished job must meet above-average office standards. The extent to which the student masters the business facts and the efficient office procedures described in this text will largely govern the quality and the quantity of the student's production on the assignments.

For convenience, the assignments appear only in the accompanying workbook, which also contains the business forms needed in carrying out the assignments. The number of assignments given for each section is sufficient to enable the instructor to train students to meet varying office conditions and dead lines as well as to take care of individual differences in learning ability and interests.

The secretary's constant contact with the public makes special emphasis on voice training essential. The printed page is inadequate for this purpose, and modern science must be utilized to supplement the printed page. An album of three phonograph records is available for both individual and group training in handling callers, telephoning, and in applying for a position. These voice records serve to emphasize the completeness and up-to-dateness of the Gregg secretarial program. This program is described in detail in the Teacher's Handbook.

Grateful acknowledgment is made to various business concerns who have generously contributed information and illustrations, especially in the fields of business machines, office supplies, communication, transportation, and banking. Special thanks are also due Miss Bertha M. Weeks, of the Chicago School of Filing, and Miss N. Mae Sawyer, of the American Institute of Filing, Buffalo, New York, for their contribution to the section on filing; to the Menasha Products Company, of Menasha, Wisconsin, for many business forms and procedures; to the Jam Handy Organization, of Detroit, and the George S. May Business Foundation, of Chicago, for personnel material; and to Miss Dorothy M. Johnson, of our Editorial Department, for preliminary research, compilation of factual data, many of the assignments, and for preparing the suggestions on business letter writing.

THE GREGG PUBLISHING COMPANY

CONTENTS

ORGANIZATION CHART FOR ROBERTS & JONES, INC.

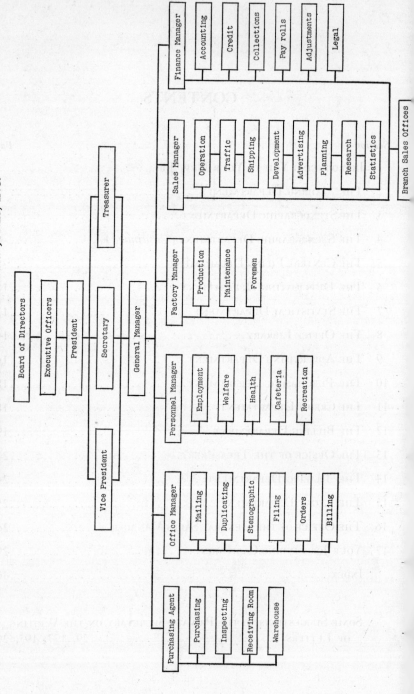

1

INTRODUCING YOU TO YOUR NEW JOB

You have completed most of your formal training in shorthand, typing, and several other business subjects and are now ready to put the knowledge and skills you have thus far acquired to the test in a business office. A breaking-in period on the job, however, is costly both to the employer and to the new employee and often results in unhappy experiences, which linger both in the memory of executives and on the personnel records of the company. This undesirable and expensive procedure can be eliminated by transferring the breaking-in period from the business office to the school in the form of an intensely practical finishing course, which for students of shorthand and typing duplicates as far as possible the working of actual stenographic and secretarial assignments from the executives of an up-to-date, efficiently managed business. Such is the purpose of the course you are now starting.

With the aid of this text, which is filled with business information of special importance to stenographers and private secretaries, and the accompanying workbook containing assignments and the business forms to be used with the assignments, you will be given the opportunity of demonstrating to your instructor and to yourself your ability to take dictation and convert it into mailable transcripts according to accepted business production standards. You will also be given the opportunity of carrying out numerous secretarial assignments that will test your judgment; your patience; your thoughtfulness and consideration for others; and your understanding of the customary office procedures in handling, buying, and selling transactions.

To make this course as businesslike as possible, assume that you have just been employed as a stenographer by the firm of Roberts & Jones, Inc., after having passed successfully a series of tests and a personal interview with the personnel director of the company. You have obtained your Social Security card and reported for work.

Courtesy Transcontinental & Western Air

A BUSY OFFICE

You are informed that for the first few days you will be given the opportunity of becoming acquainted with your new employer, and learning about the business of the company, its policies and business methods, and other details that will enable you to give the maximum service in the shortest possible time and in an atmosphere of mutual understanding and co-operation. The personnel director of the company, Mr. T. M. Wells, gives you a booklet entitled "Information for the Benefit of New Members of Roberts & Jones, Inc."

Here is the information contained in that booklet. Read it carefully and ask Mr. Wells (your instructor) any questions you wish regarding the content. The company desires that you thoroughly understand the meaning and purpose of its policies and procedures.

INFORMATION FOR THE BENEFIT OF
NEW MEMBERS OF ROBERTS & JONES, INC.

New members of Roberts & Jones, Inc., should acquaint themselves with the information following in order to become familiar with the policies of the company.

This company is a general manufacturing concern having its main office at 270 Madison Avenue, New York 16, New York. It has branch offices in the principal cities of the United States and Canada.

Salaries. Salaries are paid on the first and sixteenth of each month to members on the permanent pay roll. Deductions for Social Security benefits, income tax, hospitalization, and other pay-roll deductions will be fully explained to you upon request. Ask the treasurer's office.

Working Hours. The official working hours for all departments are, at present, from 9 a.m. to 5 p.m. Monday through Friday and from 9 a.m. to 1 p.m. on Saturday. Luncheon periods are one hour on Monday through Friday. There is no luncheon period on Saturday. During June, July, and August, all our offices are closed on Saturdays.

Employees are required to arrive on time. Tardiness will be deducted from the annual vacation and when repeated will affect the efficiency rating of the offender.

Group Life Insurance. The Company arranges for group life insurance for the benefit of its members. The cost is 60 cents a month per $1,000, which is paid for by deductions from salaries on the first pay day of each month. No physical examination is required.

Amounts of insurance are limited to $2,000 for nonexecutive employees; $3,000 for department seniors or quasi-executives; and $5,000 for department heads or senior executives.

Applications for this insurance should be made to the Accounting Department.

Workmen's Compensation Insurance. The Company carries Workmen's Compensation Insurance, which provides for medical expenses and partial compensation in case of accident to a member while pursuing his regular company duties.

Report accidents promptly to the Legal Department so that the insurance company may be notified.

Legal Matters, Donations, Etc. All legal matters, formal contracts, and negotiations outside of immediate departmental operation should be referred to the Legal Department.

All requests for donations, contributions, subscriptions, and the like should be referred to the office of the treasurer.

Your Health. Your health now becomes a matter of prime importance to the Company as well as to you. We wish you to take care of yourself, and we wish to help you in any way we can to maintain good health. Here are some basic health rules; observe them and most of your health problems will disappear:

Eat basic foods every day—milk; eggs, meat, fish, or cheese; vegetables, leafy and yellow; enriched bread or cereal; fruit.

Drink plenty of water—the average adult needs about 2 quarts of liquids each day.

Get plenty of fresh air and sunshine—have fresh air but no draft in your bedroom at night.

Get plenty of rest—the average adult needs about eight hours of sleep each night.

Get exercise—walking is one of the best forms of exercise.

Get recreation.

Observe good posture, standing and sitting.

Your Safety. Report immediately to the nurse in charge of the first-aid room every injury, no matter how small. Professional aid is always available and you may not benefit under the Workmen's Compensation Laws unless you report all accidents immediately. Familiarize yourself with all safety regulations posted on our bulletin boards. All emergency signals will be explained to you, and fire drills will be held regularly. The safety of the employees of the Company rests in the hands of every employee. Shoulder your part of that responsibility and aid in every way to eliminate all accidents.

Vacations. The Company allows vacations to its members in accordance with the following procedure, if such vacations meet with the Company's convenience and do not retard production or service to its customers:

1. The normal vacation season is from June 1 to September 30. This does not mean that it is compulsory that vacations be taken during this period, but this time is established for the purpose of this procedure.

2. Whoever, on July 1, shall have been in our service continuously for a period of one year shall be entitled to a vacation of two weeks with pay and whoever on that date shall have been in our service continuously for six months or more, but for less than one year, shall be entitled to a vacation of one week with pay.

3. Anyone whose length of service does not entitle him to a vacation with pay may take a vacation at his own expense if approved by the department head.

4. When a pay day falls within a vacation period, the pay check due on such pay day may be paid to the member before he departs on his vacation.

5. Employees who resign their positions or who are dismissed before obtaining their vacations, but after the start of the vacation season, shall not be entitled to receive vacation pay. When members who would be entitled to a vacation are laid off or dismissed for any reason, the or-

ganization may at its discretion give them one week's pay in lieu thereof.

Sick Leave. Sick leave is earned at the rate of one day a month and may be accumulated up to twelve days a year. This is in addition to the regular vacation period.

Promotion. The policy of the Company is to fill all vacant positions from among its present employees if the persons with the proper qualifications can be found. Your qualifications are on file in the personnel office and are scrutinized whenever vacancies occur for which you might qualify.

Other factors are also considered:

1. Your work performance.
2. Your working relations with your fellow employees.
3. Your attendance record.
4. Your devotion to duty.

The work of the Company must go on at all times, and there will be times when promotions will be delayed or postponed. We must subliminate our personal interests at such times to the greater interest of all of us—the success of our company. For only out of its success can come permanence of employment, promotion, and increased remuneration.

Character Factors. These are the character factors upon which our personnel is engaged, retained, and advanced:

1. Independence. Putting principles above personalities, following these principles regardless of where they may lead.
2. Co-operation. Developing individuality while accepting help from every quarter and giving help in every direction.
3. Optimism. Expecting the best from everybody, continuing according to the other fellow's viewpoint, unless a parting of the ways is inevitable.
4. Humility. Learning how it's now done before putting forth a new suggestion, maintaining modesty supported by confidence.
5. Idealism. Setting and maintaining high standards that are constantly set higher.
6. Aspiration. Proceeding resolutely toward perfection, always contented but never satisfied.
7. Liberality. Giving everything you possibly can and expecting adequate compensation, when time tells.
8. Equity. Dividing freely, with fairness to all, according to demonstrated capability and the proved value of each to others.

Performance Qualities. The performance of this organization is the composite of individual efforts to these ends:

1. Definiteness. Getting clear-cut understandings as to what is expected from us, and as to what we may expect from others.

2. Selection. Determining what is most important and proceeding according to priorities, which means first things first, second things second, etc.

3. Thoroughness. Knowing all that we have to do, how much of it we have done, how much remains to be done—scheduling it and checking progress through to the finish.

4. Accuracy. Checking all work of every kind against the original purpose, concept, and instructions—then securing a double check from somebody else.

5. Effectiveness. Putting effectiveness before efficiency and efficiency a close second.

6. Efficiency. Doing everything with as little expenditure of time, effort, and money as possible while doing it well—eliminating waste and making all our time count.

7. Progressiveness. Being ready for change always, when change means improvement.

8. Dependability. Getting good results on time, regardless of difficulties.

Standards. The success of this organization is founded upon personnel with these qualities highly developed:

1. Character. Individual integrity with moral force.
2. Intelligence. Ability to understand and learn.
3. Willingness. The characteristic of being prompt and ready to do.
4. Vigor. The ability to act with mental force and physical force.
5. Vitality. The capacity for endurance and sustained effort.
6. Versatility. The ability to turn with ease from one thing to another.
7. Initiative. The aptitude for undertaking and developing new things.
8. Resourcefulness. Skill in methods of practical expediency.
9. Loyalty. Wholehearted allegiance.

Principles. Roberts & Jones, Inc., operates on these principles, in the order of priority given:

1. Satisfaction. The customer is to be given what he wants.
2. Quality. The customer is to be given what he wants, in excellent quality.
3. Speed. The customer is to be given what he wants, in excellent quality, without waiting any longer than quality requires, whatever the inconvenience to us.

4. Economy. The customer is to be given what he wants, in excellent quality, at maximum speed, with all feasible economy.

5. Payment. The customer is to be given what he wants, in quality, with speed and economy, at a price that yields a fair profit above the outlay required to serve him.

6. Service. The customer is to be given all information, instruction, and co-operation necessary to assure successful use of our product and to insure him against interruption in its use.

It is well to realize that advancement in this organization depends solely on how you progress along the above lines, both in your attitude and in the opinion of the supervisors of your work. No other measurements are applied.

You will be given opportunity from time to time to indicate by marking on a scale your own conception of your present measurement in these characteristics. (The scale used in this course will be found in your workbook with the instructions regarding its use.)

Officers and Department Heads. As you work in the various departments, you will become acquainted with the officers of the Company and the department heads. Learn the names of the officers and department heads as soon as possible. (One of the first assignments in your workbook will be to type a list of the names of these persons.)

Your Desk. You may, of course, have no control over the desk that is assigned to you. It may be an out-of-date one, with drawers that stick and splinters that snag your clothing; but you will be expected to turn out efficient work just the same. Later, you may have an opportunity to request a modern secretarial desk.

Whatever the style and condition of your desk may be, its contents can be efficiently arranged and a clear working surface maintained. This means that your supplies will be neatly assigned to the most convenient parts of the various drawers and that no drawer be allowed to become a catchall for cosmetics, candy bars, personal letters, medicines, and other personal belongings. Likewise, the top of your desk will not be cluttered up with useless gadgets. So important is this matter of desk arrangement that some desk manufacturers have planned charts of suggested efficient arrangements. See page 8 for illustrations of a desk and a desk layout.

Courtesy Art Metal Construction Co.

A MODERN SECRETARIAL DESK

The typewriter folds away into a typewriter compartment, which may be either in the right or the left pedestal. It is important, when ordering, to consider the direction of the light and other control factors so that you will specify the correct pedestal for the typewriter

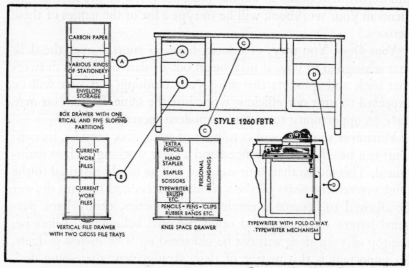

Courtesy Art Metal Construction Co.

DIAGRAM OF A SUGGESTED LAYOUT FOR THE DRAWERS OF A SECRETARIAL DESK

Other Secretarial Equipment. Your chair and your typewriter and your copy holder are also indispensable accompaniments of your daily work. A correct posture chair helps maintain a correct sitting posture and so lessens fatigue. Its additional cost is well worth the money. Study the posture illustration on page 43.

Your course in typewriting has included instructions on the proper care of your typewriter. Do not neglect this most important piece of equipment.

Office Supplies. Numerous miscellaneous office supply items are essential to efficient office routine—from paper clips to desk trays and wastebaskets. The following illustration shows a group of helpful devices. Become acquainted with their names and uses now. The larger pieces of equipment, like duplicators, check writers, and postal scales, have been discussed in the sections describing the work for which they are designed.

MISCELLANEOUS OFFICE SUPPLIES USED BY THE SECRETARY
Many of these are kept in the center drawer of the desk. See layout chart on page 8

Office Housekeeping. In addition to keeping your own desk in an orderly, efficient condition, you have a responsibility regarding the general orderliness of the office in which you and your chief work. Bookcases should be neat and tidy; accumulations of old catalogues, price lists, and newspapers kept to a minimum; and the supply cabinet kept stocked with all needed supplies.

Some businessmen like to have their own desks kept in order by their secretaries, but it is wise to ascertain the man's wishes in this matter before extending your supervision to his personal domain.

YOUR FIRST WEEK

Your first week as a new employee is a critical one. Your first impressions—of the organization, the various departments, your first job—will have an important bearing on your progress and on your daily production. The more you know now about the Company and the reasons behind its personnel policies, the sooner you will become a loyal, dependable, and efficient worker.

This getting-acquainted period is known in business, and especially in Government agencies, as the "orientation period." To orient yourself in an organization merely means to get acquainted with that organization and to understand the purposes of its various departments and their interrelationships.

In this course it would be impracticable for you to complete your orientation before you are assigned to a department. You will, therefore, continue your orientation by spending the first few days of your employment as a mailing clerk, assisting the regular mailing staff as directed. This training will stand you in good stead when you are transferred to a stenographic or secretarial position, as a thorough knowledge of handling incoming and outgoing mail is essential to all members of the secretarial staff.

After you have completed your study of mailing procedures and have finished the accompanying assignments, you will be transferred from department to department so that by the end of the course you will be familiar with the office procedures of the entire company. For practical reasons, your instructor will act as department head and will be responsible for all your assignments.

Your text describes standard practices. There is, however, often more than one way of doing a thing satisfactorily, and your instructor may ask you to perform some assignment in a different manner from that given in your text. Don't argue with him! Follow his instructions to the letter.

A final word before you take up your first assignment. You will avoid confusion and eliminate many mistakes by getting the answers to these five questions before you start a job:

1. *What* is to be done?
2. *Why* is it to be done?
3. *Where* is it to be done?
4. *How* is it to be done?
5. *When* is it to be done?

Now, to the Mailing Department, where David Rhodes, the head of the department, will be your first "boss." He will expect you, first, to obtain all the facts about mailing from your text and then to put these facts into practice through the mailing assignments given in your workbook. Good luck and happy landing.

By Ewing Galloway

THOUGHTFUL STUDY OF THE CONTENTS OF THIS TEXT WILL GIVE YOU THE ANSWER TO MANY OF YOUR PROBLEMS ON THE JOB

A BUSY MAILING DEPARTMENT

2

THE MAILING DEPARTMENT

DO YOU KNOW?

1. Your employer asks you to mail a heavy package of typed manuscript. Can you send it at the parcel-post rate?

2. You have fifty invoices to be mailed to customers. Should you address envelopes or use window envelopes?

3. Your employer gives you a 1½-ounce letter and instructs you to send it by air mail. How much postage should you put on the letter?

4. Your employer wishes to send an important letter for which he would like to have proof of delivery. How can this be done?

5. A letter is received on which action must be taken by two different departments. What should be done to avoid one department's waiting for the other to release the correspondence?

(Answer these questions if you can. Then turn to page 29.)

The receiving and dispatching of mail is a most important business activity. If mail is not properly handled as soon as it is received, delays may result that will cost both the company and its customers thousands of dollars. If mail is not properly forwarded, there are again the possibilities of delay and money loss, and occasionally the loss of an irreplaceable document. Mailing clerks quickly become acquainted with the personnel and departments of a company. For this reason some companies assign all beginning stenographers to the Mailing Department for a few days. During this period they learn the names and duties of other employees and how the work of each department is related to the work of the other departments.

The Work of the Mailing Department. Mailing Department employees are usually responsible for the following:

1. Opening, dating, sorting, routing, and distributing incoming mail.
2. Making regular pickups of outbound and interoffice mail.
3. Stamping, sealing, and sometimes folding outgoing mail.
4. Acting as special messengers when needed.

INCOMING MAIL

Opening and Sorting the Mail. Mail addressed to the company is usually opened by a mechanical letter opener. This machine slices off a narrow edge from each envelope as the envelopes are fed into the machine by the operator. Mail addressed to specific persons or departments, as well as all mail marked "Personal," is left unopened.

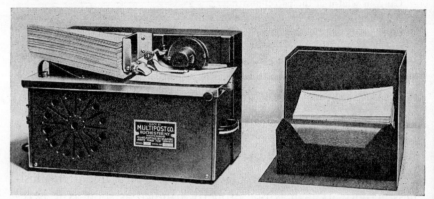

Courtesy National Postal Meter Co., Inc.

AUTOMATIC LETTER OPENER
This electrically operated machine cuts a thin slice from the top of each envelope and deposits the opened envelopes in the box at the right

The contents of each opened envelope are carefully removed. Any enclosures are attached to the letter they accompany. If an envelope contains information not included in its letter, such as a street address or "Attention of," the envelope is attached to the letter. If a letter has been sent by air mail or by special delivery, the envelope should be attached. All other empty envelopes are placed in a large box or basket. This container should not be considered a wastebasket, however, for the mail clerks must re-examine all envelopes a second time, holding each one up to the light to make sure that nothing remains inside. Then—but not until then—are the envelopes thrown away.

Every piece of opened mail is marked with a dating stamp. This stamp often shows the time of day that the letter is received, as well as the date. The mail clerk is careful to place the impression of the stamp where it will not render other writing illegible. The abbreviation for the name of the month rather than the figure for the month should be used—"Sept. 9" instead of "9/9."

The mailing clerks then quickly glance over each opened letter and decide to whom it should be delivered. If enclosures are mentioned, a clerk makes sure that they are present and firmly attached. If an enclosure is missing, this fact is noted on the letter. All notations of this nature should be initialed by the person making them.

If a letter states that something is being sent "under separate cover," a follow-up notation should be made of this, so that the expected piece of mail may be routed properly when it arrives. Such a form is shown on page 17.

Handling Remittances. Some business firms, such as mail-order houses, receive many remittances in the mail. In such offices, a

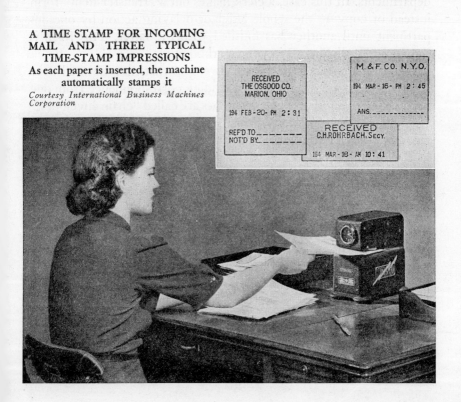

A TIME STAMP FOR INCOMING MAIL AND THREE TYPICAL TIME-STAMP IMPRESSIONS

As each paper is inserted, the machine automatically stamps it

Courtesy International Business Machines Corporation

RECEIVED
THE OSGOOD CO.
MARION, OHIO

194 FEB-20- PM 2:31

REF'D TO_____
NOT'D BY_____

M. & F. CO. N.Y.O.

194 MAR-16- PM 2:45

ANS._____

RECEIVED
C.H.ROHRBACH, SECY.

194 MAR-18- AM 10:41

ROUTING THE INCOMING MAIL

The mail clerk glances over mail addressed to the company and indicates on each piece the department or person to whom it should be delivered

Courtesy General Motors Corporation, Detroit

cashier usually works with the mail clerks, removing the remittances as the mail is opened and recording the money and checks received.

Transferring Items. Sometimes one letter concerns two or more departments. In this case, a clerk makes out a "transfer item" form instead of copying the whole letter or delaying action by one department until another has finished with the letter. This form is shown on Work Sheet 3 in your workbook.

Chain Envelopes. Large, heavy envelopes that may be used over and over again are often used for sending correspondence from one department to another. Such envelopes are called "chain envelopes."

Routing Magazines. Many firms receive a number of trade magazines and other periodicals that should be read by several persons in the organization. A single magazine may be routed to several persons or departments by attaching to it a duplicated slip bearing

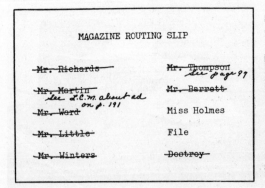

MAGAZINE ROUTING SLIP

~~Mr. Richards~~   ~~Mr. Thompson~~ *see page 99*

~~Mr. Martin~~
see J.C.m. about ad
on p. 191   ~~Mr. Barrett~~
~~Mr. Ward~~   Miss Holmes

~~Mr. Little~~   File

~~Mr. Winters~~   ~~Destroy~~

A MAGAZINE ROUTING SLIP

As each person finished reading the magazine to which this slip was attached, he crossed off his name and placed the magazine in his out box

EXPECTED UNDER SEPARATE COVER

From	Deliver	Received
Hope Engraving	David Rhodes	11-16
Triangle Stationery	Miss Holmes	11-17
Carter & Sand.	S. S. Jones	11-14
Wm. Green	Mr. Washburn	

A RECORD OF MATERIAL EXPECTED IN THE MAIL

When a letter indicates that something is being sent under separate cover, the item is entered on this record, with information as to its intended destination

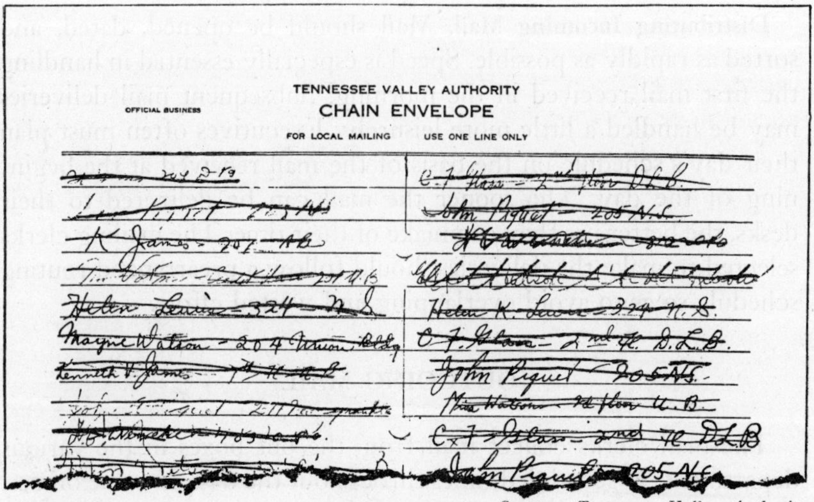

TENNESSEE VALLEY AUTHORITY

OFFICIAL BUSINESS

CHAIN ENVELOPE

FOR LOCAL MAILING   USE ONE LINE ONLY

Courtesy Tennessee Valley Authority

A CHAIN ENVELOPE

Envelopes like this are used over and over in sending papers from one department to another

the various names. Sometimes a rubber-stamp list of the various names is stamped directly on the magazine cover. As each person reads the magazine, he crosses off his name and places the magazine in his out box.

Forwarding Mail. First-class mail may be forwarded by crossing out the incorrect address and adding the new one. To insure proper forwarding of other classifications of mail, the post office should be consulted.

IN AND OUT BOXES

Mail clerks deposit incoming mail in the bottom tray and pick up outgoing mail from the top tray

Courtesy Yawman & Erbe Mfg. Co.

Distributing Incoming Mail. Mail should be opened, dated, and sorted as rapidly as possible. Speed is especially essential in handling the first mail received in the morning. Subsequent mail deliveries may be handled a little more leisurely. Executives often must plan their day's schedule on the basis of the mail received at the beginning of the day. The sooner the mail can be delivered to their desks, the better use they can make of their time. The mailing clerks selected to make the deliveries should follow a prearranged routing schedule so as to avoid overlapping and wasted effort.

OUTGOING MAIL

The mail clerks collect mail from the out boxes in the various departments at scheduled times throughout the day. In some offices, they make the last pickup just prior to closing time. In such cases, of course, the Mailing Department must continue working for a half hour or so after the other departments have closed.

FOLDING FOR NO. 6¾ ENVELOPE

FOLDING FOR NO. 10 ENVELOPE

FOLDING FOR NO. 10 WINDOW ENVELOPE

Folding and Inserting Letters. In some firms, letters are folded and inserted in the envelopes by the mail clerks. In other firms, the stenographers in each department attend to this detail before placing the mail in the out boxes.

Window envelopes, which do not require addressing, are used extensively for mailing invoices, statements, checks, and some routine letters. The typed address must appear in a predetermined place on the sheet of paper that is to be put in the envelope, so that postal clerks can read the address easily through the window of the envelope. See page 19 for illustrations of different folds.

Folding Machines. Advertising matter, letters, and invoices are often folded by machine. Several kinds of folds may be made with one machine if simple adjustments are made. Some hand-operated folding machines take up only about as much table space as a typewriter.

Sealing Envelopes. There are two much-used methods of sealing quantities of envelopes by hand. The cleaner method of moistening the glue on the flaps of the envelopes involves the use of a small metal or crockery cylinder that revolves on an axle in a container of water. Stamps and labels may also be moistened with this apparatus. The envelopes are sealed one at a time.

Another effective method of sealing envelopes by hand is illustrated on page 21. Spread ten or twelve envelopes on a padding of wastepaper sheets so that only the gummed flaps show. Run a moistened sponge over the flaps; then quickly close the flaps and exert pressure on the whole pile, sealing all the envelopes at once.

For large quantities of envelopes, a motor-driven machine is often used.

Weighing Mail. When sealing the mail by any one of these methods, lay at one side any envelopes that are bulky or seem to be heavier than the others. Then weigh these pieces on a postal scale and, in the upper right-hand corner, make pencil notations of the amount of postage required. The figures will be covered when the stamp is affixed.

Some postal scales are "self-computing"; that is, they indicate not only the weight but the amount of postage required. If you use this type of scale, be sure it is up to date.

Left: ELECTRI-
CALLY OPERATED
ENVELOPE SEALER

*Courtesy National Postal
Meter Co., Inc.*

Below: SEALING EN-
VELOPES BY HAND

Affixing Stamps.
One way of affix-
ing stamps by hand
is to moisten a
horizontal row of
stamps at a time.
Draw the strip,
with one stroke,
across a sponge or
other moistened
surface. With one
hand, put the first
stamp in place and
press it down, at
the same time
tearing the rest
of the strip loose

with the other hand. Repeat this process with the next envelope,
and so on.

When the hand stamp affixer shown on page 22 is used, rolls of
stamps are purchased. Each time the plunger is depressed, the machine moistens and affixes a stamp from the roll inside the machine.

Postage Meter Machines. Envelopes may be sealed and the amount of postage and the postmark printed, all in one operation, by an automatic mailing machine. One of the most widely used is the Postage Meter Machine. No stamps are used. Mail run through such a machine is called "metered" mail. Machines of this kind are widely used. They are clean, rapid, efficient, and economical to operate.

In one operation, postage ranging from ½ cent to $9.99½ can be printed on a piece of mail, by setting levers for the proper amount. By a quick adjustment, the machine can be made to print postage on gummed tape for

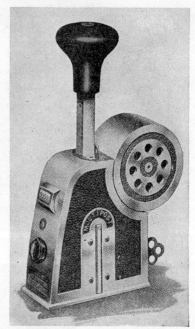

Courtesy National Postal Meter Co., Inc.

A HAND STAMP AFFIXER

AN AUTOMATIC MAILING MACHINE IN OPERATION

Above and below: Two kinds of indicia stamped on outgoing mail

Courtesy Pitney-Bowes Postage Meter Co.

affixing to packages or envelopes too bulky to go through the machine.

Visible registers, called meters, on the machine show how much postage remains on hand and how much has been used. When more postage is needed, the detachable meter is taken to the post office, with a remittance, usually a check, for the amount of postage desired—perhaps $100 worth. A postal official resets the meter to indicate the additional postage purchased and locks the meter so that it cannot be tampered with.

As the automatic mailing machine prints the postmark, together with the postage denomination, metered mail does not have to be canceled at the post office and may be sorted and routed without delay.

The machine can be equipped with special dies so that it will print an advertising slogan or trade-mark along with the postage mark.

Salesmen's Mail. Several different departments in a business may have occasion, during any one day, to write letters to the same sales representative or to the same branch office. Usually such letters are not mailed separately, but all those to one salesman or branch office are collected by the mail clerks at the end of the day and mailed together in a large envelope.

Business houses that employ a number of salesmen who are constantly traveling use various records for keeping the salesmen's mailing addresses up to date. The Mailing Department employees refer to such records daily in forwarding mail. A typical record is shown on page 24.

A man who travels a great deal sometimes moves on before his mail can catch up with him. In order that salesmen may know whether they have missed a day's mail, the daily envelopes sent them are numbered by the mail clerks. If in any month a salesman receives, for example, envelopes numbered 9, 10, and 12, but none numbered 11, he will notify his office and check back to the hotels where he has recently stayed in an effort to find the missing mail. His office may or may not send him duplicates of the lost papers, depending on the contents of the missing envelope.

FORM NO 306 ROUTE LIST FOR WEEK ENDING Sunday, May 13, 194-. WHEN IN DOUBT - CALL MAILING DEPT.							
Salesman	Monday	Tuesday	Wednesday	Thursday	Friday	Saturday	Sunday
J. H. Monroe	Chicago, Ill., Bismarck Hotel.	Same	Rockford, Ill. Faust Hotel	Same	Same	Minneapolis, Minn., Hotel Nicollet.	Same
S. S. Sorenson	Washington, D. C., Hotel Willard, 14th & Pennsylvania, Ave., N.W.	Roanoke, Va. Roanoke Hotel	Same	Same	Winston-Salem, N. C. Hotel Robert E. Lee	Same	Same
Earl Fairfax	Portland, Me. Lafayette Hotel	Same	Same	Boston, Mass. Copley-Plaza Hotel	Same	Springfield, Mass., Hotel Sheraton	Same
S. L. Rich	Denver, Colorado, Argonaut Hotel, all week						

Courtesy The Menasha Products Company

A MASTER ROUTE LIST FOR SALESMEN'S ADDRESSES
Mail clerks refer to the route list in addressing mail to salesmen "on the road"

IMPORTANT POSTAL INFORMATION

Reference Books. Every Mailing Department needs a copy of the *United States Official Postal Guide*, which is described in Section 8 of this book. It may be purchased from the local post office. The *Postal Bulletin*, which records current changes in postal regulations, will be found valuable. It also may be obtained from the local post office.

The following information should be studied carefully. Postal rules are always subject to change, however. Therefore consult your post office when in doubt about any postal matter. The alert secretary will not use more postage on a piece of mail than is necessary; neither will she affix too little postage and thus cause delay in delivery or perhaps even involve some of her superiors in explanations to the postal authorities.

First-Class Mail. First-class postage is required for the following items, whether they are sealed or unsealed: ·

Handwritten or typewritten matter.
Carbon copies.
Letters.
Postal cards.

Private mailing cards.

All other matter wholly or partly in writing.

Matter sealed or otherwise closed against postal inspection. (Parcel-post packages may be sealed only when a special label is used. See Section 14.)

Duplicated matter, *unless* it complies with strict regulations described under "Third-Class Matter."

First-class postal rates are as follows, subject to change by the United States Post Office:

Letters and other sealed matter: 3 cents an ounce or fraction of an ounce.

Postal cards: 1 cent each.

Reply postal cards: 1 cent for the card and 1 cent for the part to be detached and used for reply.

Private mailing cards (post cards): 1 cent each, whether written or printed.

Mail to Foreign Countries. Consult the *Official Postal Guide* or, if necessary, the local post office for information about mail for foreign countries.

Air Mail. For quicker delivery than ordinary mail, and at a higher rate, mail may be sent by air. Air mail may be deposited in any mailbox. Special air-mail stamps are preferable, but ordinary stamps in the proper amount may be used. The rate for air mail in the United States is 8 cents an ounce or fraction thereof.

Special air-mail envelopes are available in stationery stores, and air-mail envelopes already stamped may be purchased at the post office. Red-white-and-blue gummed strips bearing the words "Air Mail" are also obtainable. If none of these methods of identifying air mail is at hand, write "Air Mail" plainly above the address, below the stamps.

Second-Class Mail. Newspapers, magazines, and other periodicals that bear a notice of second-class matter may be mailed by *others than the publishers* at the rate of 1 cent for each 2 ounces or at the fourth-class rate, whichever is lower, to any point within the United States.

The publisher pays a special pound rate determined by a periodic geographical analysis of his entire mailing list. This analysis must be filed with the post office whenever requested.

The post office should be consulted before mailing matter by second class.

Third-Class Mail. The third-class rate is 1½ cents for each 2 ounces. Unless you are thoroughly familiar with postal regulations, consult the post office before mailing anything with third-class postage. Matter weighing less than 8 ounces may be third-class mail if it falls in one of the following classifications and if it is not first- or second-class matter:

> Printed circulars.
> Books. (See also "Books.")
> Catalogues.
> Photographs.
> Merchandise. (See also "Parcel Post" in Section 14.)
> Miscellaneous printed matter.

Questions like this will often arise, "Can we use the third-class postage rate in mailing stencil-duplicated price sheets to our salesmen?" A familiarity with the regulations concerning third-class mail rates will result in a considerable saving of money on mailings of this kind. When in doubt, consult the post office authorities.

Facsimile copies of handwriting as well as typewriting reproduced in print, on the stencil duplicator, on the hectograph, on the Multigraph, or by lithography may be mailed third class *if* a minimum of twenty identical unsealed copies is presented together at the post office. If there are fewer than twenty pieces, or if they are not identical, or if they are mailed in an ordinary letter box, they will take the first-class rate.

Fourth-Class Matter. As fourth-class mail, or parcel post, is used chiefly in shipping, it is described in Section 14, which deals with the work of the Traffic Department.

Books. A special rate of 4 cents for the first pound and 3 cents for each additional pound applies to books not containing advertising matter and plainly marked "Books." If they do contain advertising matter, they must go by parcel post. (Also consult express rates.)

Special Delivery. When a special-delivery stamp, in addition to the regular postage, is affixed to a letter, a postal card, or a package, the mail will be delivered by special messenger. Ordinary stamps in the proper amount may be used for this purpose provided the words "Special Delivery" are written on the front of the envelope or package. The fee for letters is 13 cents; the fee for packages varies with the weight of the package and its classification.

Special delivery is of little value in small towns.

Registered Mail. Valuable mail, such as money, legal documents, and securities, may be safeguarded during transmission by sending it registered. A registry fee, in addition to the regular postage, is charged for this protection. The service applies to mail in the first, second, and third classes.

The fee for registration ranges from 20 cents for an indemnity (remuneration for loss or damage) not exceeding $5 to $1.35 for an indemnity not exceeding $1,000. Mail matter without intrinsic value, such as a letter that the sender wishes delivered to the addressee in person, may be registered for 20 cents.

A return receipt, signed by the recipient of the mail, but not necessarily by the addressee, may be procured by requesting the receipt at the time of registration and paying a small additional charge. To insure that the mail is delivered only to the person to whom it is addressed, it is necessary to stipulate that the delivery be "to addressee only."

Do not sign for registered mail delivered to your office unless you know that the addressee is employed in the office and that you can effect delivery. If the addressee has moved and you know his address, supply it to the mailman so that the material may be forwarded. Do not accept a registered letter or package with the intention of forwarding it yourself. If you do, a second registration fee will be required.

Sending Remittances by Mail. Coins or paper money should not be sent by mail unless it is impracticable to obtain checks, money orders, or various other forms of remittances that safeguard the sender against loss. These forms are described in Section 13.

Insured Mail. Third- and fourth-class matter may be insured for values up to $200. The fee, which varies with the amount of insurance, provides for indemnity in case of loss or damage in transit. A return receipt may be requested for insured mail as for registered mail.

Receipts for registered and insured mail should be filed, preferably attached to the correspondence about the item.

C.O.D. Fees. Sometimes it is desirable to mail something for which payment is to be made by the recipient at the time of delivery. Before mailing anything C.O.D., consult the *Postal Guide* or the post office authorities. Certain forms must be filled out at the post office. It is impracticable, as a rule, to send C.O.D. any item costing less than $1.

Lost Mail. The post office will try to trace lost or undelivered mail if the proper form is filled out. Unregistered mail usually cannot be found, however, as the post office has no record of original mailings.

Consult the Postal Authorities. Take your mailing problems to the employees in your local post office. It is especially important to consult them when you have any of the following mailing problems:

1. If your company plans to sponsor a contest that will operate partially or wholly through the mails.

2. If printed or duplicated advertising matter is to be mailed in quantity.

3. If identical duplicated material is to be mailed in quantities of more than twenty pieces, whether it is advertising matter or not.

4. When your company is considering the use of envelopes or cards of an unusual size or shape.

5. When samples are to be accompanied by a letter requiring first-class postage.

6. When postage-paid return envelopes are to be enclosed.

After you have studied the information contained in this section, turn to your workbook and work the assignments for the section. One assignment calls for the writing of a letter of acknowledgment. Before writing it, read the suggestions concerning the writing of letters. These suggestions immediately follow this section.

Answers to "Do You Know?" (Page 13)

1. No. Typed material must be sent by first-class mail or by express.

2. Unless otherwise instructed, use window envelopes because they do not have to be addressed.

3. The postage required for a 1½-ounce air-mail letter is 16 cents (8 cents for every ounce or fraction of an ounce).

4. Send it by registered mail and request a return receipt.

5. Make out a "transfer item" form for one of the departments and copy on this form the portion of the correspondence on which that particular department is to take action.

SOME SUGGESTIONS TO THE PRIVATE SECRETARY ON THE WRITING OF LETTERS

BY DOROTHY M. JOHNSON

A secretary must know how to write letters. Your ability to write acceptable letters may be the deciding factor in your promotion. Effective letter writing can be mastered by any intelligent person.

In this secretarial course you will have an opportunity to study and practice the fundamentals of effective letter writing. When, during your advancement from a job to a career, the time comes for you to take on heavier responsibilities, by all means make a more serious and thorough study of this subject.

A businessman, seasoned by years of dictating experience, can read a letter once and immediately dictate a clear, well-worded answer. His ability to do this is the result of experience. At first, you had better write rough drafts of your letters, or at least make brief notes, before typing the finished letters on company letterheads.

The advisability of avoiding the use of longhand in writing your rough drafts cannot be overemphasized. Longhand is too slow, for one thing. For another thing, the use of longhand robs you of opportunities to practice the basic skills of your trade—shorthand and typewriting. The very words you are reading here were written first in shorthand.

Personality in Letters. Businessmen who write many letters try to make them individual by injecting a certain amount of personality into them. The letters written by a secretary, however, should be

TYPICAL LETTERS WRITTEN BY THE SECRETARY

impersonal. There is good reason for this rule. The secretary writes only as a representative of her employer, not as an individual. As a rule, she writes only routine letters, usually because it is not convenient or possible for her employer to write them when needed.

It is easy for the beginner in business to overstep the bounds of good taste or to become overenthusiastic. Do not attempt to be witty or clever in business communications until you have worked with other people's letters long enough to be able to judge how far it is safe to go with originality of expression.

Plan your letter. Be sure you know exactly why you are writing it.

The "You" Approach. Appeal to your reader on the basis of his own interests. Remember that *u* comes before *i* in "business." The reader's interests, not the writer's, should be emphasized.

A manufacturer, for example, has made up a large number of display cabinets for use in retail stores. He will not sell them direct to retailers, but to wholesalers. The wholesaler will never use the cabinets himself. He will only sell them. The manufacturer knows that the wholesaler wishes two things: fast sales turnover, and reasonable profit.

In writing a sales letter to a wholesaler, therefore, the manufacturer will stress the wholesaler's known interests. His sales approach to the wholesaler will be something like this: "Your investment will be small, but your profits will be gratifying. You will find that this display cabinet is just what your retailers have been wanting for the summer season."

When to Avoid the "You" Approach. There is an important exception to this rule about using the word "you" in business letters. When you must lay the blame on the recipient of your letter, be very impersonal. In this case (and in almost no other), remember the passive voice and use it. Omit all direct reference to *you*.

Wrong: Apparently you misunderstood our order. Anyway, you shipped the wrong thing.

Right: Apparently our instructions were misinterpreted, with the result that the wrong article was shipped.

Always Be Courteous. The admonition to be courteous may seem obvious, but what you write with perfect good will may easily be misunderstood by the reader unless you keep his reaction constantly in mind.

Be Careful. Never write anything in a business letter that you would not wish to see printed over your name in the daily newspapers.

Letters of Acknowledgment. Every secretary must be able to write letters of acknowledgment. These fall into two general classifications: letters that simply acknowledge the receipt of something, and letters that explain why a complete answer will be delayed.

Acknowledging Receipt. A letter acknowledging receipt may be like either of these:

1. The sample desk calendar arrived in this morning's mail and has gone to work already on Mr. Wilson's desk. Thank you very much.

2. The papers relating to the Miller case have been received. Thank you for sending them.

Explaining Necessary Delay. Letters that cannot be answered fully are acknowledged at once by the secretary so that the correspondent will understand that he is not being ignored. If such acknowledgment is not made, the dictator will have to make embarrassing apologies when he does answer fully.

Do not promise that your superior will answer at once. He may be too busy to do so. You can, however, safely say that the matter will be brought to his attention at once.

Here is an example of an acknowledgment written because of absence:

This acknowledges your letter of June 4, asking about the Belknap contract. Because of the absence of several of our men, who are attending a convention, no final decision has been made on this, but as soon as there is something definite to report, you will hear from Mr. Wilson.

Other reasons than absence may require that a letter of acknowledgment be written to explain a delay. For example:

This acknowledges your inquiry of April 7 about flooring. Your letter has been sent to our San Francisco office for attention, because the records that will have to be consulted are kept there. You will hear from that office soon.

When you acknowledge a letter that must be sent on to another department or office, attach a carbon copy of your acknowledgment to the letter so that the person who follows the transaction through will know what has been done.

Letters of Transmittal. Secretaries often compose routine letters of transmittal for the employer's signature. Typical transmittal letters are as follows:

1. Enclosed is the price list about which you inquired in your letter of September 2. We can supply copies for your branch stores if you would like to have them. Will you let us know?

2. Two copies of the lease for the property at 147 Park Boulevard are enclosed. Will you please sign and return both copies to us? The carbon copy will be returned to you after the owner affixes his signature.

Here is a letter of transmittal to be signed by the secretary.

Mr. Blank has asked me to send you our book, "How to Save Money on Insurance," about which he spoke to you. The book is being mailed separately today.

A letter of transmittal simply tells the recipient that something is being sent to him, and sometimes it tells him why. A man who has asked for a catalogue may have forgotten it by the time the catalogue arrives unless a letter of transmittal reminds him of his request.

Continued on page 177

Top: A section of a central stenographic pool. Center: The supervisor of the pool. Below: These two girls, equipped with telephone headset and mouthpiece, type telephoned dictation

read
7/ better Bur. Bureau
telegram

3

THE STENOGRAPHIC DEPARTMENT

DO YOU KNOW?

1. A dictator for whom you are working for the first time reads the complete address, rather rapidly, for each letter he dictates. Should you write it all down or depend on getting the addresses later from the correspondence?

2. Your chief uses a technical term that is unfamiliar to you. Should you ask him to repeat it as soon as he finishes dictating the letter, or should you try to find out its meaning after you begin to transcribe?

3. Your employer uses a letter form unlike any you have seen during your business training. Would you immediately suggest that he adopt one of the more common letter forms?

4. You must make a change on a carbon copy. Would you use a soft pencil eraser or an ink eraser?

5. You have finished transcribing the morning's dictation, and your employer is ready to sign the letters. If he finds errors in your typing, what have you neglected to do?

MANY large business firms have central Stenographic Departments, or stenographic pools, as they are sometimes called, from which stenographers and typists are called when needed. A central Stenographic Department somewhat resembles your business practice room, with many persons at work and one person supervising their activities. Members of the central Stenographic Department are sent to executives in various departments for dictation and other assignments. They also take dictation from the head of the Stenographic Department and help in keeping the department records up to date.

Your shorthand writing will not be timed. You will be expected to write what the dictator says, as fast as he says it, and to transcribe it acceptably. Each day you will learn more about the vocabulary of the firm's business, its policies, the names of its customers, and the special requirements of your various dictators.

How to Use Your Notebook. Every morning, date an unused page in your notebook. When you take dictation from more than one

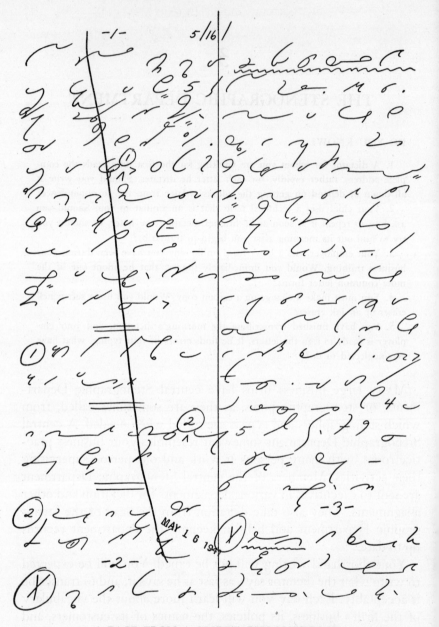

A PAGE FROM A SECRETARY'S NOTEBOOK

Changes and additions are marked by circled figures, and an X in a circle is used to designate "rush" assignments. Letters are numbered in the middle of the column. The secretary draws a vertical line through each letter after transcribing it.

person, write the dictator's name, preferably with colored pencil, at the beginning of his dictation. Otherwise, you may give one dictator's letter to another dictator for signature.

If you take dictation regularly from two or three persons, you may find it convenient to use a separate notebook for each dictator.

Number in your notebook, in sequence, all the letters taken during a dictation period. Then, if your dictator should ask how many letters you have left to transcribe, you can easily tell him.

Adopt some clear way of indicating the end of each letter. Then, when you begin to transcribe, you can easily judge the length of each letter and its proper placement on the letterhead. Some stenographers draw a horizontal line across the notebook column at the end of each letter.

After a letter has been transcribed, draw a line downward through the notes for that letter. It is very important to be certain that each letter has been transcribed.

Keep a rubber band around the used leaves of your notebook so that it will open at once to the first unused page when you are called to take dictation. Be sure to put the rubber band around only the pages that have been *completely* transcribed. Use another rubber band, if necessary, around the pages on which there are untranscribed notes.

On the cover of each new notebook, write your name and the date on which you begin to use the book. When the notebook is full, add to the cover notation the date on which you took the last dictation it contains.

The dictation of some executives is so important that all stenographers' notebooks are preserved for several years. This precaution is taken in case file copies of transcripts should be lost or a question arise regarding the accuracy of a transcript.

Date: May 1 through May 14, 194-
Dictator: W. R. Ripperger
Transcribed by Mary Patterson

Index of Contents

Anderson Supply Co.		14
Andrews, Graves & Hardy		3
Barnes Wholesale Grocery		78
Brant Market, Inc.		43
Burnett, Martin J.	1, 15,	39
etc.		

AN INDEX FOR A FILLED NOTEBOOK

Whether or not you find this rule in effect in your first stenographic position, it would be wise to keep your notebooks during your first year.

It takes very little additional time to prepare an alphabetic index of the contents of each notebook and to paste a typed copy of the index on the inside of the front or back cover. For ease in locating letters, it is advisable to number notebook pages and include page numbers in the index. See the one shown on page 37.

Take Care of Your Office Tools. Every morning, and after every prolonged dictation period, check to see that your fountain pen is filled. Black or purple ink is preferable for note taking. Have several sharp pencils always at hand for emergency use, including at least one colored one. It is desirable to use a colored pencil in marking special instructions regarding your shorthand notes.

Your Typewriter. Your typewriter is an expensive and efficient machine. Take pride in it and in the product you turn out with it. Also select the proper ribbon for your machine. Typewriter ribbons are made in many varieties. Among the factors to be considered in selecting a typewriter ribbon are its inking (light, medium, heavy, extra heavy) and the fabric (silk or cotton) of which it is made. Light to medium inking is generally very satisfactory for a machine equipped with elite type, and medium to heavy inking for a machine with pica type. The sharpness of the impression made by the keys will also depend on whether the typist taps the keys with a light or a heavy stroke.

Generally speaking, cotton ribbons are entirely satisfactory—they are more durable and less expensive than silk ribbons. Silk ribbons make an exceptionally clear impression and, if obtainable, should be used when unusual neatness is a job requirement.

Taking Dictation. When you are called for dictation, whether the call comes by buzzer, telephone, or messenger, respond at once, ready for work. Have your notebook open; some men begin dictating at once, whether the secretary is seated or not. Be prepared to write with the notebook on the edge of a desk or on your knee if necessary. If you take notes from a factory official, you may have to write shorthand while walking beside him, with machinery almost drowning his voice.

Take dictation without fidgeting and without calling attention to yourself in any way. There may be long pauses in the dictation while the dictator searches for the exact word or phrase he needs. Do not offer to help him unless he asks for a suggestion or unless you are thoroughly familiar with his particular work.

When the dictator pauses, use the time to read over your notes, making notations about punctuation, capitalization, and paragraphing. Study carefully the details shown in the frontispiece.

To Stop or Not to Stop. Every beginning stenographer has the problem of deciding what to do when the dictator uses an unfamiliar word or term. Is it better to interrupt immediately or wait until he has dictated the entire letter? You must be guided by his personal preference, and the only way to learn this is to ask him.

Then there is the problem of deciding what to do with awkward sentence structure. Some dictators prefer to stop dictating at once and avoid trying to patch a confused sentence later when it may have been forgotten. Others prefer to wait and not risk losing the trend of thought of the whole letter.

If the dictator prefers not to be interrupted until the end of the letter, you will need to devise some method of turning to the places in the notes about which you have questions. As you write, draw a large circle around the notes in question; also, quickly turn over the corner of that page of the notebook.

Of course obvious mistakes in grammar or in names may be corrected without referring them to the dictator. In fact, it is much more tactful *not* to call his attention to them. He has more important things on his mind; and, anyway, it is part of your job to take the burden of details off his shoulders. Until you have become accustomed to your work, however, it will be much safer not to make the more drastic types of changes, such as shifting sentences about or changing wording, but to assume that the dictator is right. Some letters that do not make sense to you, because of your limited business experience, may still be entirely correct.

In any event, any questions that you do have should be asked *before* you leave the dictator's desk, not when you begin transcribing. If you wait until then, the dictator may assume that you are unable to read your notes; also, it may be impossible to ask him later.

Do not be overtimid about asking questions. It is far better to ask questions than to place on the dictator's desk a letter that does not make sense just because you hesitated to clear up something that was not clear to you. No dictator will accept transcripts that do not make sense. Also, you waste the company's time and stationery when you have to retype an entire letter.

If the dictator gets too far ahead of you, your course is obvious: ask him to wait until you can catch up with him, and, if necessary, repeat part of what you missed. To have to stop the dictator is embarrassing, but to leave out parts of the letter is very much worse. If this situation arises often, obviously you should practice to increase your speed, either by attending evening school or by having someone dictate to you at home.

Names and Addresses. Most dictators do not give the address or even the full name of the addressee when dictating an answer to a letter. When the dictator says, "Letter to Al Brown," the stenographer, if she does not know Mr. Brown, is expected to refer to the correspondence (which the dictator will give her or which is in the files) and obtain from it Mr. Brown's complete name and address.

Make a habit of writing names and addresses in shorthand, using longhand only to indicate peculiar spellings of unfamiliar names. As fast as you can, become familiar with the names and addresses of regular correspondents. A card index kept on your desk is most helpful and sometimes necessary. By referring to this index, you can avoid going to distant files to consult correspondence. But be sure to keep the index up to date. A secretarial "Who's Who" card is shown on page 277.

It is impossible to overemphasize the importance of writing names, titles, and addresses absolutely correctly. There are no rules for the spelling of proper names as there are for spelling other words. Do not guess. What you type on the envelope determines whether or not the letter it contains will reach its destination with the least possible delay. Work Sheets 26 and 27 contain an assignment that includes helpful hints on spelling names and addresses.

Always Write Down Instructions. When special instructions are given, take time to note them in shorthand. Make such notations at the *beginning* of the shorthand notes to which they refer, even if you have to turn back several pages to find the beginning. If you place them at the end, you may forget to look for them and may neglect to carry out instructions at the right time—such as instructions to make extra copies, to include form paragraphs, or to telephone for certain needed data before transcribing a letter.

If you write memoranda of all kinds in shorthand—on your calendar pad, on your follow-up sheet, on correspondence to which

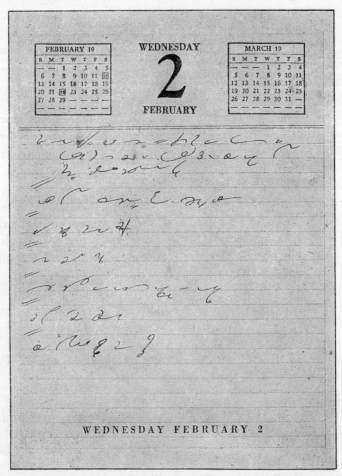

A PAGE FROM A SECRETARY'S CALENDAR PAD

you are to compose replies—you will gain shorthand speed and fluency and will save many minutes that soon count up to hours.

Some letters are more important than others. In one dictation period, you may take an air-mail letter and a telegram that should go at once, an interdepartment memorandum that can wait until tomorrow, and a dozen or more letters that should go out in the last mail that day. You should mechanically signal them by some such device as a clip on the side of the sheet containing rush items or by folding over those pages that are to be transcribed first. If you use a colored pencil to note the special instructions the dictator gives you about these, or that you yourself know should be indicated, the notations will stand out prominently so that you will not miss them when transcribing.

Your Shorthand Vocabulary. The dictation you receive at first will probably include some terms that are new to you. Note such words and expressions. If you cannot conveniently obtain a special vocabulary of shorthand "short cuts" pertaining to your business, make special shorthand outlines for those frequently used technical terms peculiar to your business but that take too long to write in full.

How Fast Should You Be Able to Write Shorthand? If you can take dictation of unfamiliar matter for at least five minutes at 100 or 120 words a minute, you will have little difficulty with ordinary dictation in your first position. Always remember that your value to your firm will be based more on the amount of finished, usable work you produce than on your shorthand speed.

Your *transcription speed* will determine your productiveness. Try continually to increase it. No matter what your speed is, refuse to be satisfied with it. You can always improve it and increase your productiveness and your value to your employer.

Transcribing. In order to transcribe intelligently and well, you must be able to do these five things:

1. Read shorthand notes quickly and accurately.
2. Interpret your shorthand notes for sense. You may have misheard or misunderstood the dictator. He may have become involved in a complicated expression of thought and said something in a way he did not intend. Your transcript must make sense.
3. Know English thoroughly—spelling, punctuation, capitalization,

sentence structure, and grammar. You need, also, to understand the meaning of expressions peculiar to business in general and to your firm's business in particular.

4. Judge quickly from the length of your shorthand notes how to place the transcript attractively on the typed page.

5. Type from shorthand notes rapidly, accurately, and artistically.

Copyholder. Wherever practicable, use a copyholder for your notebook while transcribing. This device will enable you to read your notes from the correct angle and from the right distance, thus lessening eyestrain.

Posture. Incorrect posture will surely make you tired and may harm your health. You will not have much to say about the height of your typewriter or of your desk top or about the style of your chair, but sometimes adjustments can be made. If you should find yourself tiring every day, consider speaking to your superior about it in an endeavor to correct the height at which you work.

Keep your shoulders back while standing, sitting, or walking, and you will tire less easily. If you walk with runover heels, your posture will suffer, and you will tire as a consequence.

CORRECT OPERATING POS-TURE AT THE TYPEWRITER

Note the low wrist, naturally curved hand and fingers, forearms slanting upwards, upper arms forward, trunk slightly forward. Note also posture chair with back rest at proper height

Keystone View Company

Standard Letter Forms. The three most commonly used letter forms are: (1) the indented form; (2) the modified, or semiblock, form; and (3) the block form. These forms are illustrated in the model-forms section of your workbook. A less common form is the hanging-indention form. Usually, a uniform letter style is used throughout an organization. When you are given a certain style to follow, do not try to introduce variations or what you consider to be improvements. Uniformity increases efficiency, because the mechanical part of your work will soon become automatic, leaving you more time for actual production. Later, of course, when you become experienced, you may be able to suggest improvements; and you should feel free to do so.

Letter Placement. In learning to place typed letters attractively on a page, your problem is to judge, from the amount of space taken up by your shorthand notes, how much space the typewritten

DICTATING AND TRANSCRIBING LETTERS BY MEANS OF DICTATING MACHINE EQUIPMENT

Courtesy Ediphone Company

transcript will fill. A little practice will enable you to decide this for each transcript without counting words.

A working secretary does not take time to count words or do any preliminary figuring. She glances at her shorthand notes and knows, from experience, where to set the typewriter margin stops and how far down on the page to place the inside address so that the letter will be attractively centered.

The following letter placement table [1] may be used for a short time while you are learning to place your transcripts attractively. As soon as possible, learn to visualize the placement of letters and dispense with the table.

LETTER PLACEMENT TABLE

(Single-spaced letters)

Number of words in body of letter (actual count)	50	75	100	125	150	175	200	225 to 275 *
Number of line spaces from:								
Top edge to date line	19	17	15	16	15	14	14	14
Date to inside address	6	6	5	5	4	4	3	2
Length of line in body of letter—spaces	40	40	40	50	50	50	50	60
Average number of paragraphs in body	2	2	3	3	3	4	4	4

*A letter exceeding 275 words should be typed on two or more pages, the letter being divided so that at least four or five lines of the body of the letter appear on the last page.

Erasures. Neat erasures can easily be made, except on certain grades of paper, if proper precautions are followed. If a soft pencil eraser is used first on the original to take off the excess ink, and then a hard ink eraser is used, much of the original coating of the paper will be retained. Hold the eraser firmly and, using short strokes, apply it lightly to the paper. After the erasure has been made, smooth the area by rubbing the area in a circular motion with the fingernail or a paper clip.

[1] From *Gregg Typing*, Third Edition, by SoRelle, Smith, Foster, and Blanchard, The Gregg Publishing Company.

On a particularly important letter or document, you will want to add this step: after the eraser has been used, cover the spot with ordinary white chalk and brush off the excess chalk dust before typing over the spot. In most cases, this procedure will insure a correction that can scarcely be detected.

Never use an ink eraser for carbons; use a soft eraser.

Paper. The secretary should be familiar with all the commonly used business stationery and other office supplies and should know when to use and how to buy these supplies economically.

Paper has a multitude of uses in the business office. Probably the most frequent use is for correspondence. Most business letterheads are printed or engraved on bond paper, although parchment, ledger, and many book papers have been found suitable. Bond paper has tough, strong fibers that withstand rough handling. A bond paper may always be distinguished from other papers by the watermark that appears on each sheet. A watermark is a faint figure impressed in the paper. It is easily seen when the sheet is held to the light. Many concerns have their trade-marks watermarked into their stationery.

For carbon copies, a manifold paper is used. This kind of paper has most of the characteristics of bond paper, but it is lighter in weight. It may or may not be a bond paper. A very lightweight paper, known as onionskin, is often used for carbon copies. Many offices use a manifold paper on which the word "Copy" is printed in large outline letters. A cheap grade of manifold paper, often called a "second sheet" and obtainable in many colors, is also used for carbon copies.

Ledger paper is of exceptional strength and has a fine writing surface. As its name implies, it is used mainly for accounting records.

For stencil duplicating, a paper sometimes called "impression paper" is available. This paper has a soft surface so that the ink penetrates and dries quickly.

The most common size of paper used for letters, second sheets, and duplicating work is $8\frac{1}{2}$ by 11 inches. The baronial size, $5\frac{1}{2}$ by $8\frac{1}{2}$ inches, and the monarch size, $7\frac{1}{4}$ by $10\frac{1}{2}$ inches, are sometimes used by executives.

Envelopes. Envelopes should match in quality, color, and weight of paper the letterheads they accompany. The style of printing in the "card" (the return address in the upper left corner or on the flap) should harmonize with that of the letterhead.

Two sizes of envelopes are made for the usual 8½- by 11-inch letterhead: (1) The commonest size is the No. 6¾ size. It measures 6½ by 3⅝ inches. (2) The No. 10 size, 9½ by 4⅛ inches, is used when a letter consists of several sheets or when several enclosures are to be inserted.

Envelopes of the proper size are also provided for baronial- and monarch-sized letterheads.

The window envelope is much used in sending out bills and statements. It is not ordinarily used for general correspondence, however. This style of envelope contains a transparent address section so that the inside address on the statement may also serve as the envelope address. The object of this arrangement is to save time and avoid an opportunity for error. Window envelopes come in all standard sizes.

Return envelopes, or self-addressed envelopes, are often enclosed with requests for information, to make it easy for a person to reply or mail an order, and for many other occasions. Return envelopes are slightly smaller than the standard-sized envelopes and are known as No. 6 and No. 9 respectively.

Carbon Copies. One or more carbon copies are required of nearly every letter. Always ascertain how many will be needed.

When many sheets of paper and carbon must be inserted together into the machine, the sheets seldom emerge evenly. You can even the sheets by using the paper release and your fingers; but that method is slow and uncertain. Here is a better method:

Cut a strip of paper 3 inches deep by 8½ inches wide. Fold the strip in half the long way. Place the folded strip over the paper and carbons. Insert the edge protected by the fold into the machine, give the platen a turn, and the "book" of sheets is in place.

Use a backing sheet, such as half a manila file folder, behind the last carbon copy. (Special backing sheets may also be purchased.) This sheet will often enable you to make even your final multiple copy legible.

Many firms, particularly Government agencies, require from five to ten clean, legible copies of nearly every typed form. The typist must strike the keys sharply and accurately, as erasing is extremely costly.

Carbon Paper. Carbon paper is thin tissue paper that has been coated with a composition of ink, adhesive, and wax or other suitable surfacing. Carbon paper is manufactured in many weights, styles, and finishes so that it is possible to get just the right kind for the typing job you are doing.

If you are inclined to strike the typewriter keys heavily, use a hard-coated carbon. A soft-coated carbon is intended for typists who tap the keys with a light touch. This kind is also best for use with Noiseless typewriters.

Carbon paper should be handled carefully, for it is easily damaged. When not in use, the sheets should be laid flat and preferably with the carbon (shiny) side down. The usability of a carbon sheet may be prolonged by turning it from top to bottom each time the sheet is used. When you are making several carbon copies in one operation, it is advisable to change the order of the sheets after each typing. This plan will help to distribute the pressure and make the sheets wear more uniformly. A minimum of twelve consecutive, single-spaced, legible copies may be expected from a standard sheet of carbon.

The manufacturers of carbon paper have perfected various features of their papers. On some makes, corners are clipped for the quick removal of the sheets without soiling the fingers. On other makes, the typist can clip the corners himself. One make of carbon paper comes with the right edge of the paper carbonless. On this white edge is printed a scale of figures from 1 to 66, corresponding to the number of single-spaced lines on a letter-sized page. By means of this handy scale, which is always visible in the typewriter, the typist knows at any time the number of lines that have been typed and how many more may be typed on the sheet. The typist who regularly makes a large number of carbons of all her work should have a hard-surfaced platen substituted for the ordinary typewriter platen.

Enclosures. Sometimes a stenographer, when working under pressure, forgets to insert the enclosures that have been indicated in the dictation. Of course it is important to type the letters dictated, but the enclosures are sometimes even more important. "Enc.," with a figure representing the number of enclosures, typed below the identifying initials at the bottom of a letter serves to warn the stenographer, as well as the person who signs the letters, that something is to go in the envelope with the letter.

Another warning signal is a bright-red gummed seal, bearing the word "Enclosure" in white. This seal may be attached below the identifying initials. It is especially useful where the enclosures are to be put into the envelope by another person, as when certain advertising folders, referred to in a letter, are to be inserted by a mail clerk after the letter reaches the Mailing Department. If the person who transcribes the letter also includes the enclosures, it is hardly worth while to attach this seal, since "Enc." may be typed on the letter more easily.

The Finished Transcript. Finished transcripts may be presented to the dictator for signature in various ways. Here is one way of doing it. Follow this procedure unless you are instructed otherwise.

From the top to the bottom of the pile of completed letters, the papers are arranged thus. (See illustration on page 50.)

1. The addressed envelope is on the top of the pile, right side up, with the flap tucked under the top edge of the finished letter. In the envelope are all enclosures mentioned in the letter except those for which the Mailing Department is responsible.

2. The top of the finished letter is covered by the envelope, but the space for the dictator's signature is not.

3. Under the letter to be mailed are extra carbons, if any, properly addressed to other departments or persons; any follow-up copies; also accompanying envelopes for carbons to be mailed.

4. Under the extra carbons (which are usually on thin onionskin paper) is the file copy, attached to the original correspondence. On this file copy are the notations indicating that enclosures were actually sent, that extra copies were sent to persons interested, that arrangements have been made for any material that is to be sent separately, and any follow-up notations.

Some dictators prefer to have all the outgoing letters and their envelopes together in one pile, with the original correspondence

Courtesy Underwood Elliot Fisher Company

THE SECRETARY PROOFREADS HER WORK
Note that she is proofreading the material while it is in the machine

and carbons in a separate pile. This arrangement prevents the backs of outgoing letters from being smudged with carbon; but it makes it difficult for the dictator, when he is signing his mail, to look through the correspondence if he wishes to check something.

If the dictator has given you permission to sign his name, in his absence, to letters that he has dictated, sign his name and write your initials neatly underneath and close to the end of his name.

Addressing Envelopes. Several styles of envelope addresses are illustrated in your workbook.

Window Envelopes. The method of folding letters for insertion in window envelopes was shown on page 19. When a letter is typed for enclosing in a window envelope, the address must be carefully arranged. Invoice forms and some letterheads have small guide marks printed on them. The invoice forms in your workbook have these guide marks.

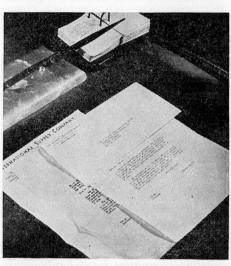

A LETTER READY FOR SIGNING

Final Inspection. Check every letter you type before giving it to the dictator for signature. If you are to sign the letter or if you have to release the outgoing mail in the dictator's absence, additional checking may be necessary. Check these points in the letter:

1. Are the addressee's name and address correct on both letter and envelope?

2. If you signed your employer's name in his absence, did you sign your own initials below it? (This is customary. You cannot then be suspected of forging his signature.)

3. Did the original correspondence include a key number or department reference (such as "Address reply to Dept. B") to which the answer was to be addressed? If so, does the reply carry this key or reference on the letter and on the envelope? It should.

Check these additional points on the envelope:

1. If the letter is to go by air mail, have you typed this instruction in capital letters on the envelope or affixed an "air-mail" sticker?

2. Have you attached a colored signal to letters addressed to foreign countries, so that the mail clerk will affix special postage?

3. If the letter is addressed "Attention of . . . ," is the envelope also addressed that way?

Check these points about carbons and enclosures:

1. Have you addressed the extra carbon copies to the proper persons?

2. Have you made the same corrections on the carbons that were necessary on the original?

3. Did you note on the carbon that the enclosures actually were enclosed?

4. If material was promised "under separate cover," have you made provision for sending it and noted this fact on the carbon?

FORM LETTERS

A form letter is either a letter that is written in advance and copied whenever needed, or a letter that has been duplicated in advance so that it is ready to be sent out when needed, with the inside address filled in. Usually, each form letter is known by a number.

Form paragraphs are often used, too. Like form letters, these are numbered. A dictator may dictate a paragraph in a letter replying to an inquiry, and then say, "Use form paragraphs 3 and 17, and end it, 'Sincerely yours.'"

The Use of Form Letters. Form letters save a great deal of time. Assume, for example, that your company has a new product, trade-named Blocktex. Your salesmen send names of prospective customers to the office on their daily reports. A dozen names may be received each day; and letters must be written to all of them, describing Blocktex and its superior qualities and what it will do for the user.

If a dictator takes the time to compose an entirely new letter for each prospective customer, he may not always describe the product in the most effective way. Therefore, he writes one really good letter and takes the time to polish it, as he can seldom do when he is dictating under pressure. This letter is then numbered—for example, Form Letter 382. Whenever a list of prospective purchasers of Blocktex is received, a typist is assigned to write letter No. 382 to each of them. The dictator's time is freed for the writing of individual letters on individual problems.

The typing of form letters is more or less mechanical—in fact, it may be almost entirely mechanical and automatic if one of the automatic typewriters is used.

A DICTAFORM FILE

Form letters and form paragraphs, filed by number, can be found readily in this desk-top file

Courtesy Meilicke Systems, Inc.

Form Letters As Fill-in Work. Many business firms do not find it worth while to purchase machines especially for writing form letters. Instead, they have the letters written by their typists and stenographers in slack periods. Numbered form letters and form paragraphs are often kept in a loose-leaf file like the Dictaform, illustrated on page 52.

The typing of form letters may become monotonous, but remember that good judgment must be exercised continually. You may have to make slight changes in the form letter from time to time in order to make it fit a particular situation.

The easiest way to type form letters is *not* the right way. The right way—the safe way—is to type each one from a master copy. The wrong way is to type each one from the one before it. If you make a mistake or leave something out of one, you may not notice it; and the error or omission will be repeated in every letter that follows.

Answers to "Do You Know?"

1. To be safe, write down addresses that are dictated. It will be most disconcerting if you discover later that the dictator has no intention of giving you the correspondence for reference, or that he is initiating correspondence, in which case there will be no letter to refer to.

2. You would be wise to ask for necessary explanations of technical terms immediately after a letter containing them has been dictated.

3. No; you would use the employer's letter style without comment. He probably has some good reason for his preference.

4. You would use a soft eraser for carbon copies.

5. You have neglected to proofread the letters and to correct all errors before submitting the letters to the dictator.

CORRECT AND INCORRECT METHODS OF SPEAKING INTO THE TELEPHONE

The lips should be not more than half an inch from the mouthpiece. When the transmitter is dropped below the lips, the telephone instrument can pick up sounds only one-tenth to one-fiftieth as well as when it is in the correct position

4

THE STENOGRAPHIC DEPARTMENT
(*Continued*)

DO YOU KNOW?

1. Your New York office must have some information from your Chicago office within eight hours. You estimate that approximately a half hour will be required for the Chicago office to compile the information. How would you communicate with that office at the least cost?

2. It is now 11 a.m. Your chief, in New York, must place an order with a manufacturer in Detroit before noon. What method of communication should he choose?

3. Your company's sales representative in Seattle must have $100 expense money within twenty-four hours. How can your New York office send it to him in time?

4. A station-to-station long distance call is cheaper than a person-to-person call. Why is a person-to-person call sometimes preferable, in spite of the higher cost?

5. Why is the tone of your voice particularly important in business telephone conversations?

THE most rapid forms of business communication—the telegraph, the cable, the radio, and the telephone—are of utmost importance because of the time element involved. The more important the transaction, the more likely is the use of the most rapid means of communication. It is essential, therefore, that you not only master the information in this section but that you have that information at your finger tips for immediate use in emergencies.

Communication Services Compared. In your work in the Mailing Department you became familiar with the chief means of communication, the postal service. Communication by telegraph, cable, radio, telephone, and other means is described here.

You should understand clearly the relative advantages of the various types of telegraphic and telephonic services in comparison with mail service so as to be able to use each type effectively and economically.

Ordinary Mail. Slower but less expensive than any of the following methods of communication.

Air Mail. Much faster over long distances, weather permitting, than ordinary mail; also, more expensive.

Telegrams and Cablegrams. Faster than air mail; also, more expensive. Straight telegrams and cablegrams can usually be delivered within a few hours. Slower types of telegraphic service, which are cheaper than straight telegrams, are described in subsequent pages of this section.

Telephone Calls. The fastest and most-used type of communication for business purposes. Even long-distance telephone connections can usually be completed in a few minutes after the call is placed. Long-distance calls are much faster than telegraphic service and usually more expensive. The additional expense, however, is often more than offset by the ease, speed, and effectiveness of conversing by telephone.

Time Zones. The purpose of using the telegraph or long-distance telephone is to insure faster delivery of a message than would be possible if the mails were used. When telegraphing or telephoning to distant points, therefore, always take into consideration the differences in time in various parts of the United States, which is

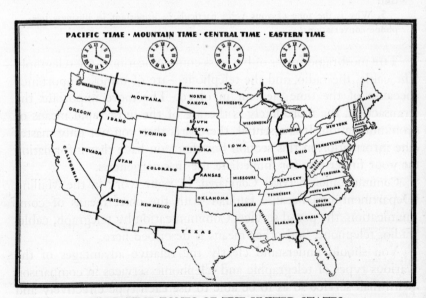

FOUR TIME ZONES OF THE UNITED STATES

divided into four zones; namely, Eastern time, Central time, Mountain time, and Pacific time. The accompanying map shows the territory included in each zone. There is a difference of one hour between zones. Thus when it is 4 P.M. in San Francisco, it is 5 P.M. in Denver, 6 P.M. in Chicago, and 7 P.M. in New York City. Therefore, even the fastest message sent from the West Coast to the East Coast in the late afternoon could not reach its destination until after the usual office closing time.

Daylight saving time, first established in 1916 as a measure to utilize for work as many daylight hours as possible and thus conserve electric power, is generally used only during the summer months starting the end of April and extending through September. It is not used in all cities in the United States except during periods of national emergency. However, when sending messages from one section of the country to another, it is necessary to know whether daylight saving time is used at the receiving end, so that the additional hour may be taken into consideration.

TELEGRAPHIC SERVICES

Types of Messages. Telegrams may be sent to all points in the United States as well as to Mexico, Canada, and Alaska.

Telegram. The straight telegram (sometimes called "a fast wire") is the fastest and highest-priced telegraphic service. It takes precedence over the lower-priced services. The initial rate is based on a minimum of ten words, and there is an extra charge for additional words. Many messages must be longer than the ten-word minimum in order to convey the required information.

Day Letter. The day letter is not quite so fast as the telegram, but it is less expensive for long messages. The time between transmission and delivery is usually about two hours. Be sure to take time zones into consideration when sending day letters to distant cities.

Night Letter. A night letter is deliverable the morning after it is sent. The cost for a minimum of twenty-five words is less than for a ten-word straight telegram. Additional words are charged for in groups of five words. As the wordage increases, the cost per group of five words becomes progressively lower.

COMPARATIVE RATES, NEW YORK TO DENVER

Classification	Rate Based on	Minimum Charge
Straight telegram..................	10 words	$ .99
Day letter........................	50 words	1.49
Night letter......................	25 words	.72

Special Business Services. Several telegraphic services have been developed especially for business purposes.

Serial Messages. An office that sends many telegraphic messages each day to one recipient may save money by requesting the serial rate. In using this rate, all the day's telegrams to one person or concern are charged for as a single long message even though they are sent separately. Each installment must be marked "Ser." If the first installment of the message is sent marked as a serial but no further messages are sent during that day, the first message is charged as a full-rate message.

Serial messages receive the same fast handling as regular telegrams. Each installment of a serial is rated at a minimum of fifteen words, and a minimum charge is made for an aggregate of fifty words in any one day.

Note: The rates quoted do not include taxes. Types of messages and the extent of telegraphic services are subject to governmental curtailment and restrictions during wartime and other national emergencies.

Special Telegraphic Equipment. Special equipment, such as the teleprinter, the teletype, the telautograph, and the automatic telegraph, has been developed to meet the needs of business.

Teleprinter. A company that sends a large volume of telegraphic messages may install a teleprinter in order to do away with the use of messengers. This machine, which resembles an electric typewriter and has a

Above: A TELAUTOGRAPH TRANSMITTER-RECEIVER

Courtesy TelAutograph Corporation

Below: A TELEPRINTER

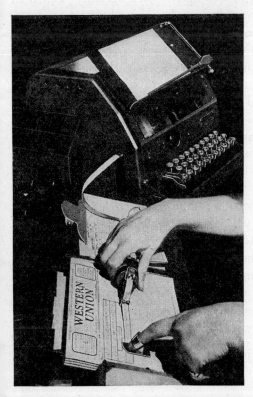

somewhat similar keyboard, sends messages direct to the telegraph office and receives them direct.

The operator simply types the message on the teleprinter. The message appears on a continuous paper tape that emerges from the machine, and the identical message is typed simultaneously on a tape by a machine at the receiving end. The tape is gummed, so that it may be moistened and applied in strips to telegraph blanks. The company operator keeps the pasted-up message to show what was sent. The messages that she receives are delivered immediately to the proper departments or persons.

Teletype. The teletype provides a direct connection with another teletype machine and is used like a private telephone line, except that communication is by means of typed rather than spoken words. The teletype resembles the teleprinter, but teletype messages come from the teletype machine on sheets of paper, not on paper tape.

Telautograph. The telautograph transmits handwriting instantaneously to another department or building. Both sender and receiver have permanent, identical records on a roll of paper. This machine is used in large institutions, such as banks, factories, hotels, and large railroad stations.

Automatic Telegraph. The Telefax, or facsimile telegraph, is a new development that is likely to supplant present telegraphic methods. The automatic telegraph sends exactly what it "sees"; the material may be handwritten or typewritten and may include drawings.

Dictated Telegrams. The secretary should always keep a notebook and pen where they can be picked up and used instantly. When an executive wishes to dictate a telegram, he is in a hurry.

Whenever telegrams are dictated along with letters, during a regular dictation period, they must, without fail, be transcribed first. Use a colored pencil and a paper clip to mark "rush" parts of your shorthand notes for immediate attention. (See pages 36-37.)

Sometimes you may need to ask the dictator at the time of dictation whether he wishes the message to go as a straight wire or at a special rate. When you have questions about the best classification for a certain message, consult your telegraph office for detailed information.

As a secretary, you may have to compose telegraphic messages yourself. Omit unnecessary words, but make sure the meaning is clear. The word "Stop," which used to cause much merriment because of the misunderstandings resulting from its use in telegrams, is no longer required to show the end of a sentence because the telegraph company now transmits periods and other ordinary punctuation marks at no cost to the sender. For the same reason the words "quote" and "unquote" are no longer used.

Here are some suggestions to follow in preparing a telegram:

1. Be sure that everything in it is accurate and legible. Time spent in reading over the message for accuracy is not wasted.

2. Avoid abbreviations. They can be garbled in transmission, and they do not lessen the cost of sending.

3. Be sure to indicate the "Class of Service Desired" in the proper place on the blank telegram form.

4. Use ordinary, sensible punctuation marks. Do not count them as words.

5. Do not divide a word at the end of a line.

6. Telegrams to persons, in care of a company, should preferably be addressed to the company, with the person's name following if desired; for example, a wire for Peter S. Reed, Northwestern Supply Company, should be addressed "Northwestern Supply Company, Peter S. Reed," followed by the street and city address.

7. Indicate whether the message is to be sent "Paid," "Collect," or "Charged." On the copies, but not on the original, place the dictator's and transcriber's initials, as you do on a letter.

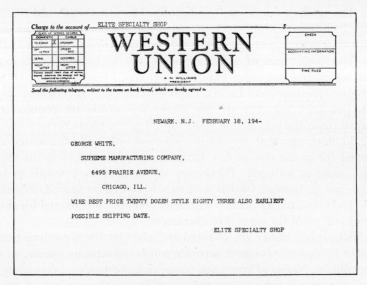

A PROPERLY TYPED TELEGRAM

Carbon Copies. Be sure you know how many copies are to be made of a telegram. Usually, three copies are required. Copy No. 1 goes to the telegraph company (or to the company's teleprinter operator); No. 2 is the file copy (on this copy, type the number of words in the message); and No. 3 is mailed to the addressee as a confirmation. If the company has a charge account with the telegraph company, a fourth copy will be needed by the Accounting Department for checking the telegraph bill. A timesaving hint: cut carbon paper into a convenient size for immediate use with telegram blanks and keep several sets of telegram blanks and carbon sheets assembled in your stationery drawer.

How to Count Words. The following rules govern the counting of words in telegrams:

1. Groups consisting of combinations of letters, figures, and other characters are counted together at the rate of five characters per word.

2. Punctuation marks (period, comma, colon, semicolon, hyphen or dash, question mark, apostrophe, quotation marks, and parentheses) are not counted or charged for.

3. The symbols $ & % # ' (indicating feet or minutes) and " (indicating inches or seconds) are counted as one character in the groups in which they appear. For example, $100 is counted as one word.

4. The single count of words applies only to dictionary words in the eight authorized languages (English, German, French, Italian, Dutch, Portuguese, Spanish, and Latin). Expressions in common commercial or correspondence use that are not dictionary words are counted and charged for at the rate of one word for every five characters.

5. Trade names that are not dictionary words will be counted and charged for at the rate of five letters a word, instead of at the single word count as formerly. Dictionary or nondictionary words in languages not authorized, initials written without being spaced, abbreviations, and mutilated dictionary words are counted and charged for at the rate of one word for every five characters.

6. All proper names are counted and charged for according to the number of separate words, or separate words and separate initials, which they contain. Names of countries, states, cities, towns, etc., consisting of more than one word are counted according to the number of words they contain. Initials in any proper name, or as an abbreviation for a proper name, may be written together without space between and when so written are counted as a letter group at the rate of five letters per word. Periods may be inserted and will not be counted. If initials are spaced, each initial is counted as one word.

Delivery Report. If it is necessary that the sender know whether a message has been delivered, type the words "Report Delivery" conspicuously at the top of the blank. The telegraph company makes a charge for this added service.

Repeat Back. If, for the sake of absolute accuracy, it is desirable for the receiving operator to repeat the message, type "Repeat Back" at the top of the blank. There is a charge for this added service.

Paying for Telegrams. Telegrams may be paid for in these ways:

1. One at a time, when sent.
2. Monthly, through the use of a charge account. In many localities, telephone subscribers may send telegrams by telephone and have the cost of the telegrams included in the regular telephone bill.
3. By the person who receives the message, when the message is sent "collect."

How to Send a Telegram. In most cities, a person wishing to send a telegram may take the message directly to the telegraph office; telephone for a messenger; or telephone the message, having it charged on his telephone bill. The telegraph company will install a "call box" for a person or a concern that sends many messages. By turning a knob or pulling a lever on this mechanism, the operator or secretary notifies the telegraph company that a messenger is wanted.

A CALL BOX FOR SUM-MONING MESSENGER

Tie lines—direct wires from a business office to the telegraph company—are sometimes arranged. They may be operated by telephone, by teleprinter, or by Morse operators.

Telegraphic Money Orders. Money is often sent by telegraphic money order when mail is not fast enough. The sender fills out a money-order application like that illustrated on page 64 and pays the telegraph office the amount of money that is to be sent, plus a

A TELEGRAPHIC MONEY ORDER APPLICATION WITH
MESSAGE

A TELEGRAPHIC MONEY ORDER

fee for the service. At the receiving telegraph office, the designated person can collect the money after showing satisfactory identification. The sender, if he wishes, however, may waive identification. The cost of a telegraphic money order is based on the standard message rate for the distance between the sending point and the point of destination, plus a service charge for handling the money. For an additional charge, a message may be included.

Miscellaneous Telegraphic Services. Except in times of national emergency, Western Union provides uniformed messengers to run errands for a small fee. Special services available in normal times include low-rate greeting messages, the delivery of parcels and flowers, and the performance of other tasks.

CABLEGRAMS AND RADIOGRAMS

For rapid telegraphic communication with countries other than Mexico, Canada, and Alaska, cablegrams or radiograms are used. The cost is the same for these two types of service.

Radiograms may also be sent from a ship to a point on shore and vice versa. The rate is the same as for cable messages transmitted at the full rate.

Types of Cablegrams and Radiograms. The following classifications of service apply to both cablegrams (which are sent over heavy metal cables laid on the ocean floor) and radiograms (which are transmitted by radio).

Full Rate (Ordinary). Plain or cipher language or a combination of both may be used for this class of message. Plain-language words are counted at the rate of fifteen letters to the word; cipher is counted at five letters or five figures to the word.

Code Rate. Code words at this rate must contain no more than five letters. The minimum charge is for five words.

Deferred. Deferred messages must be in a language that can be written in letters of the English alphabet. Code is not allowed in the text, but registered code addresses may be used.

Night Letter. A night letter sent by radio or cable must be written in plain language. It will be delivered on the day after filing.

Addresses. Firms that do much foreign business usually have a one-word registered address, such as "Gregpubco" for the "Gregg Publishing Company." The use of such an address is an economy, because *all* the words, including the address and the signature, are counted when the charge is computed. (This is not true of telegrams.)

Plain Language, Code, and Cipher. Here are some definitions:

Plain language consists of words used with the meaning that they have in the language to which they belong.

Code language consists of real or made-up words not more than five letters long. One word may express a phrase or a sentence. In addition to many private codes used by business firms, several commercial codes exist. Commercial codes are not secret. Their value is in condensation. When a thought can be expressed in a single code word, the sender saves money, because every word counts.

In using commercial code, the appropriate indicating symbol must be included in the preamble of the message. Some of the standard commercial codes and their symbols are as follows:

Name of Code	Symbol
ABC Sixth Edition	ABC
ACME Code and Supplement	ACME
Bentley's Complete Phrase Code	BENCOM
Lombard General Code	LOMGEN
Lombard Shipping Code and Appendix	LOMSHIP
New Standard Half Word Code	STANHAF
New Standard Three Letter Code	STANTER
Peterson's Third Edition	PET

Here are some examples of code words and their meanings:

Word	Meaning
Drake	Draw with bill of lading attached.
Inset	For your private information only.
Islip	Your instructions are having every attention.
Frame	Until further orders.

Cipher language is formed of groups of figures or words having a secret meaning. Words, names, expressions, or letters that do not comply with the conditions of plain language or code language are also considered to be cipher language. Governments use cipher language for secrecy.

How to Send Radiograms and Cablegrams. Special rules govern the sending of radiograms and cablegrams. Secretaries who have occasion to use radio and cable from time to time should study the restrictions and rules with especial care and check carefully with the communications companies when in doubt about any detail. One way in which foreign communications differ from telegrams is that punctuation marks may be included in telegrams at no extra cost, whereas each must be spelled out in a radiogram or cablegram and paid for.

Special instructions for preparing radiograms and cablegrams may be obtained from the communications companies. In times of national emergency, such as the World War, service to civilians is restricted, and many of the rules stated here are not in force.

Radiograms. Firms that send radiograms often may obtain special radiogram blanks like the one illustrated here. Ordinary telegram

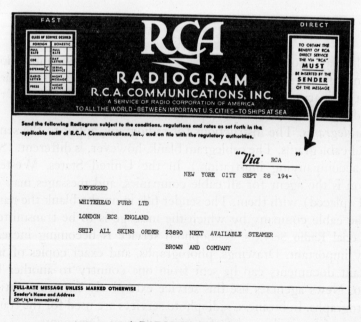

A RADIO MESSAGE

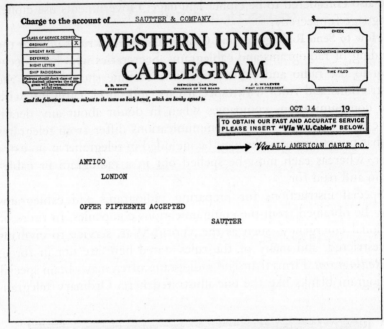

A CABLEGRAM WITH A CODE ADDRESS

blanks may also be used. In cities where R. C. A. Communications has no offices, radiograms may be sent through Western Union. If an ordinary telegram blank is used for sending a radiogram, the words "Via RCA" must be typed on it.

Cablegrams. The instructions for radiograms apply to the sending of cablegrams. The cablegram blank, however, is different. (See the accompanying illustration.) In the United States, Western Union is the agent for all cable companies, and messages may be filed (placed) with them. The sender fills in on the blank the name of the cable company by which the message is to be transmitted.

Special Radio Services. Radiophoto service is becoming increasingly important. Drawings, photographs, and exact copies of important documents can be sent from one country to another by radio. News agencies use this service extensively for transmitting photographs. In business, radiophoto services are used for the transmission of facsimile copies of many important documents.

THE USE OF THE TELEPHONE

The proper use of the telephone will constitute one of your most important secretarial duties. The telephone calls that you handle establish a direct contact between your company or your chief and those with whom business is transacted. Therefore, at this stage of your training, make every effort to master the technique of telephoning.

The Telephone Voice. Your telephone voice may have a great effect on other persons. If you become careless, you may unintentionally sound tired, annoyed, smug, peevish, bored, busy, chilly, brusque, frightened, or even stupid. As no intelligent business employee would intentionally speak in a way that would deserve any of these descriptive adjectives, the conclusion is that most of the obvious defects in telephone voices are unintentional and avoidable.

A person who is interrupted by a telephone call when he is working at a task demanding concentration may sound tired, busy, or annoyed.

Very young employees who are trying hard to seem at home in the office sometimes sound smug, bored, or brusque. A thoughtful person avoids these attitudes.

A timid, inexperienced person, in telephoning, may sound frightened; unfortunately, the same person may also sound stupid. Timid telephoners simply need more telephone practice. If you are one of these, here is a word of comfort: Some personnel men who hire applicants for switchboard operators' jobs say that a timid beginner will develop into a better operator than one who is overconfident.

All these faults may be corrected easily and immediately. They are due to carelessness and lack of realization of the effect of the telephone voice on the person at the other end of the wire.

Keep your voice cheerful and speak distinctly. Here are some suggestions. See also the illustrations on page 54.

1. Lower your voice a little below the usual pitch.
2. Speak only as loudly in telephoning as you do in normal face-to-face conversation.
3. Speak directly into the telephone, with your lips not more than half an inch from the mouthpiece.

4. Pronounce numbers with especial distinctness. Telephone operators are trained to exaggerate the pronunciation of numbers to avoid misunderstanding, but exaggeration is not necessary for telephone users.

5. Be very careful of your speech. Do not use slang. You represent the company.

INCOMING CALLS

Answering the Telephone. Your chief may want you to answer his telephone whenever it rings; learn his wishes in this matter. Find out, also, how he wishes you to answer. Here are some often-used answering phrases: "Mr. Hansen's office," "Mr. Hansen's desk," "Advertising Department." Avoid answering with "Hello" or "Yes." These words waste time because they require further explanation.

If your chief requests you to answer his telephone for him, he will probably also wish you to be able to tell him, when you transfer the call, who is at the other end of the wire. If the calling party does not give you this information at once, ask him. This inquiry must be tactfully phrased, but more important than the phrasing is the intonation you use. Your voice should be warm and helpful. You may use one of these questions: "May I ask who is calling, please?" "May I have your name?" "Who shall I tell him is calling?"

If your voice gives the effect of warmth and graciousness, the calling party will not be annoyed. If there is a hint of brusqueness or of suspicion in your voice when this question is asked, then you need a little more telephone practice. The secret of asking pleasantly is always to raise the voice, not lower it, when asking these questions.

Persons who refuse to identify themselves are usually not important or welcome callers.

Transferring Calls. In a large organization, you are likely to receive calls that can be answered only by someone else. Tell the calling party courteously that you must transfer his call to another person or telephone, and be sure that you transfer it to the proper place. A caller who has to talk to three or four persons before reaching the right one is justified in being annoyed at what may seem to him "passing the buck." One way of phrasing this information would be:

"Mr. Hansen is in another office just now. I'll ask the operator to transfer your call to him there." Then signal the operator and say, "Will you please give this call to Mr. Hansen in the Engineering Department."

Another would be:

"Mr. Hansen is out of town, but Mr. Watkins has that information for you. Just a moment, please." Signal for the operator and say, "Will you transfer this call to Mr. Watkins and tell him that Mr. Alexander would like to know the closing date for bids on the factory addition."

If your chief is not in the office, say, "He isn't in his office just now. May I take a message?" If there is a message, take it at once, in shorthand; and if the message can wait until he returns, put a transcript of it on his desk immediately. If you feel the message is urgent, relay it to him by telephone if you know how to reach him.

If he is in conference—and, cartoons and jokes to the contrary, many conferences are very important and are not to be disturbed —say, "Mr. Hansen is attending a meeting just now. May I take a message for him?"

If your office is separate from his and he wishes you to answer all his calls, you should practice phrasing messages concisely and clearly when you have to ask him whether he wishes to talk to the calling party. Here are some ways of phrasing telephone messages:

Mr. Orrin, of Consolidated Motors, would like to see you this morning. You have no appointment for ten o'clock.

Your daughter will meet you here at five o'clock.

Thomas Malone is on the wire. Can you meet him Wednesday for luncheon at the Statler Hotel?

M E S S A G E
For _Mr. Andrews_
Date _June 2_ 19___ Time _9:15_
Simon Porter
Of _Rogers Peet_
Address_____
Phone No._____
Called on the phone [×]   in person [ ]
Message _The factory has delivered the suit ordered. Come in for fitting any time today or tomorrow._
Received by_____ _A. S. P._

A MESSAGE FORM

A reporter from the *Times-Tribune* would like to see you this afternoon for an interview about the new testing laboratory.

You may communicate such messages in person or by using a direct-wire telephone or a Dictograph if your office has one. (The Dictograph is explained later in this section.)

If your desk is in the same room with your chief's, you may need to cover the transmitter with your hand while you ask him for instructions. In this case, be careful, because the calling party may be able to hear what you say. Do not hold the transmitter against your chest while speaking to your employer, because this will almost certainly enable the calling party to hear you.

Occasionally, a caller will refuse to tell his name or reveal his business with your chief. If you have clear instructions not to put through calls of this kind, all you can do is tell the calling party courteously that you are not permitted to put through calls without having the information for which you are asking.

Much of your secretarial success will depend on the way in which you handle telephone calls. Experience and your own intelligence and increasing understanding of human nature will help you to divide the welcome from the unwelcome callers and to make even the unwelcome callers feel that they have received courteous treatment.

Requests for Information. Be sure that, in your effort to be courteous and obliging, you do not reveal any confidential information to outsiders—and even to insiders.

If you have occasion to quote prices or estimates or to give important information by telephone, you may find it advisable to follow conversations of this kind with a letter of confirmation, so that there will be no question as to what you said.

If it is necessary for you to look up information, make it clear to the caller whether he is to remain on the line, call back, or wait for your call to him. Understanding saves time and tempers. If you cannot obtain the desired information, do your best to help the caller find it.

Personal Calls. Avoid incoming and outgoing personal calls. You have not much control over incoming calls, but you can always remind your friends that you are forbidden to have personal calls if this is the rule in your organization.

OUTGOING CALLS

Most-Used Telephone Numbers. You will find that most of the calls that you and your superior make are to a few numbers. Instead of looking up each number in the directory each time you need it, make an alphabetic index for your own use. This can be a card file, showing names and addresses as well as numbers, or you may use an alphabetically arranged booklet or such a device as is pictured here.

Unlisted Numbers. In the larger cities, many telephone subscribers, especially persons of prominence or those who frequently come in contact with the public, arrange with the telephone company not to have their numbers listed in the telephone directory. Only persons to whom the subscriber has given his number can call it. "Information" will not divulge the number.

Occasionally, a businessman has an unlisted telephone as well as his extension of the company telephone on his desk.

In answering an unlisted telephone, depart from the usual correct business practice of announcing your chief's name. Say rather, "Hello." This will not inform the calling party of the identity of the person being called until you are certain that the call is acceptable.

Using the Directory. Familiarize yourself with the telephone directories available in your office. In small cities, all sections of the directory may be in one book. In larger places, the directory is issued in three parts—the general telephone directory, the suburban telephone directory, and the classified telephone directory. Many offices keep telephone directories of several important cities on file.

The general telephone directory contains the name, the address, frequently the business connection, and the telephone number of every subscriber (except unlisted subscribers), arranged alphabetically by name:

Check Protection Co 3OW54..............Green 9-6129

In locating names, you will save time by referring to the index reference printed in bold type at the top of the directory page. This reference gives the first and last names appearing on the page.

The telephone directory also contains much other valuable information, such as toll charges and definite instructions for telephoning. It is a most useful office reference book because of its list of subscribers' street addresses.

Classified Directory. The classified telephone directory is described in Section 8.

Getting Numbers Through "Information." When you wish to call a number (either local or by long distance) that you cannot find in the telephone directory, call "Information." On dial telephones, a special number is assigned for calling the Information operator. This operator will provide the number desired if you will give her the name and address of the person or firm. (Unlisted private numbers are, of course, an exception.)

This service should not be abused, however. Do not call upon Information for information that you can locate yourself, with a reasonable amount of effort.

Enunciate carefully when talking with Information because a mistake of *b* for *d* when you have asked for a Mr. Darnley's number, for example, will result in her telling you something like this: "There is no telephone listed for Mr. Barnley of South Main Street."

Toll Calls. A toll call is another name for a long-distance call; it is a call made to a telephone outside your community or telephone service area. The charge made for such a call varies with the distance of the called point, the type of service, the time of day, and the length of the call.

There are two kinds of toll calls: station-to-station and person-to-person calls. If you understand the rules governing toll charges, you can expedite your chief's work and save your company money.

Person-to-Person Calls. In placing a toll call, if you ask the operator for a particular person or for a particular extension or department reached through a private switchboard, you will be charged at the person-to-person rate, which is slightly higher than the station-to-station rate. If someone else answers the telephone and the telephone company relays to you a message, such as "Mr. Jones is out of the city," a small report charge may be assessed; but no other charge is made. Person-to-person calls should be chosen when you wish to speak with a certain person and no other.

Station-to-Station Calls. When you give the toll operator the telephone number or address only, you are placing a station-to-station call, on which the charge is lower than for a person-to-person call. This class of service is usually a little faster than person-to-person because there is no delay in having a particular person called to the telephone. No matter who answers, you will be charged for the call. Use this service when it is not necessary to talk with any particular person.

Procedure for Making Out-of-Town Calls. To determine which out-of-town calls should be placed with the local operator and which with "Long Distance," consult the information pages of your local telephone directory.

On a nondial telephone, place the call with the local operator or ask for "Long Distance." (Your directory will tell you which procedure to follow in each of these cases.) State the details of the call clearly and at a moderate speed so as to give the operator time to record the information you give her.

The operator will ask for the following information:

1. The city you are calling.
2. The telephone number and the person's name. (In placing a station-to-station call, say "Anyone" in place of the person's name.)
3. If you do not know the telephone number, give the firm name or the name of the telephone subscriber and the street address.
4. The number of the telephone from which you are calling.

You may be asked to hold the line until the call is completed. If the call covers a very long distance, the operator may tell you that she will call you back.

If you wish to find out immediately the cost of a toll call, without waiting for the monthly bill to come through, say to the operator as soon as you have given her the information mentioned above, "Quote charges, please." She will then give you this information when you have finished your long-distance conversation.

If a long-distance operator tells you her number, remember it and ask for her by number if you must call her back while the call is being put through.

The following examples show how to give the details of the various kinds of out-of-town calls.

Station-to-Station Calls. You wish to call the Walton Hardware Company, 417 Appleton Avenue, Asbury Park, New Jersey. You are willing to talk with anyone who may answer.

1. If you know the telephone number, place the call this way: "Asbury Park, New Jersey, 9971."

2. If you do not know and cannot find out the number, place the call in this manner: "Asbury Park, New Jersey. Anyone at the Walton Hardware Company, 417 Appleton Avenue."

Person-to-Person Calls. You have business with the Walton Hardware Company that can be transacted only with Herbert Walton.

1. Use this phraseology if you know the number: "Asbury Park, New Jersey, 9971. Herbert Walton."

2. Place the call in this way if you do not know the number: "Asbury Park, New Jersey, the Walton Hardware Company, 417 Appleton Avenue. Herbert Walton."

Reversing the Charge for Toll Calls (Calling Collect). The calling party is charged for his toll call at the time that he makes the call. The charge, however, may be reversed—that is, the called party may be charged—upon the request of the calling party. The toll operator will not make the connection for a collect call until she has obtained the consent of the party called. To reverse the charges, say "Collect" before giving the other details described in the foregoing paragraphs. Salesmen sometimes call the home office collect in order to report or ask for instructions.

Putting Through a Call. The time of everyone concerned is saved when executives place their own telephone calls. More and more executives are making this a practice. If the custom in your office requires you to place your superior's calls for him, however, be sure that he is ready to talk when you get the called party on the line.

If he says, "Get Watson for me at the First National," and then is called out of the room, it is advisable to wait before taking action. Upon his return, ask him whether he is ready to talk to Mr. Watson. If he is, place the call.

The person who initiates a call should be ready to talk before the called person answers. The secretary who is placing a call will usually say to the answering secretary, "Mr. Blank is calling Mr. Watson. Is he busy?"

Telephoning a Message. When you are asked to telephone a message, put the call through as usual. When you have reached the proper person, say, "This is Mr. William J. Brown's secretary. Mr. Brown has asked me . . ." and so on.

Obtaining Information. When you are instructed to ask for information, be sure that you know exactly what you are to find out. State your request clearly and briefly, and obtain all the information so that you will not need to call again for further details. Do not forget to thank the person from whom you obtained the information.

When you must obtain information from a large firm and do not know what department to ask for, you will probably have to state your question to the switchboard operator and then to one or two other persons before you reach the right one. This repetition becomes annoying, but all you can do is be patient about it.

When answering incoming calls that are made under similar circumstances, remember your own experience and do all you can to help the inquiring person obtain his information without wasting time.

The Office Switchboard. Many firms have their own private telephone switchboards. Such a switchboard is known as a PBX board, meaning "private branch exchange."

There are two

Underwood & Underwood

A CORD-STYLE PBX BOARD

A CORDLESS PBX BOARD
Often the switchboard operator also
acts as receptionist

Keystone View Company

types of PBX boards, the cord and the cordless. The cordless type is often used when the number of extensions is small.

A PBX operator is often expected to perform various clerical tasks and typing jobs while sitting at the switchboard. It is not uncommon for a PBX operator to act also as receptionist and to receive and send telegrams on a teleprinter.

The private telephone lines within the company, which connect with the PBX, are known as "extensions."

Incoming Calls. The PBX operator answers all incoming calls and, after ascertaining the person or extension number desired, makes the necessary connection.

Outgoing Calls. Some companies keep a record of all outgoing calls. In such cases, the calling employee tells the PBX operator what number he wishes, and the operator places the call with the main switchboard of the telephone company.

In other organizations, the employee says "Outside" when the

PBX operator comes on the line. After the outside connection has been made, the calling employee gives the number to the telephone company operator himself.

Inside Calls. When an employee calls another extension within the organization, the PBX operator makes the connection through her own board, and the call does not reach the telephone company.

The secretary should know how to operate a PBX, as it may be necessary to make or answer calls when the regular switchboard operator is off duty.

Interoffice Communications. In some business organizations, the Dictograph system is the means of communicating between offices. This system is a variation of the telephone extension system, the difference being that it is an independent system, thus leaving the switchboard clear for incoming and outgoing calls. Instant contact can be made with any and all departments at the same time by the pressure of a key. A conference may be held and business involving several departments may be dispatched quickly without requiring anyone to leave his desk.

Courtesy Dictograph Sales Corp.

A DICTOGRAPH WITH TELEPHONE ATTACHMENT FOR PRIVACY

ANSWERS TO "Do You Know?"

1. Two telegrams will be required, the first asking for the information and the second giving it. Telephoning would be more expensive.

2. A telephone call could be completed within the time limit specified, but a telegram might not be delivered within that time.

3. Send the money by telegraph. No other method would achieve the purpose over so great a distance within the time available.

4. If you must speak with a particular person and yet put in a station-to-station call, you pay for the call even though you fail to reach your party.

5. Because your facial expression cannot be seen in telephoning, your voice has to carry the whole burden of expressing good will.

Courtesy The Shaw-Walker Co.

A CENTRAL FILING DEPARTMENT

In the offices of this company all requests for filed material are received at the service counter. Persons from outside the Filing Department do not have access to the files. Floor space is saved by the use of five-drawer files

5

THE CENTRAL FILING DEPARTMENT

DO YOU KNOW?

1. You have been given correspondence from A. Smith, Albert Smith, and A. Benson Smith to file. In what order should the letters be filed?

2. The signature on a letter you are to file is "Sister Marguerite." Will you file it under S or under M?

3. You are filing letters by "subject." You have received a letter covering several subjects. What will you do?

4. In reading over one of the letters you are to file, you find that it is to be brought to the attention of the personnel manager at the end of the month. What will you do?

5. The sales manager requests a piece of correspondence. Before you take it to him, you prepare an "out" card. What will you do with it?

NEARLY every business transaction is initiated by correspondence of one type or another. The correspondence may be received through the mail—an order, an inquiry, a telegram, or a bill; it may be interoffice correspondence; it may be a penciled memorandum from an executive to his secretary. Such correspondence becomes the written record of the activities of the business and is often referred to even after the work it initiates has been completed.

The problem of storing a vast amount of important data over a period of years and of arranging the material so that a single piece of correspondence may be located with dispatch when needed has brought about the development of modern filing methods. Filing is simply a system of properly classifying all business data and records and of placing them in receptacles where they may be referred to with precision. Filing may be compared with other conveniences with which we already are familiar; for example, the dictionary is a filing system for words, telephone and city directories are filing systems for names, and public libraries are filing places for books.

The complexity of the filing problem in any office depends on the size of the organization and the nature of the business. The tendency, in large organizations especially, is to have records filed in a centralized department, by file clerks selected for their liking for detail, sense of orderliness, analytical type of mind, and willingness to serve. Separate files are often maintained, however, for individual executives and departments. The secretary to an executive or to a department head usually has charge of such files.

FILING EQUIPMENT AND SUPPLIES

Filing Cabinets. Correspondence and other papers that are to be filed are placed first in folders, to prevent the material from becoming torn and wrinkled and to permit convenient grouping of small units of the material; then the folders are filed on edge in the drawers of filing cabinets. Such cabinets are called "vertical" filing cabinets.

The most commonly used cabinet contains four drawers, one above another. For special purposes, however, other arrangements are available—five-drawer cabinets are desirable when floor space is at a premium; a row of three-drawer cabinets forms a convenient counter; and two-drawer cabinets are sometimes used beside a desk. Most cabinets stand on a base, which raises the lower drawers to a convenient working height.

Cabinets are made of wood or of steel and in various finishes—

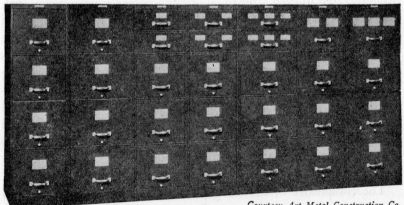

Courtesy Art Metal Construction Co.

A BATTERY OF FILES RANGING FROM CARD SIZE TO JUMBO SIZE

olive-green, oak, ma-
hogany, or walnut—
to harmonize with
other office equip-
ment.

The drawers come
in standard widths
according to the
type of material to
be filed—letter, le-
gal, bill, check, and
several card sizes.

To be satisfac-
tory, a file drawer
must be easy to pull
out and close and
yet must remain se-

Courtesy Art Metal Construction Co.

A FILE DRAWER SHOWING FOLLOWER BLOCK

curely closed when shut. The drawers of confidential files are provided with locks.

The contents of each drawer are marked on the outside on a
label provided for that purpose.

Inside the drawer, toward the back, is a compressor block, or
follower block. This block may be moved forward to make the
contents of an unfilled drawer more compact and to keep the folders standing upright. The block may be moved backward to provide additional space when the material expands.

File Folders. For ordinary purposes, folders made of manila or
kraft are durable enough. For valuable papers to be kept for a
long time, folders made of leatheroid or pressboard are preferred.

The back edge of a folder usually has a projection, or tab, on
which a number, a letter, or a name may be placed, according to
the needs of the filing system being used. Because it is difficult to
insert a folder in a typewriter, the information that is to appear on
the tabs is typewritten on gummed labels, which are pasted on the
tabs. These labels come in perforated strips or rolls. Different colors
may be used for different purposes; for example, buff labels may
denote wholesale customers and white labels retailers.

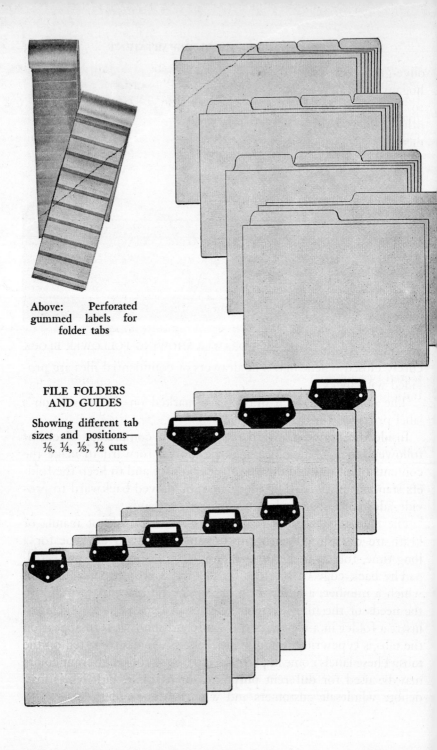

Above: Perforated gummed labels for folder tabs

FILE FOLDERS AND GUIDES

Showing different tab sizes and positions— ⅕, ¼, ⅓, ½ cuts

Folders are variously cut so that the tabs will fall in different positions, as shown in the accompanying illustration. In a five-position arrangement, for example, the tabs on five folders will fall at five different positions across the width of the file drawer, thus aiding visibility. In this arrangement, the tabs are described as "one-fifth cut." Similarly, the tabs in a three-position arrangement are referred to as "one-third cut," and so on.

At the bottom of the front flap of the folder is a scored line (sometimes there are two, three, or more scorings). The flap of the folder may be bent at these scorings, thus forming a flat base for the folder and preventing the folder from buckling.

Guides. Guides are stiff cards, usually of pressboard, which are inserted between groups of folders to aid in filing and finding and to prevent the folders from slipping.

Each guide has a tab, or projection, on which appears the division of the alphabet or some other notation, depending on the filing system in use. These guide tabs are cut to fall in various positions, like the tabs on the folders. The tab projections are usually protected by celluloid or by a metal rim. See the accompanying illustration.

Methods of Filing. There are three basic methods of filing:

1. Alphabetically according to the name of the correspondent—called *name filing*.
2. Alphabetically according to the name of a place (state, city, county)—called *geographic filing*.
3. Alphabetically according to the subject of the correspondence—called *subject filing*.[1]

The nature of the material to be filed and the use to be made of the material determine which filing method is best adapted to the particular business.

In each method, note that material is arranged alphabetically. Alphabeting is the basic process in filing. You must, therefore, first be sure that you are thoroughly familiar with the standard order of the letters of the alphabet—that you do not have to stop to think whether *r* comes before or after *t*, for example.

[1] Some authorities consider numerical filing a fourth basic method, but in this text it is treated under subject filing.

NAME FILING

Probably 90 per cent of office filing is according to names. This method is the simplest of all filing methods. If you understand it thoroughly and can apply the rules you are about to study, you will be able to operate the files in almost any office in which you may work. Refer to the illustration on page 87 while reading this description.

Guides. The first feature of the name filing system to become acquainted with is the system of guides. The tabs of the guides appear at the left side of the file drawer. Sometimes the tabs are staggered in two or three positions to the left.

The tabs bear the divisions of the alphabet and may range in number from 25 for a small file to 10,000 for an extensive file. Names are not distributed evenly over the alphabet; for example, 51 per cent of the names in a normal file would begin with *B, C, H, M, S,* and *W.* Therefore, these letters require many more subdivisions than do other letters.

The assignment of the subdivisions is done by experts employed by the equipment manufacturers and is based on a wide knowledge of names. To show how these divisions vary with the size of the file, here are the divisions for the two letters *A* and *B* in files of 25, 30, 40, 60, and 125 divisions:

25 Divisions	30 Divisions	40 Divisions	60 Divisions	125 Divisions
A	A	A	A	A
B	B	B	Am	Al
	Bi	Bi	B	Am
		Br	Be	Ar
			Bi	B
			Br	Bar
			Bu	Be
				Ben
				Bi
				Bl
				Bo
				Br
				Bro
				Bu
				Bur

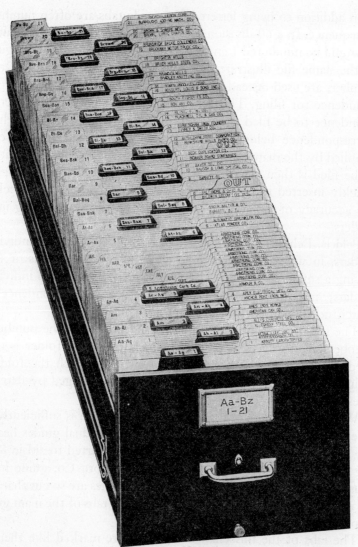

Courtesy Yawman and Erbe Mfg. Co.

A DIRECT-NAME FILE

In addition to being lettered, the guide tabs are often numbered in sequence. In a 60-division file, for example, the first guide under *A* would be numbered 1 and the last guide under Z, 60. The guides in the name file illustrated are numbered. In many offices, these numbers are used instead of letters of the alphabet to "code" correspondence for filing. The file clerk places on each piece of correspondence to be filed the number of the guide behind which the correspondence belongs. This number is obtained from a chart supplied by the manufacturer of the filing equipment. The material to be filed is then arranged in numerical order, and each paper is quickly inserted in its proper position. Coding acts as a check on the accuracy of alphabeting and speeds up the actual filing in the folders.

Folders. Behind each guide are two types of folders—individual folders, in which are filed papers for individual persons or firms having a sufficient amount of correspondence to require individual folders; and miscellaneous folders, to hold correspondence for which no individual folders have been provided.

The tab of an individual folder bears the letter (the number, if numbers are used) of the guide behind which the folder is to be filed and the name of the person or firm to which the folder is assigned. Inside these folders, the papers are arranged by date, the latest on top.

When correspondence with a person or a firm is sufficiently active to require several individual folders, individual guides bearing the name of the correspondent are usually inserted to aid in locating material quickly. (See the Armstrong Cork Co. guide in the illustration.) The tabs of these individual guides are so cut that they do not fall at the same positions at which the tabs of the main guides appear.

The tabs of the miscellaneous folders are marked like their respective guide tabs. Miscellaneous material is filed in alphabetic order in these folders. Usually an individual folder is prepared as soon as five or six papers accumulate for any one name.

Determining the Name under Which to File. The selection of the name under which any piece of correspondence is to be filed is the most important operation in filing, for upon this selection depends the quickness with which a piece of correspondence may be located should it be required. Remember—the purpose of filing is finding. The technical term for this process of name selection is "indexing."

The name that should be chosen may be the name in the letter-head, as it often is for incoming letters; it may be a name in the inside address, as it often is for carbon copies of outgoing mail; or it may be some name that is mentioned in the body of the letter. In other words, the selection cannot be made blindly without considering the subject matter of the letter.

Of course the secretary is already familiar with outgoing mail (carbon copies) that she files because she has written the letters. Other letters must be quickly scanned in order to select the important name. This does not mean that each word in a letter must be read, however.

It is not possible to give exact rules for choosing the names under which correspondence should be filed. The following suggestions will be found helpful in many cases, however:

1. Correspondence relating to business with a company is filed under the name of that company, not under the name of the employee with whom the correspondence is carried on.

2. Personal letters are filed under the name of the person with whom the correspondence is carried on, not under the name of the company that employs him.

3. Interoffice correspondence about a *specific* matter is filed according to the subject matter of the memorandum. With interoffice correspondence about *general* matters, the department that receives the original letter files it under the name of the department from which it came; the department that wrote the letter files the carbon copy under the name of the department to which it is addressed.

Cross References. If it seems probable that the correspondence may be sought under more than one name, then the correspondence should be filed under what seems to be the most important name and a cross reference sheet made out for the other names.

A cross reference is a device that refers anyone who may consult the file to another heading for part of or all the material. A cross-reference sheet is shown on page 90.

Cross references are also used when a company changes its name;

when a company
is referred to by a
shortened name or
a nickname; when
a name is unusual,
so that correct
reference to it
might be uncer-
tain; or when a
name is spelled in
several ways.

**A CROSS-REFER-
ENCE SHEET**

*Courtesy The Shaw-
Walker Co.*

CROSS REFERENCE SHEET

Name or Subject _Office Specialties Co., Fargo, North Dakota_

SEE

Name or Subject _Gaffaney's Office Specialties Co._

_____Fargo, North Dakota_____

Date____4/1/4-_____

Correspondence preceding_____July 1, 194-_____

Filed

___Office Specialties Co._____

An incoming letter:

STRONG & EDWARDS REALTY COMPANY

365 Madison Street, Brooklyn 15, N. Y.

April 10, 194–

Mr. Edward Blunt
    85 Main Street
        Waterville, Maine
Dear Mr. Blunt:
    We have had an inquiry regarding farms in your section of New England;
and our good friend, Mr. Thomas Sloan, of this city, has suggested that you
might be able to locate just the property we seek.
    Our client wishes a small house in good repair, with modern conveniences,
and a small acreage—just large enough for one man to work with comparative
ease. He is interested in a property valuation of about $3,000.

Sincerely yours,
(*Signed*) Philip Strong

Two Specimen Letters. To illustrate the application of these principles of name selection in filing, consider the preceding letter and the following interoffice memorandum.

In Mr. Blunt's office, this letter, with the carbon copy of Mr. Blunt's reply attached to it, should be filed under "Strong & Edwards Realty Company," not under "Philip Strong."

Also, a cross-reference sheet should be made out for Thomas Sloan.

An outgoing interoffice memorandum:

Mar. 1, 19—

To: Chicago Office
From: D. C. Hurd
Subject: Vacations

Henceforth, all offices of the Company are to observe the same rules regarding employees' vacations.

1. The normal vacation season is from June 1 to September 30. This does not mean that it is compulsory that vacations be taken during this period, but this time is established for the purpose of this procedure.

2. Whoever, on July 1, shall have been in our service continuously for a period of one year shall be entitled to a vacation of two weeks with pay; and whoever on the date shall have been in our service continuously for six months or more, but for less than one year, shall be entitled to a vacation of one week with pay.

3. Anyone whose length of service does not entitle him to a vacation with pay may take a vacation at his own expense if approved by the department head.

4. When a pay day falls within a vacation, the pay check due on such pay day may be paid to the member before he departs on his vacation.

5. Employees who resign their positions or who are dismissed before obtaining their vacations, but after the start of the vacation season, shall not be entitled to receive vacation pay. When members who would be entitled to a vacation are laid off or dismissed for any reason, the organization may at its discretion give them one week's pay in lieu thereof.

D. C. Hurd
Personnel Manager

In the Chicago office, this memorandum would be filed under "Personnel Manager." If a subject file is maintained, a cross reference would doubtless be made to "Vacations."

RULES FOR ALPHABETING NAMES

The next step in learning to file is to become acquainted with the rules for arranging names alphabetically.

In most alphabetic name files, papers are filed according to the exact spelling of the name. *Cain* would be filed under *C* and *Kane* under *K*, for example. (But see page 97 for a description of the Soundex system.) The following simple rules should be mastered. They are applicable to both large and small files.[1]

NAMES OF PERSONS

1. Arrange personal names in strict alphabetic sequence, considering the surname as the first unit, the given name or first initial as the second unit, and the middle name or middle initial as the third unit.

1st Unit	2d Unit	3d Unit
Cass	Edward	L.
Cassidy	Albert	F.
Johnson	S.	Frank
Johnston	E.	Philip

A hyphened surname is considered as the first unit.

Name	1st Unit	2d Unit	3d Unit
J. Leonard Merritt	Merritt	J.	Leonard
Edward S. Merritt-Smith	Merritt-Smith	Edward	S.

2. File each name according to the exact sequence of its letters; as:

Bryan	Scarlett
Burns	Scartella
Byrnes	Scartly

3. File nothing before something; that is, in a group of the same surname, file names that have only an initial as the second unit before those that have a given name starting with that same initial; as:

Fernald
Fernald, A.
Fernald, Andrew

Also, in a group of surnames that are otherwise identical in spelling, but some of which have and some do not have a final *e*, a final doubled letter, and so on, "file nothing before something."

Clark	Curtis
Clarke	Curtiss
Clarkson	Curtissville

[1] Accurately speaking, of course, the correspondence or cards are filed, not the names. For simplicity's sake, however, these rules give directions for "filing" names.

4. Disregard all titles and designations in filing personal names.

Name	1st Unit	2d Unit	3d Unit
Professor John H. Howard	Howard	John	H.
Dr. Leslie Upjohn	Upjohn	Leslie	

If necessary in order to make it possible to distinguish between two otherwise identical names, however, such designations may sometimes be considered.

Jones, Robert R. (Jr.)
Jones, Robert R. (Sr.)

Note: In typing names for a card index, however, any titles and designations are included, in parentheses.

Madden, William (Captain)

Where the title and only one name are given or where the surname is omitted, file under the title.

Name	1st Unit	2d Unit	3d Unit
Duke of Gloucester	Duke	Gloucester	
Father Riordan	Father	Riordan	
Sister Mary Celeste	Sister	Mary	Celeste

The legal name of a married woman—as (*Mrs.*) *Mary Ann Blair* or (*Mrs.*) *Mary Davis Blair*—is the one considered in filing.

Name	1st Unit	2d Unit	3d Unit
Mary Ann Blair	Blair	Mary	Ann
Mary Davis Blair	Blair	Mary	Davis

The husband's name may be cross-referenced.

Blair, S. C. (Mrs.)
See: Blair, Mary Ann (Mrs.)
or   See: Blair, Mary Davis (Mrs.)

5. Treat abbreviations as if they were spelled out. (*Wm.* should be filed as *William; St. John* as *Saint John.*)

6. Treat a surname containing a prefix as if the name were one word. Some prefixes are *De, de, d', le, l', Mac, Mc, O', St., Ten, van,* and *Von.* Arrange such names in their logical alphabetic order.

De Castro
de Land
d'Esopo

Mabry
MacCord
Madden
McAfee
Melvin

NAMES OF COMPANIES

7. When a company name includes a given name as well as a surname, select the surname as the first unit and the given name as the second unit. Names of companies that include a surname but no given name are filed as written.

Name	1st Unit	2d Unit	3d Unit
Clifford Hedges Company	Hedges	Clifford	Company
Hedges Company	Hedges	Company	
John Hedges Company	Hedges	John	Company

8. File coined or trade names as written. (*Ye Olde English Inn* should be filed under *Y*.)

9. When a firm name is composed of initials, each initial is considered as a unit.

Name	1st Unit	2d Unit	3d Unit	4th Unit
A C Spark Plug Co.	A	C	Spark	Plug
AWR Drapery Supply Co.	A	W	R	Drapery
Alice Aaquist	Aaquist	Alice		

Each letter of the name of a radio station is considered as a unit. This rule is simply an application of Rule 3.

10. The words *a, an, the, and* (&) are disregarded in filing.

Name	1st Unit	2d Unit	3d Unit
The Mercury Fan Company	Mercury	Fan	Company
Stevens & Company	Stevens	Company	

Note: If *The* is spelled with a capital (indicating that it is a part of the corporate title), the word is enclosed in parentheses in typing such names on cards or in lists.

Mercury Fan Company (The)

11. Names containing numerals are filed as if the numeral were spelled out in words.

Name	1st Unit	2d Unit	3d Unit	4th Unit
33 Church Street Building	Thirty Three	Church	Street	Building

12. In filing names containing a possessive, disregard the letter following the apostrophe. (This rule applies to the singular possessive principally, because the regular plural possessive is formed by adding the apostrophe to the plural form.)

Name	1st Unit	2d Unit	3d Unit
The Boys' Clothing Co.	Boys	Clothing	Company
Children's Wear, Inc.	Children	Wear	Inc.
Gould's Book Shop	Gould	Book	Shop

13. Names that contain abbreviations are treated as if the words were spelled in full.

Name	1st Unit	2d Unit	3d Unit	4th Unit
N. J. Laundry Service	New	Jersey	Laundry	Service
N. D. Advertising Co.	North	Dakota	Advertising	Company
Y. W. C. A.	Young	Women's	Christian	Association

14. Each name in a hyphened firm name is considered as a unit when the names do not contain a given name.

Name	1st Unit	2d Unit	3d Unit
Hill-Cannon & Co.	Hill	Cannon	Company

When hyphened firm names do contain a given name, the hyphened name is considered as one unit and the given name or names as the second and third units.

Name	1st Unit	2d Unit	3d Unit
Walter Hill-Cannon & Co.	Hill-Cannon	Walter	Company

15. When a name contains a word that is sometimes spelled as one word and sometimes as two words, the word is treated as one unit.

Name	1st Unit	2d Unit	3d Unit
Northeast Fisheries	Northeast	Fisheries	
North East Fuel Co.	North East	Fuel	Company

NAMES OF INSTITUTIONS, GOVERNMENTAL UNITS, MISCELLANEOUS

16. Names of hotels, schools, hospitals, libraries, and similar institutions should be filed under their distinctive titles if they have them.

Name	1st Unit	2d Unit
Hotel Astor	Astor	Hotel
Harvard University	Harvard	University
Morgan Library	Morgan	Library

But if such institutions lack a distinctive title, the names should be filed under the location.

Name	1st Unit	2d Unit	3d Unit
Public Library, Newark	Newark	Public	Library
University of Michigan	Michigan	University	
High School, Canton, Ohio	Canton	High	School

17. In filing material from various departments, bureaus, offices, and other subdivisions of the Federal, state, and city governments, the name of the government is considered as the first unit.

Name	1st Unit	2d Unit	3d Unit	4th Unit
Dept. of Education, State of Connecticut	Connecti-cut	State	Education	
New York City Police Department	New	York	City	Police
United States Weather Bureau	United	States	Weather	

Note that in compound geographic names each word is considered as a unit.

Name	1st Unit	2d Unit
New York	New	York
North Dakota	North	Dakota

18. In filing identical names with different addresses, the name is considered first and then the city.

Name	1st Unit	2d Unit	3d Unit	4th Unit
Montgomery Ward & Co., Atlanta	Montgomery	Ward	Company	Atlanta
Montgomery Ward & Co., Birmingham	Montgomery	Ward	Company	Birmingham
Montgomery Ward & Co., Charleston	Montgomery	Ward	Company	Charleston

19. In filing bank names, the city is considered as the first unit because of the great number of bank names beginning with identical words.

Name	1st Unit	2d Unit	3d Unit	4th Unit
First National Bank, Chester, Pa.	Chester	First	National	Bank
First National Bank, Flint, Mich.	Flint	First	National	Bank
First National Bank, Lansing, Mich.	Lansing	First	National	Bank

Variations in Name Filing Systems. When you start your filing work in the office, you may encounter some features in the name filing system in use that have not been described here. Each manufacturer of filing equipment naturally incorporates in his product certain distinctive features. By consulting his literature, you will understand how to make the best use of the equipment. Some varieties of the name filing systems are the Direct-Name, the Variadex, and the Tailor-Made systems.

Soundex System. The Soundex name filing system is entirely different from other name filing systems. It brings together in one group all names with similar sounds but different spellings. There are, for example, thirty-six ways to spell "Baer." "Baher" and "Beyer" are two of the ways. In the standard alphabetic name file, these two names would be widely separated— one in the *Ba*'s and the other in the *Be*'s. In the Soundex system they would appear in the same group.

Soundex counteracts

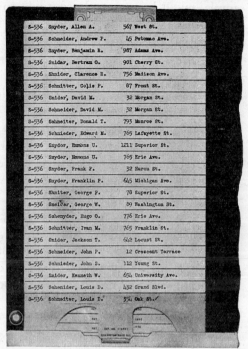

Courtesy Remington Rand, Inc.

INDEX TO A SOUNDEX FILE

many of the more common mistakes in spelling names and in the misreading of handwriting.

Case records filed by Soundex brought to light the fact that public aid was being paid to both Davalsky and Dybolsky, two ways of spelling the name of one man.

This system of filing is used extensively where records contain many names. Hospitals, insurance companies, welfare agencies, public utilities, and branches of the Government use this system. The vast name file required for Social Security records is so arranged, by this method, that the record for any person can be located in less than a minute.

FILING BY PLACE

In some businesses, geographic location is more important than names for filing purposes. The files of a sales organization, for example, might be arranged according to the location of the branch offices or salesmen's territories. Mailing lists are invariably arranged by location because postal regulations require second- and third-class matter to be sorted by states before it is delivered to the post office. Real-estate offices arrange material pertaining to a town by street or lot number. Public-utility files and many Government files are arranged geographically.

Geographic files are most commonly arranged either by state or by town. When the arrangement is by states, the state names, which appear on the main guides, are arranged alphabetically—*Alabama*, *Arizona*, *Arkansas*, and so on. Usually the state names appear on the first-position guides.

The town and city names are arranged alphabetically behind the state names. In some systems of filing, the town and city names appear on the second-position guides; in other systems, in two or three positions. Within each town or city, the names of firms in that locality are arranged, again alphabetically. For example:

> ILLINOIS
>> Abington
>> Alton
>> Belleville
>> Cairo
>>> Atwood Lumber Co.
>>> Tideman Electric Mfg. Co.

As in name filing, individual folders are assigned to active correspondents, and miscellaneous correspondence is placed in miscellaneous folders. The tabs of folders usually fall at the right side of the drawer. (See the accompanying illustration.)

Sometimes, geographic files are arranged alphabetically by name of city or town, regardless of the state name, and then alphabetically by firm name; thus:

> **ABERDEEN** (South Dakota)
>> Adams & Brown
>> Jones Bros.
>> Mason Can Company
> **ABILENE** (Kansas)
>> Carr, L. J.
>> Johnson Wagon Co.
>> Williams Bros.

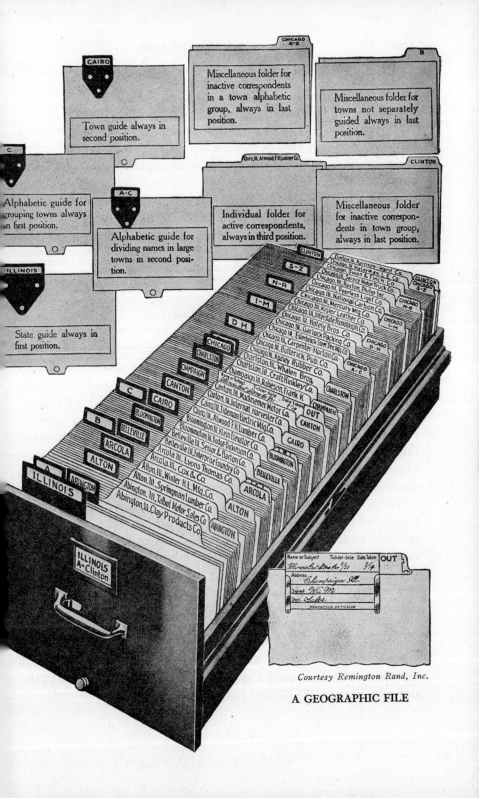

Labels visible in the illustration:

- CAIRO — Town guide always in second position.
- Miscellaneous folder for inactive correspondents in a town alphabetic group, always in last position.
- Miscellaneous folder for towns not separately guided always in last position.
- C — Alphabetic guide for grouping towns always in first position.
- A-C — Alphabetic guide for dividing names in large towns in second position.
- Individual folder for active correspondents, always in third position.
- Miscellaneous folder for inactive correspondents in town group, always in last position.
- ILLINOIS — State guide always in first position.

Card/tab labels within the drawer:

CLINTON · S-Z · N-R · I-M · D-H · CHICAGO · CHARLSTON · CHAMPAIGN · CANTON · C · CAIRO · B · BLOOMINGTON · BELLEVILLE · ARCOLA · ALTON · A · ABINGTON · ILLINOIS

CLINTON · CHICAGO S-Z · CHICAGO N-R · CHICAGO I-M · CHICAGO D-H · CHICAGO A-C · CHARLSTON · CHAMPAIGN · OUT · CANTON · CAIRO · BLOOMINGTON · BELLEVILLE · ARCOLA · ALTON · ABINGTON

Clinton, Ill. Harrison-Ward L. E. Co.
Chicago, Ill. Waterman L E Co.
Chicago, Ill. Swan & Finch Co.
Chicago, Ill. Service Motor Truck Co.
Chicago, Ill. Ruxton Philip Inc.
Chicago, Ill. Peerless Light Co.
Chicago, Ill. National Carbon Co.
Chicago, Ill. Mercury Mfg. Co.
Chicago, Ill. Kisler Leather Co.
Chicago, Ill. Interstate Phonograph Co.
Chicago, Ill. Hotely Bros Co.
Chicago, Ill. Garlock Packing Co.
Chicago, Ill. Esterbrook Steel Pen Mfg Co.
Chicago, Ill. Carpenter-Morton Co.
Chicago, Ill. Butlerick Pub. Co.
Chicago, Ill. Apsley Rubber Co.
Charlston, Ill. Whalen Bros.
Champaign, Ill. Craft Hinkley Co.
Champaign, Ill. Robeson, Frank K.
Canton, Ill. Mackmemer Motor Co.
Canton, Ill. Internat Harvester Co.
Cairo, Ill. Tideman Electric Mfg Co.
Cairo, Ill. Atwood F. H. Lumber Co.
Bloomington, Ill. Klein Elevator Co.
Bloomington, Ill. Bodge-Dickinson Co.
Belleville, Ill. Senior & Barton Co.
Belleville, Ill. Enterprise foundry Co.
Arcola, Ill. Lyons Thomas Co.
Alton, Ill. Cox & Co.
Alton, Ill. Winter H. L. Mfg. Co.
Abington, Ill. Springman Lumber Co.
Abington, Ill. Talbot Motor Sales Co.
Abington, Ill. Clay Products Co.

ILLINOIS A-Clinton

Name or Subject · Tickler date · Date Taken · OUT
Illinois Est. Store Co. 7/21 · 9/4
Address · Champaign Ill.
Signed · H. C. M.
Dept. · Sales
REQUISITION OR TICKLER

A GEOGRAPHIC FILE

ADAMS   (Massachusetts)
         Hubb Sport Shop
         Nelson & Nelson
         Pratt Jewelry Store

When there are two or more towns of the same name in different states, the town folders are filed in the alphabetic order of their respective state names.

Geographic filing supplies have not been standardized to the same degree that alphabetic filing supplies have, largely because the individual requirements of firms vary so widely.

Cross references in geographic filing are handled in the same way as in name filing.

SUBJECT FILING

Sometimes the subject matter of correspondence is more important than the names or the locations of the correspondents. This is true commonly for office memorandums, interbranch correspondence, and the correspondence of various executives who are responsible for and deal chiefly with matters of policy. Such correspondence is usually filed by the subject filing method. Printed matter—reports, pamphlets, clippings, surveys, speeches, for example—is often filed by the subject filing method; and in some subject files, correspondence and printed matter are filed in the same file.

Subject-matter filing is the most advanced—and the most interesting—of all types of filing. To set up a subject file, a person must not only understand the operating procedure of the particular business but must have a broad general knowledge of related fields as well. The construction of a subject file is usually the work of a file expert. And, after the file has been constructed, persons using the file must exercise a great deal of judgment and discretion in assigning material to the proper classifications and in preparing cross references.

Most subject files are arranged alphabetically by topics and subtopics. The main topics appear on the first-position guide tabs and subtopics on the second-position tabs.

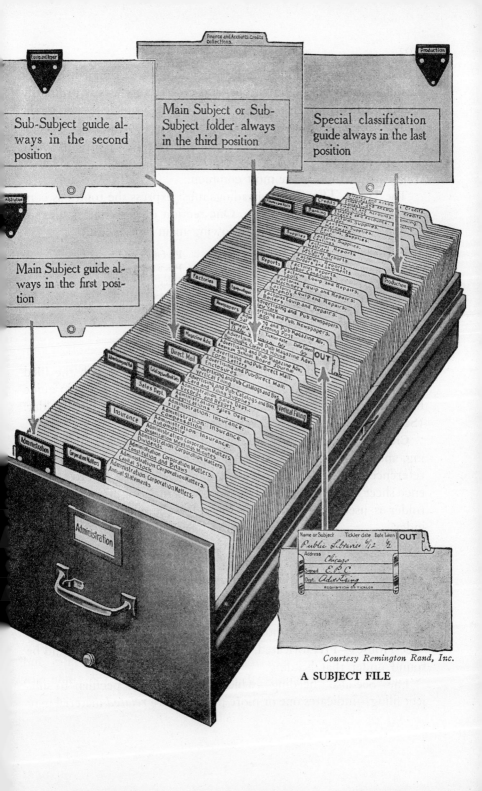

Sub-Subject guide always in the second position

Main Subject or Sub-Subject folder always in the third position

Special classification guide always in the last position

Main Subject guide always in the first position

Courtesy Remington Rand, Inc.

A SUBJECT FILE

Index. A separate index, or classification list, of the main subject headings, divisions, subdivisions, and cross references is ordinarily maintained for a subject file in order to give a quick review of the contents of a file when choosing new headings and to help in locating materials requested under unusual headings. Such an index may be kept in a bound book, in a loose-leaf binder, or on 5-by-3 cards. The card method is the most common.

The Topics. The subject headings must express the topics as concisely and exactly as possible. One section of a technical file, for example, might contain the following main and subguides.

Power	Prefabricated houses
Electric power	Price control
Hydroelectric power	Price fixing
Water power	Prices
Precious metals	Basing point system
Gold	Regulation
Platinum	Retail
Silver	Wholesale

Behind the subguides are placed the folders in which the filed material is placed. The broad tab of the folder bears the main guide head, the subguide head, and the heading of the individual folder. (See the accompanying illustration.)

Cross References. A paper is filed under the most important heading, and cross references are made for other headings. These cross references are kept by various methods. Sometimes a cross-reference sheet is filed in the folder; sometimes the back flap of a tabbed folder is used; and sometimes the reference appears only in the index.

There are two types of cross reference. One type reads simply "See," while the other type reads "See also." "See" references indicate that no material is to be found under the heading to which the cross reference is attached, but that *all* the material appears under the heading referred to. In the subject headings listed above, for example, "Prefabricated houses" might bear a single cross reference, "See Houses—Prefabricated," indicating that all material would be found under that heading.

The "See also" heading—which, by the way, is peculiar to subject filing—indicates one or more places where *related* material may be found. The heading "Price fixing," for example, might bear a cross reference, "See also Prices—regulations," where additional material would be found.

It is not unusual for a heading to contain several cross references.

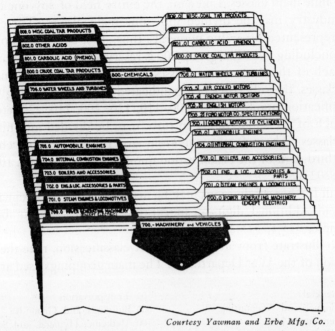

Courtesy Yawman and Erbe Mfg. Co.

NUMERIC SUBJECT FILING BY THE DEWEY DECIMAL SYSTEM
An alphabetic card index is used in conjunction with this file

Special Points to Watch. A person who files material in a subject file must be constantly on guard against filing similar material in several places under synonymous headings. Then, too, letters often cover several subjects. As a paper can be filed in only one place, additional cross references must be prepared and inserted in the proper subject folders. To avoid this additional work, many companies require that their branches, salesmen, and agents limit each letter to one subject. Of course it is impossible to exercise this control over outside companies.

Another pitfall to be avoided is the overuse of such headings as "General" and "Miscellaneous."

Numeric Subject Files. Some subject filing systems are arranged numerically. The Dewey Decimal system is the best known.

This system is based on Melvil Dewey's system of classifying library books, in which he classified the field of human knowledge into nine main classes. Likewise, the entire field of any one business or industry may be divided into nine main classes. These classes are represented by arabic numerals, thus: 100, 200, and so on up to and including 900. The group 000 is reserved for general items.

Each of these nine main classes, in turn, is subdivided into nine subclasses, the subclasses being indicated by the second digit in the classification number, thus: 100, 110, 120; 200, 210, 220; etc.

Each of the subdivisions, in turn, may be divided into nine sub-subclasses. These further divisions are represented by changing the third digit of the classification number, thus: 100, 101, 102; 200, 201, 202; etc.

Still further subdivisions may be made by affixing a decimal point and an additional digit to an existing classification number; for example, 315.1, 315.2, etc.

To illustrate from an actual subject classification, take the classification of the War Department. The main groupings used are:

000 General	500 Transportation
100 Finance and Accounting	600 Buildings and Grounds
200 Personnel	700 Medicine, Hygiene, and Sanitation
300 Administration	800 Rivers and Harbors
400 Supplies, Equipment, and Services	900 (Open for future expansion)

The following outline shows how a main division may be broken down:

```
400   Supplies, Equipment, and Services
 450   Supplies for Transportation
  451   Vehicles
   451.2   Motor and Auto trucks
    451.21   Parts and Accessories
```

An alphabetic index to the topics is a necessity. Each topic, together with its classification number, is recorded on a card; and the cards are arranged in alphabetic sequence. The appropriate classification number is placed on each piece of correspondence, and then the correspondence is filed in numerical sequence. A person wishing to locate correspondence in the file first finds the card in the card index and notes the classification number. He then goes to that numbered section of the files and obtains the correspondence.

FOLLOW-UP FILES; CHARGE-OUTS; TRANSFERRING

Follow-up Files. A follow-up file is really a system of reminders. It serves to bring up various matters for attention on dates determined beforehand. Most secretaries maintain their own follow-up systems, referring to this special file at the beginning of each day's work and removing all letters, memos, and other papers marked for the dictator's attention on that day.

One simple method of follow-up filing is to prepare, in addition to the usual file carbon, a follow-up carbon of each letter that may need attention at a later date. The follow-up copy is often on paper of a different color from that used for the file copy.

On the follow-up, the secretary notes the date on which action should be taken. She usually writes this in rather large figures in either the upper or the lower right corner. She files this copy in a special follow-up file containing twelve guides for the months and thirty-one folders for the days. Each morning, she removes the carbons from that day's folder and sends each carbon to the proper person for attention.

For example, on January 15 Mr. Harrington dictates letters A and B. Concerning Letter A he says to his secretary, "Follow this up about March 15." The secretary writes "3/15" in the upper or lower right corner of the follow-up copy and files it behind the March guide, in the folder marked "15." On March 15, he will find that copy in the regular routine of business.

Letter B, dictated by

Courtesy The Shaw-Walker Co.

GUIDE CARDS FOR A FOLLOW-UP FILE

Mr. Harrington, asks a question for which an answer is required. Mr. Harrington has reason to doubt whether his correspondent will answer at once, and so he says, "I'll follow this one in two weeks." The secretary writes "1/29" in the upper or lower right corner of the follow-up copy and places it behind the January guide, in the folder for the twenty-ninth day.

Meanwhile, the complete correspondence is kept in the regular file where it can be found when it is needed.

According to another method, cards are substituted for the follow-up carbon copy. The notation for follow-up is indicated on the file copy, and a 5-by-3 card is then prepared. The information as to what is wanted, by whom, with the date, is noted on the card. The cards are then arranged by dates, and the correspondence is filed. Each morning the cards for that day are removed, and the material called for is located in the file and sent to the proper person for attention.

Pending, or Suspense, Files. Sometimes follow-up files are referred to as "pending" or "suspense" files, but the names are really not interchangeable. A true pending, or suspense, file is maintained for papers being held for further information.

Charge-Outs. Executives frequently call for previous correspondence pertaining to current matters. Some system for controlling the loan of such papers is necessary.

A common method is to record the paper borrowed, the subject matter of the paper, the person by whom borrowed, and the date on a letter-sized "out" card, usually of manila and bearing a tab reading "Out." This card is substituted for the papers removed and remains in the file until the papers are returned, the same card being used over and over again until no more space remains for entries.

Another method is to use out guides bearing a small metal frame in which a card bearing the same information can be inserted.

If an entire folder is lent, an out folder is often inserted in its place so that any incoming papers for that correspondent can be placed in the out folder until the regular folder is returned.

The accompanying illustration shows some of the commonly used charge-out forms.

The secretary should follow up charge-outs more than ten days or two weeks old to see whether the papers have been stored in someone's desk.

Transferring Correspondence. Periodically it becomes necessary to remove material from the files in order to make way for new papers. This process is called "transferring." It is usually done at least once a year at the close of the fiscal year. Sometimes correspondence is transferred twice a year.

The simplest method consists of removing *all* folders, both individual and miscellaneous, to transfer cases. As the old folders are removed, new ones, properly labeled, are put in their places. Guides are not transferred.

As frequent reference to the old file is necessary during the early weeks of the new period, it is an advantage to keep the transferred material in an accessible place if possible. A convenient plan, when four-drawer cabinets are used, is to keep the current files in the two top drawers and the files containing the transferred material for the last transfer period in the two bottom drawers of the cabi-

Courtesy Remington Rand, Inc.

CHARGE-OUT FORMS

Top: Out guide to replace folder in use. Below: Two out cards to replace correspondence temporarily removed from folder

net. Then, at the following transfer period, the transfer material in the two bottom drawers can be removed to a storeroom, making room for the new material to be transferred.

Cabinets made especially for transfer purposes are available. They are usually constructed of cheaper materials and are less durable than regular files. Transfer cabinets are also made in the form of individual drawers of steel, wood, or a composition of wood and pasteboard. This type of transfer file is especially suitable for holding material that is to be stored in a storeroom.

How Long Should Correspondence Be Held? One of the most responsible filing duties that the person in charge of the files exercises is the destruction of old records. A policy must first be established to determine what may or may not be destroyed.

Doubtless such a policy will already be in existence in the office to which you will go. If it is not, it may be necessary for you to help in planning the policy. The first step will be to study all the records filed and to determine the individual value of each type of form. With these facts in hand, a schedule for the retention of the papers may be drawn up. The schedule should be approved by the company's attorney, because there are laws governing the preservation of certain records.

The length of time that records should be held depends on: (1) the kind of record, (2) the type of business, and (3) the Statute of Limitations.

Kinds of Records. Records may be classified as (1) vital, (2) important, (3) useful, and (4) unimportant.

1. Vital records (minutes of meetings, charters, bylaws, audit reports, general ledgers, and similar documents) should never be destroyed.

2. Important records (expired contracts, for example) should be kept for at least twenty years, and then brought up for final decision before being destroyed.

3. Useful records (as correspondence and orders) should be kept for about seven years. This is an average length of time for preserving this type of materials.

4. Unimportant records (letters of acknowledgment and transmittal, duplicate copies of correspondence—all material that appears in permanent form elsewhere) may safely be destroyed in a few months.

The Type of Business. The length of time that papers are required depends on the nature of the business. A concern manufacturing heavy machinery, for example, will receive orders for replacement parts for years to come and must keep copies of the original orders far longer than would a company selling a perishable product, such as food.

The Statute of Limitations. The statute books of all states bear a law known as the Statute of Limitations fixing the time within which legal action must be brought in order to collect an account. These statutes vary in the different states, the time ranging from three to fifteen years. Papers supporting an account that is outlawed by the Statute of Limitations need not be retained in the files, subject to the final approval of the company's attorney.

THE COMPLETE FILING ROUTINE

Filing should be done every day, not left to accumulate; and a definite procedure should be followed. The complete routine is outlined here.

PREPARING CORRESPONDENCE FOR FILING
Note the pencil ready for instant use and the calendar at hand for reference to follow-up dates. (Page 111.) The file clerk uses a stapler to fasten sets of papers together and removes unwanted staples with the staple remover shown beside it. As she finishes with each set of papers, she puts it into its proper place in the alphabetic sorter at her right, from which she will take all papers and file them

1. *Inspecting the Correspondence.* Notice first whether the correspondence bears the signal used in your office to show that it is released for filing. This release signal may be a line drawn through the correspondence (as in the illustration), a large check mark across the face of the correspondence, the initials of the person releasing it, the word "File," or some special indication adopted in your office.

2. *Reading, Indexing, and Coding the Correspondence.* Read the correspondence to determine the name of the person, place, or subject matter under which the correspondence is to be filed, and underline the name in colored pencil. In the illustration, the name is International Supply Company. Also, if a file or code number is required in the filing system used, insert the number in the upper right corner.

3. *Cross-Referencing.* If a letter contains a reference to any name, place, or subject that might be looked up in the files, make a cross-reference card for that topic and mark the correspondence accordingly. In the illustration, the underline opposite the X calls for a cross reference to The Mazzini Galleries.

4. *Preparing the Follow-up.* If the correspondence bears a notation of a follow-up date, prepare the reference that will assure that the matter will come up for attention on the date indicated.

5. *Stapling.* When correspondence consists of several pages that are pinned or clipped together, remove the pins or clips and staple the pages together, placing the latest letter on top. One staple in the upper left-hand corner is usually sufficient.

6. *Sorting.* Next, make a preliminary sorting of the correspondence, dividing it into small groups, to facilitate filing. A sorter is of great help in this operation. A sorter contains far fewer guides than do the regular file drawers. Each piece of correspondence is simply placed behind its corresponding guide. In name filing, only the first letter of the name under which the correspondence is to be filed need be noted in making this preliminary sorting.

7. *Actual Filing.* You are now ready to take the final step—to place the correspondence in the file. Remove one group of correspondence at a time from the tray and sort it in strict alphabetic (or numeric) order to the last letter or number. At this time you will apply the rules on pages 91-96. Begin with the first group and insert the letters in their proper places in the file. Proceed straight ahead—do not go back over your tracks. If you overlook any group, leave it until you have finished the other groups in their order, and then go back to it.

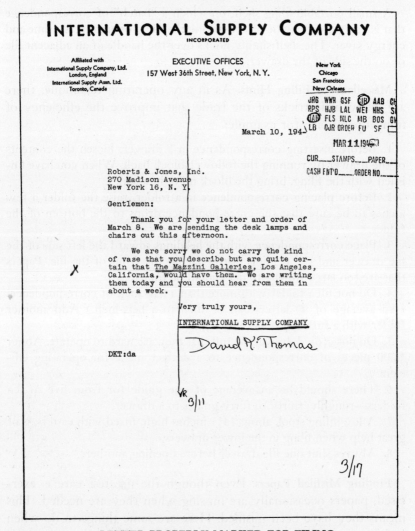

A LETTER PROPERLY MARKED FOR FILING

The vertical line indicates that the letter has received proper attention and has been
released for filing. The underline in the signature indicates that the letter is to be
filed under that name. The X in the margin calls attention to the name under which
the letter is to be cross-referenced. The date in the lower right-hand margin shows
that the letter is to come up for attention on March 17

A small portable filing shelf, on which a "batch" of correspondence that is being filed may be placed during the filing operation, is a time and energy saver. The shelf simply hooks over the handle of an adjacent file or on the side of the drawer.

Miscellaneous Filing Hints. As in any operating technique, there are many little tricks of the trade that improve the efficiency of filing operations; for example:

1. Before inserting correspondence in a drawer, loosen the contents of the drawer by running the follower-block back. When you have finished with the filing, bring the block up tight again.

2. Before placing correspondence in a folder, raise the folder a few inches to be sure that the correspondence drops to the bottom of the folder.

3. Place correspondence with the headings toward the left side of the file drawer and the reading matter facing the front of the file. Papers that are too large for the folder should be folded.

4. Do not fill a folder with more than a half inch of correspondence. (An average of 90 letters can be filed to a half-inch.) Add another folder with a further division.

5. Do not crowd drawers so full that they are hard to operate. About 4,000 pieces of correspondence to a drawer make for operating efficiency.

6. There should be an average of one guide for from five to ten folders—roughly, thirty to forty guides to a drawer.

7. A low filing stool, about 14½ inches high, fitted with casters, is of great help when filing in the lower drawers.

8. Always shut one file drawer before opening another.

Finding Misfiled Papers. Even though the greatest care is exercised, papers occasionally are missing when they are needed. This means they have been misfiled. Here are some things to do when making this unhappy search:

1. Look in the folder preceding or following the one in which the correspondence belongs.

2. Look between the folders and on the bottom of the file drawer under the folders.

3. In a name file, look through folders containing correspondence with similar names.

4. In a numeric file, look over the index for similar names, and then check through each folder to see whether a wrong file number was assigned to the paper. Also, look over folders bearing numbers that might be easily transposed; for example, if a paper is missing from folder 76, see if it was filed in folder 67.

5. Look up previous correspondence to see whether it contained a cross reference that may give a clue.

6. In a subject file, see if the paper may have been filed under some synonym of the subject.

7. Watch out for paper clips. Papers sometimes become attached to the wrong correspondence. If so, they will generally be found on the bottom of the correspondence that is clipped together.

CARD FILING; VISIBLE FILING; MICROPHOTOGRAPHY

Card Filing. Card filing is simply an extension of the principles of correspondence filing to record keeping by means of cards. It is principally used for indexes to numeric files and in recording names and addresses for a mailing list, in preparing a similar record in connection with numeric filing, or for cards to be used as a "tickler," or follow-up, file. The cards are placed in a drawer that is provided with a set of index guides similar to those used in name filing.

Cabinets for holding cards are obtainable in the same styles of units as those for the large-sized filing drawers. The tickler file is equipped with a set of month and day guides. Cards, as well as guides, may be procured in various colors, weights, rulings, and sizes. The nature of the material to be recorded and the method of recording determine the spacing between rules. If cards are filled in on the typewriter, the line spacing should be typewriter spacing. The commonest card sizes are 5 by 3, 6 by 4, and 8 by 5 inches.

Card drawers are commonly arranged in horizontal or vertical rows in cabinets. The drawers are sometimes placed in a type of desk known as a tub desk, which enables the file clerk to reach the cards easily without rising or stooping.

Visible Filing. All types of files described up to this point may be described as "blind" files; that is, papers are hidden and must be

Courtesy Art Metal Construction Co.

A ROTARY VISIBLE FILE

found and abstracted from the file when needed. Where speed of reference is essential, as in sales records, personnel records, purchasing data, stock and inventory records, and similar cases, "visible" files are preferred because the information may be seen at a glance.

Some of the most commonly used visible files are pictured here. Although they are constructed differently, they are similar in one particular—the pockets or holders into which the record cards fit are so arranged that the bottom of each card is visible. On this bottom margin a name or an item is typed, and the margin is protected by a transparent "window."

Microphotography. Microphotography is used extensively in some filing departments in order to save space and to make permanent records of various papers. Banks, for example, return canceled checks to their makers; and, until microphotography came into use, the bank had no record of the details of checks that had been cashed.

and returned. For many years, some banks have used microphotography to make permanent photographic records of all checks.

Documents to be recorded on microfilm are photographed in miniature. So great is the reduction in size that the microfilm must be enlarged when it is to be read. The film is viewed by means of a magnifying apparatus, such as is pictured here.

A particular advantage of microphotography in filing is the small space required to store records. The original material, after it is photographed in miniature on microfilm, may be destroyed.

A large business firm in Pittsburgh effected a saving of one acre of floor space and tons of filing cabinets by reducing to microfilm two

Courtesy Recordak Corporation

Records preserved in miniature on film by microphotography are enlarged on the screen of a "reader," the device shown here

million sheets of sketches and records dating back to the early 1880's. The census records of the United States for an entire century have also been recorded on microfilm.

ANSWERS TO "DO YOU KNOW?"

1. A. Smith, A. Benson Smith, Albert Smith.

2. "Sister Marguerite" should be filed under *S*.

3. Prepare cross-references for each subject except the one under which the letter will be filed.

4. Prepare a follow-up.

5. Place it in the file, in the exact place from which the correspondence was removed.

Courtesy E. W. Alexander, Hadley Technical H. S., St. Louis

A DUPLICATING DEPARTMENT

Various pieces of duplicating equipment described in this section are shown here

6

THE DUPLICATING DEPARTMENT

DO YOU KNOW?

1. Can a stencil be saved and run again if additional copies of the duplicated material are needed later?
2. If you make an error in typing a stencil, can it be corrected? If you make an error in typing a master sheet for a gelatin duplicator, can it be corrected?
3. What kind of duplicating machine would you recommend for duplicating several hundred letters so that they would resemble individually typed letters?
4. How can you justify the right-hand margin with an ordinary typewriter?
5. If you were asked to cut a stencil on which several different type faces and sizes were to be used, which of the following machines would you use for cutting the stencil—typewriter, Vari-Typer, Multigraph?

A SECRETARY should understand the various kinds of duplicating processes, their limitations, and the kind of work to which each is best adapted. The simplest duplicating process is the making of carbon copies. Other kinds of office duplicating processes require more elaborate equipment and supplies and considerable skill in preparing the copy and in operating the duplicator.

STENCIL DUPLICATION

The Mimeograph, the Niagara, and similar duplicating machines make multiple copies by means of stencils on which the copy that is to be duplicated has been written or drawn. Lettering and illustrations may be traced on stencils with a sharp instrument called a stylus. The sharp type or the point of the stylus pushes aside or presses through the coating on the stencil sheet, leaving the fibrous portion exposed. When copies are being "run off," the duplicating machine forces ink through this fibrous portion.

Some of the common uses for stencil duplicating are for bulletins, announcements, price sheets, instruction sheets, and ruled forms.

It is possible to produce a stencil-duplicated piece of work that resembles original typing very closely.

Typing the Stencil. Clean the type on your machine before typing a stencil. Unless the type is clean, some letters will fill up with the stencil coating, and the impressions will not be sharp and clear. Use a stiff cleaning brush instead of cleaning fluid for this operation because cleaning fluid may injure the stencil.

Before typing, throw the ribbon lever to the "off," or "stencil," position. Use a firm, even touch in typing. The letters *o*, *c*, and *e* may be cut out of the stencil unless struck lightly. Strike the capitals *W*, *M*, and *E* with a touch somewhat heavier than normal.

After you have become an experienced stencil typist, you will be able to type a stencil almost as rapidly as you can type on paper; but while you are a beginner, you should type rather slowly until you acquire the firm, even touch that produces the desired results.

On every stencil sheet, or on the backing sheet attached to it, are printed markings to show the margins beyond which the duplicating machine cannot reproduce. The typing or drawing must not extend beyond these margins.

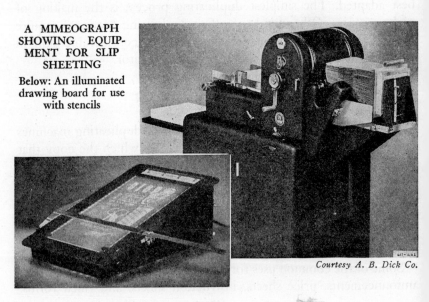

A MIMEOGRAPH SHOWING EQUIPMENT FOR SLIP SHEETING

Below: An illuminated drawing board for use with stencils

Courtesy A. B. Dick Co.

Correcting Errors. Errors in stencil typing can be corrected if a few simple instructions are followed:

wa wa was

| Burnish the error | Apply correction fluid | Retype |

STEPS IN CORRECTING AN ERROR ON A STENCIL

1. Rub the error lightly with the flat part of your fingernail or the round end of the burnishing tool that accompanies correction fluid. (If the stencil has a cellophane cover sheet, this must be pulled back, of course, before the correction is made.)

2. Allowing only a small quantity to remain on the brush, apply a thin but complete coating of correction fluid over each incorrect character, with a single vertical stroke of the brush.

3. Let the fluid dry from 30 seconds to a minute before retyping. Wipe the brush clean.

4. Using a touch slightly lighter than normal, strike the correct letter over the coated error.

Two common faults that result in mussy corrections are the use of too thick a coat of fluid and too heavy a touch in typing the correction.

Proofread the finished stencil by holding it against the light or by reading the impression of the type on the cushion sheet, which is between the stencil and the backing sheet.

Tracing and Lettering. When tracing or lettering is to be done, the stencil sheet is clamped to a glass-topped drawing board illuminated from below. An operator who prepares complicated copy usually has a kit of tools, including several styli, curved rules, screen plates, and lettering guides.

Two-Color Stencil Duplicating. Two or more colors can be used on stencil-duplicated work. The production of color impressions is somewhat technical, however, and will not be discussed here. This information may be obtained, if needed, from the local representative of the company manufacturing the duplicating machine used.

How to Fold a Stencil Sheet. If the material to be duplicated must go lengthwise on the sheet, the stencil sheet may be inserted lengthwise into the typewriter. Fasten both lower corners of the stencil sheet to the backing sheet, using cellulose tape if available. This prevents the stencil from wrinkling when the typewriter platen is turned.

Fold the stencil to fit the carriage length, and slip a fold of paper over the edge that is to go into the machine. This will keep the edge of the stencil sheet from curling.

Reruns of Stencils. Used stencils may be saved and run again when needed. The ink must be removed, however, or it will harden in the stencilized letters. A quick but not very satisfactory way of preparing used stencils for filing and subsequent use is to blot them between large sheets of absorbent paper or newspaper. A better way is to clean them with kerosene, using a soft brush to wash off the ink, and then blot them dry.

Paper. An absorbent grade of paper that will absorb ink almost instantly is preferred for use with the stencil duplicator. A hard-finished, nonabsorbent paper may be used if necessary; but the ink is likely to smear unless the excess ink is taken up by a process known as slip-sheeting.

Slip-Sheeting. Slip sheets are sometimes large blotters, but usually they are extra-long sheets of absorbent paper that are inserted between freshly duplicated sheets. The sheets of absorbent paper are preferable to blotters because the blotters absorb the ink and produce gray instead of black copies. The blotters, however, can be used many times. As a duplicated copy comes out of the machine, the operator lays a slip sheet on the paper and then runs another copy. A skilled operator can insert slip sheets by hand while the machine is running at a reasonable rate of speed.

Mechanical slip-sheeters, which can be attached to the machine, are available. After a pile of sheets has stood for several minutes, the operator shakes out or pulls out the long slip sheets. (See illustration on page 118.)

The slip-sheeting method slows up production, but it is necessary when a stencil must be run on hard-finished paper—for example, on a letterhead or other printed form.

OTHER TYPES OF DUPLICATING MACHINES

Gelatin Duplicator. The gelatin duplicator, or hectograph, is somewhat cheaper to use than a stencil duplicator; but it produces fewer copies. The finished work is usually of a purple color; but red, green, blue, and some other colors can be used. Up to one hundred copies may be produced from an original.

Many large organizations use either the gelatin or the direct-process duplicator instead of making several carbon copies—for example, when orders must be entered and copies must go to several departments. These duplicated copies are usually clearer than carbons and are quickly made.

The original for the gelatin duplicator, called the "master," is usually made by typing through a special ribbon or special carbon paper. Special colored pencils and special fluid inks can also be used for writing or drawing on the master. As many as seven different colors can be used on one master and reproduced, all at one impression, on the copies made from it.

Paper with a special finish is recommended for this duplicating process; but ordinary paper may be used, with less satisfactory results both in the quality of the copy and in the number of copies that may be run.

To type a master for the gelatin duplicator, arrange two sheets of paper and a sheet of carbon just as if you were going to make an ordinary carbon copy. Special carbon pa-

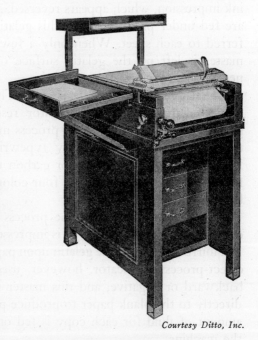

Courtesy Ditto, Inc.

A FLAT-BED GELATIN DUPLICATOR

per must be used, and the carbon copy (or master) should be made on hard-finished paper especially made for this process. (Carbon paper of good quality can be used for several masters before it wears out.) The top sheet of paper, on which you type directly, has two uses: you can proofread from it, and it protects the carbon paper from being cut as you type. If this top sheet is of thin paper, the master will be clearer.

Making Corrections. Unlike stencils, masters for the gelatin process can be erased. Using an erasing shield, apply a plastic cleaner to remove excess dye. Then erase completely with a typewriter eraser.

Another way of correcting is by blocking out the error with a special wax pencil, and then typing the correction directly over the blocked-out area.

Running the Copies. The master is pressed down on a moistened gelatin surface on the duplicating machine and is left there for not more than one minute; then it is removed. The gelatin absorbs the ink impression, which appears reversed, as in a mirror. Blank sheets are fed under pressure across this gelatin, and the image is transferred to each sheet. When only a few copies are to be run, the master is left on the gelatin surface one second for each copy needed—ten seconds for ten copies.

Liquid or Direct-Process Duplicator. The work produced on the liquid or direct-process duplicator resembles that done on the gelatin duplicator. The direct-process method differs, however, in that neither ink nor ordinary typewriter ribbons can be used. Either special carbon paper or carbon typewriter ribbon is satisfactory. These are available in four colors—purple, red, green, and blue.

Another difference is in the process involved. For the gelatin duplicator, the positive image is impressed on gelatin in reverse, as in a mirror, and from the gelatin upon paper as a positive again. The direct-process duplicator, however, uses a master that is already backward or negative; and this master is applied by the machine directly to the blank paper to produce positive copies. The proper amount of fluid for each copy is fed on to the blank paper from the machine.

The direct-process duplicator has two advantages over the gelatin process: (1) it produces more copies from one master, and (2) the master may be saved and run again at a later date.

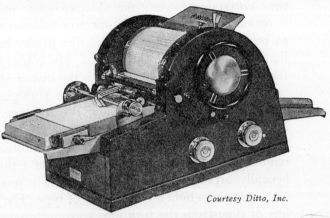

Courtesy Ditto, Inc.

A DIRECT-PROCESS DUPLICATOR

Making the Master. The master for the direct-process or fluid duplicator is made like any other carbon copy, except that the carbon paper must be placed with the carbon toward you. A negative master *on the back* of the first sheet will result—a "mirror" copy like that you sometimes make by accident in typing carbon copies.

Courtesy Ditto, Inc.

ARRANGEMENT OF PAPERS FOR TYPING A DIRECT-PROCESS DUPLICATOR MASTER

Making Corrections. Always use an erasing shield when making corrections for the direct-process duplicator. Either (1) cover the error with a wax block-out pencil, or (2) scrape most of the carbon impression away with a razor blade or knife and remove the remainder with art gum. Over the blocked-out or erased portion, place a small piece of unused carbon paper (facing you), and type the correction over the blocked-out or erased portion.

Running the Copies. The operator attaches the master directly to the drum of a rotary duplicator. Blank sheets, moistened by liquid, are fed through the machine; and copies are produced when they come in direct contact with the master sheet.

The Multigraph. The product of the Multigraph resembles individually typed material, because this machine uses type and an inked ribbon.

The operator uses a grooved tool, called a composing fork, to remove typewriter type, one character at a time, from an alphabetically arranged type holder called a typesetter. This fork is long enough to hold an entire line of type. The operator slides the line of type from the fork into a groove on a metal cylinder and continues this operation line by line until an entire letter or page is set. This cylinder is technically called a segment.

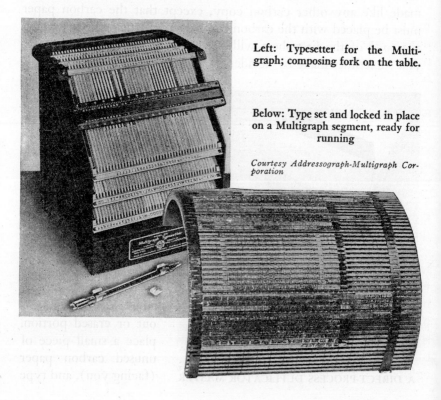

Left: Typesetter for the Multigraph; composing fork on the table.

Below: Type set and locked in place on a Multigraph segment, ready for running

Courtesy Addressograph-Multigraph Corporation

The cylinder of type is then affixed to the Multigraph frame and covered with an inked ribbon as wide as the cylinder itself. The cylinder is applied to page after page with a rapid, rolling motion. Colored ribbons are available.

Signatures can be automatically printed on letters, in what looks like actual pen writing, from plates made from original signatures.

Advantages of the Multigraph are: (1) it produces work that looks like typewritten material, and (2) a very large number of copies may be run from one type setup.

By using ink instead of ribbon, and type like printer's type, the Multigraph may be used for real printing jobs if the printing does not cover much space on the page. The process is widely used for imprinting dealers' or store names on previously printed advertising matter.

Considerable mechanical aptitude and training are required to become a Multigraph operator. Not many secretaries are called on to run this machine, but they should know what the machine will do.

Offset Printing. The following terms describe various forms of offset printing and mean approximately the same thing: photo offset, photolithography, and planography.

Courtesy Addressograph-Multigraph Corporation

AN ELECTRICALLY DRIVEN MULTIGRAPH

To the untrained eye, offset printing looks like printing done on a printing press. Letterheads and office forms can be produced by offset often more cheaply than by regular printing.

An offset machine widely used in large offices is the Multilith. This versatile machine will print from copy produced by typewriter, pen, crayon, brush, carbon paper, or by a special photographic process. It is unlike any of the other office duplicating machines described here, in that it can reproduce photographs, with all their lights and shadows, in addition to turning out simple duplicating jobs very quickly.

Flexible metal masters are used for many Multilith jobs, especially those involving photographs; but a newer development is the paper master, called the Duplimat, which is more economical than the metal master. Copy can be typed or drawn on it.

The Multilith has an advantage over ordinary (or letter-

Courtesy Addressograph-Multigraph Corporation

AN ELECTRICALLY DRIVEN MULTI-
LITH DUPLICATOR

A FLEXIBLE METAL MASTER
FOR MULTILITH

press) printing in the running of office forms because the forms can be ruled by hand. Ruled forms printed on the letterpress are much more expensive.

Typing Copy for Offset. Although as a secretary you are unlikely to be required to learn to run a Multilith, you may be called upon to prepare copy for this machine and other offset presses. Here are some facts to remember.

A one-color letterhead may be reproduced in the same operation that prints the letter itself. Simply type the letter on one of your company's letterheads. The entire sheet then will be reproduced. You can paste on drawings, too, if they are needed.

Typing with an ordinary black ribbon may produce thick, black letters. You can produce sharper copy by typing with a special ribbon made of tough carbon paper, which is used only once. If no carbon ribbon is available, place a sheet of new carbon over the paper on which the master copy is to appear, and remove the ribbon or set the ribbon lever at "Stencil." The type must be clean.

Typed copy for offset printing must not be erased, but corrections may be pasted on. When you are reading proof on the typed page, indicate in the margin, with a *light-blue* pencil, any necessary corrections. On another sheet, retype enough of the material to make a patch large enough to handle. Use tweezers and your fingers very delicately to attach this in place with rubber cement. Rub the excess rubber cement away with your fingers.

Justified Right-Hand Margin. Typewritten copy for bulletins, booklets, and other important publications should have the right margin justified—that is, as even as the left one. Even-margin typing is practical only for work that is to be reproduced by one of the duplicating processes; it takes too long to be used for everyday letters.

Special typewriters are available that make it possible to produce even-margin copy automatically on the second typing, each line being expanded or condensed to a predetermined length.

By using care, you can justify a right-hand margin on an ordinary typewriter. The accompanying illustration shows the way the material is typed the first time, inside ruled lines, with check marks added to indicate the points where spaces should be distributed;

Indicate the ✓width of ✓the typed//
column by drawing parallel vertical
rules with a pencil.
    Now✓type ✓a line✓of ✓copy ✓at a/t̷i̷m̷e̷
time, never going outside the rule.
Fill each short line with some sel-
dom-used ✓symbol, ✓such as ✓the ob-///
lique line. Go over the copy✓with/
a pencil, ✓filling✓each line✓with///
as many check marks (denoting extra
spaces needed in the final✓typing)/
as you✓have ✓symbols. ✓ Distribute///
these spaces✓so that no noticeable/
gaps appear. Then retype.

Indicate the width of the typed
column by drawing parallel vertical
rules with a pencil.
    Now type a line of copy at a
time, never going outside the rule.
Fill each short line with some sel-
dom-used symbol, such as the ob-
lique line. Go over the copy with.
a pencil, filling each line with
as many check marks (denoting extra
spaces needec in the final typing)
as you have symbols. Distribute
these spaces so that no noticeable
gaps appear. Then retype.

METHOD OF TYPING COPY TO GET AN EVEN RIGHT-HAND MARGIN

and the completed second typing, which incorporates the changes indicated.

The Vari-Typer. The Vari-Typer, like the typewriter, is not in itself a duplicating machine, but it is widely used in conjunction with duplicating machines because several faces and sizes of type can be used on it.

The Vari-Typer has a standard typewriter keyboard. Many different and interchangeable type faces are available. All the characters needed for a particular type face are contained in one type plate, and the machine holds two type plates at a time. Type plates can easily be interchanged by the operator.

Multifax. Business firms that require a great deal of duplicating work use an additional machine called the Multifax, which automatically prepares stencils, metal-plate master copies, or hectograph masters from printing, writing, drawings, or blueprints. In this machine, an electric eye actuates a tiny hammer that copies the original design, dot by dot, on stencils or master sheets.

The Multifax, which is made by Western Union, has two outstanding advantages: it can produce complicated masters and stencils more quickly than they could be made by hand, and it can actually transmit these by automatic telegraph from one city to another.

One of the four of the F
especially adaptable to

A beautiful, modern F
spacing. Especially

A good print face type
spacing. Also has matcl

Wherever emphasis is needed this type se
for footnotes, explanatory matter, or a

Combining compactness with good legibilit
Where the conservation of space is highly

An excellent type for headings
faced effect in copy. Reproduc

Above: Inserting Type
Plate in Vari-Typer.

Left: Styles of Vari-
Typer Type (Actual
Size)

Courtesy   Coxhead   Vari-
Typer Co.

Answers to "Do You Know?"

1. Yes, if it is cleaned properly.
2. An error on a stencil can be corrected by the use of a burnishing tool and correction fluid. An error on a master for the gelatin duplicator can be erased or blocked out.
3. The Multigraph or the stencil duplicator.
4. By typing the copy twice and inserting extra spaces during the second typing.
5. Vari-Typer.

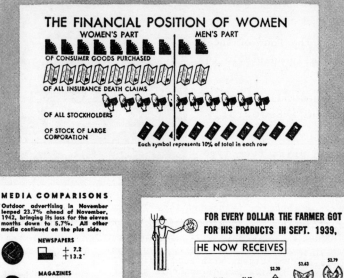

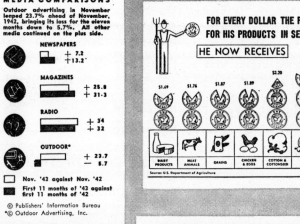

STATISTICS ARE EASILY UNDERSTOOD WHEN SHOWN IN PICTURES

Top and Bottom: Pictograms (Pictograph Corp.). Left: Bar graphs used in advertising. Right: The circle graph used in a pictogram

7

THE STATISTICAL DEPARTMENT

DO YOU KNOW?

1. You think the name of a book referred to in a footnote of an article you are typing is "Ten Years in Business." The book is in an office down the hall from where you are working. Would you take time to look up the exact title?

2. In a report you are typing, you find a superior figure 4 (like this: [4]), indicating that the reader is to refer to a footnote. There is no footnote numbered 4, however. Will you renumber the footnotes or ask the author for instructions?

3. You are to copy exactly a quotation from a very old book in which a word is spelled wrong. How will you show, in your typed material, that the error is intentionally copied?

4. One of the stenographers in your office is typing a long manuscript on onionskin paper, single spaced. She explains that she is doing this so as to save postage when the manuscript is mailed to a publisher. What would be your comment on her choice of paper and spacing?

5. Your chief wishes to include, in a book he is writing, a cartoon from a current magazine. Should he simply reprint the cartoon without asking anyone?

MANY business organizations employ efficiency experts who are continually studying ways of improving manufacturing methods, products, services, and the office management of the company. The department conducting this study is known as the Statistical —or Research, or Planning—Department.

Much of the work of the Statistical Department consists of typing reports, many of them very technical. Some of these will come to the typist written in longhand (and what longhand!); some will be typed in rough draft by the executives themselves; and some will be dictated from outlines and notes. This work requires patience, accuracy, and alertness. A report may have to be retyped several times because of additions, deletions, and changes. You cannot afford to try for originality in work of this kind, because meanings may easily be changed.

Copying from Rough Draft. When a manuscript is changed a great deal, having additions pinned to some sheets, paragraphs changed from one page to another, and other paragraphs crossed out, you may be able to copy it more efficiently and with less chance of error if you cut apart the sections affected and paste them in their proper order. You will watch very carefully, of course, to see that you do arrange them in the correct order.

Paper. Reports that are to be kept in typewritten form are usually typed on plain white paper of good quality. Onionskin is not strong enough to stand the handling that typed reports usually receive, and it should never be used for original copies of manuscripts. (See page 46.)

Spacing and Margins. Manuscript and advertising copy—anything that is to be set up by a printer—should be typed double spaced. Some writers even require triple spacing, to allow plenty of room for changes.

As in any typing, make the right-hand margins as even as possible without, of course, taking time to justify them. Margins in your first draft should be extra wide. If any page of the report is shorter than the others (if, for example, a graph should appear at the foot of a page but must be put on the following page because of space requirements), center the word "More" in the space below the last line of the short page.

If the pages are to be bound at the side, make your left-hand margins wide enough for the form of binding to be used.

The accompanying table indicates accepted standards for the margins of final drafts of completed manuscripts.

Numbering the Pages. Number each page of a manuscript or a report. If the sheets are to be bound at the top, place the page numbers at the bottom. If the sheets are to be bound at the left, insert the numbers in the upper right-hand corner or center them at the top.

Carbon Copies. You can produce better-than-usual carbon copies by using a flexible backing sheet under the last carbon copy, against

Minimum Manuscript Margins
(In inches)

Margin	Bound at Top	Bound at Side	Unbound
Top margin:			
First page *...............	2½-3	2	2
Other pages...............	2-2½	1-1½	1½
Side margin:			
Left.....................	1½	2-2½	1½
Right....................	1½	1	1½
Bottom margin.............	1¾	1¼	1¾

* The first page of each chapter and of the preface, table of contents, index, or appendix.

the typewriter platen. Such sheets are provided with some kinds of duplicator stencils. They may also be purchased separately.

Judging Page Length. How to tell when you are close to the end of a page is sometimes a problem. If you are using the type of carbon paper that has a protruding right-hand margin bearing a numbered scale, you can tell at a glance how many lines there are left. With ordinary, unmarked carbon paper, try pasting a very small strip of colored paper near the bottom of the carbon paper, so that it will project a little, for a signal indicating that you should end the page.

Headings. Main headings are usually centered in all capitals. They may also be spaced out and underscored. There should be more space above a center head than below it.

Subordinate headings may be written in several ways, as shown in the accompanying illustrations. A center head or a subordinate

RUN-IN HEADINGS

The typical American community usually has the following kinds of stores:

Retail stores may be either independent or chain stores, but they all sell directly to the consumers.

Department stores are retail stores that are so expanded as to have separate departments that are "small stores within the great store."

Independent stores are usually owned by an individual or a partnership. They have no connection with any other store. The independent store may be a member of a large association that charges a membership fee for sending out window displays

head that is not on the same line with the material it introduces is not followed by a punctuation mark unless it is in question form.

Copper The change from the use of stone to the use of metals did not take place rapidly. Gold was scarce and was used only for ornament and decoration. Copper, which was more abundant than gold, could be hammered into knives, axes, and daggers; but it bent too easily to make strong tools and weapons.

MARGINAL HEADINGS

Bronze Someone made a happy discovery when, by melting a mixture of nine-tenths copper and one-tenth tin, it was found that the cooled product was much harder than either copper or tin alone. This combination of copper and tin is bronze. Knives, axes, spears, and other implements could then be given hard, sharp edges. Bronze enabled man to further his culture, or mode of living--he could kill game, cut down trees, and protect himself more easily with his better tools and weapons.

There are several definitely marked steps that should be carefully observed in retail selling.

SEPARATE-LINE FLUSH HEAD-INGS

Starting the Sale

This means meeting your customer, who is a guest in your store. "Good morning," "May I serve you?" or some such pleasant greeting usually opens the way to start the sale. Make the customer feel that you are immediately interested in his problem. Give yourself the advantage of a good start.

Learning the Customer's Wants

The next step is learning what the customer wants. Some people have only a general idea of what they want, while other people know exactly what they want. Study your customer, consider his point of view, and induce him to talk.

Displaying the Goods

Show the customer what you think will best fill the need. Handle your merchandise carefully and, if possible, show how

Liability insurance indemnifies the insured against liability for injury to other persons. Public liability automobile insurance is one kind of liability insurance. Owners of **LIABILITY INSURANCE** trucks, teams, threshing machines, road-building machinery, taxicabs, busses, railroads, street cars, steamships, ferries, and airplanes usually carry liability insurance of some kind. Through employer's liability insurance the employer is indemnified against loss arising from accidental injury to an employee while in the service of the employer.

INSERTED HEADINGS

Rather recent laws in various states compel an employer in certain occupations to pay benefits to employees who are injured while at work. Such employers are required to carry **WORKMEN'S COMPENSATION INSURANCE** workmen's compensation insurance with an insurance company or with the state insurance department, so that an employee or his family is sure to receive the indemnity prescribed by law for injuries or death. Every workman injured in the field of industry is entitled to such compensation (pay); or if he dies as a result of injuries received on the job, his family becomes the beneficiary (the one benefited).

Outlines. Outlines should be planned and numbered consistently. Here is an accepted outline form for a business report.

```
INSURANCE AND RISK BEARING

I. INSURANCE ON PROPERTY:
   A. What insurance is.
   B. The principle of insurance.
   C. The insurance policy--a contract:
        1. The insurer.
        2. The insured.
        3. The premium.
        4. The amount of the policy.
        5. The conditions of the policy.
   D. Fire insurance:
        1. Cost of fire insurance.
```

STANDARD FORM OF OUTLINE

Merely numbering and lettering divisions of a topic does not make an outline. Outlining is really the intelligent planning, step by step, of major and minor divisions of thought, and the arrangement of these thoughts in the order of their importance.

Parallel ideas should be expressed in parallel form, and they should always be clearly expressed.

Poor: Reasons for increase in competitor's sales:

1. Has streamlined the product, making it more attractive.
2. Sets low prices.
3. Closer to Chicago.

Good: Reasons for increase in competitor's sales:

1. Streamlined, attractive product.
2. Low price.
3. Low transportation costs because of location close to Chicago.

Quotations. Quotations must be accurately copied. For reference books in which quotations may be checked for accuracy, see Section 8.

In typing quotations, follow these rules:

1. Enclose short quotations—up to four typed lines—in quotation marks and "run in" on the same line with the sentence that introduces them. (See Figure 1.)

Figure 1

```
     It was, of course, interesting and fairly easy for these boys
to build the edifice and to construct the furniture and fixtures.
One boy wrote in his notebook:  "I was elected foreman and had
charge of the construction work.  A committee appointed by the
business teacher laid out the floor plan for the offices and
departments."
```

2. Start a new paragraph when beginning a long quotation—one of four or more typed lines. Single space long quotations and do not use quotation marks around them; the single spacing will stand out in a double-spaced manuscript. (See Figure 2.)

```
Miss Jane Rathburn, office manager of Treadwell Systems, Inc.,

describes the orientation plan this way:
```

```
    Beginners here have an opportunity to adjust themselves to
other personalities and the job itself through what we call an ori-
entation plan.  The new employee receives an office manual (we re-
vise this twice a year) and additional duplicated instructions
pertaining to the particular department in which he is first as-
```

Figure 2

If the copy is already single spaced, make the quoted paragraphs stand out by indenting them. (See Figure 3.)

```
            Miss Jane Rathburn, office manager of Treadwell Systems, Inc.,
            describes the orientation plan this way:
```

Figure 3

```
                Beginners here have an opportunity to adjust them-
            selves to other personalities and the job itself through
            what we call an orientation plan.  The new employee re-
            ceives an office manual (we revise this twice a year) and
```

3. Copy quotations exactly as in the original, even if the original seems wrong. Antique spelling and old-fashioned punctuation must be followed exactly. When words are obviously misspelled or other obvious errors occur, the word *sic*, enclosed in parentheses, may be typed immediately after the error to indicate that the original has been followed exactly. *Sic* is a Latin word meaning "thus." In preparing typed copy for the printer, use a pen to underscore *sic* and to change the parentheses to brackets. (See Figure 4.)

4. Quotations from copyrighted material must not be reprinted without permission from the publisher and the copyright owner. The legal outcomes of copyright infringement may be serious and expensive.

Footnotes. Footnotes are used to refer to authorities for statements made in reports or manuscripts. (See footnote 1 in Figure 4.)

Occasionally, footnotes are used to present facts that are pertinent but not closely related to the text. (See footnote 2 in Figure 4.)

There are two possible locations for footnotes. In reports that are to be kept in typewritten form, type the footnotes at the bottom of the page. (See Figure 5.) Stop typing far enough above the bottom of the page to leave room for them.

In manuscripts that are to be set in type, place the footnote immediately after the reference, no matter where it falls on the page, typing a line the entire width of the page above the footnote and a similar line below it. (See Figure 4.)

Figure 4

> That Dr. Morley was absent from his home for long periods in 1899 and 1901 is indicated by letters written by the children's nurse, Margaret Appleby, to William Farmer, whom she later married. In her letter dated December 25, 1899,[1] she wrote, "Dr. Morly [sic] has been away so long I wounder wheather the little ones will know him when he does come back."[2]
>
> --
>
> [1] Letter quoted by courtesy of Melinda Farmer Hendricks, Cross Plains, Wisconsin.
>
> [2] Dr. Morley's youngest daughter, Agnes, told the writer that the three younger children did not recognize him and that she herself burst into tears because she was "afraid of his whiskers."
>
> --
>
> Not until after his death in 1913 did the correspondence he had carried on with Fights on Horses, an Indian of the Salish tribe, come to light. Fights on Horses, also known as Jeremiah Buck, was a college graduate, who at the time of the correspondence was living on the Flathead Reservation in Montana.

Footnote data should be arranged in the same order in all the footnotes in any one report or manuscript. The standard order for the items in a footnote in a reference to a book is: author, title, place of publication, publisher, date, and page reference; and to a magazine: author, title of article, magazine, volume, page reference, and date. (See Figure 5.)

Figure 5

> and what knowledge are valuable to students of arithmetic, several surveys have been made.
>
> Phillips[2] and Henderson[3] investigated the general use of arithmetic among the adult population of several different states. Data
>
> _____
>
> [2] Elmer L. Phillips, A Survey of the Uses of Arithmetic, New York, Doberman-Wesley Publishing Company, 1942.
>
> [3] P. Louis Henderson, "Occupational Arithmetic," Weekly Business Survey, 20:118-136, October, 1943.

When a footnote refers to the work mentioned in the preceding footnote, use *ibid.* instead of repeating the full reference. *Ibid.* is an abbreviation of a Latin word *ibidem*, meaning "in the same place." Example:

4

<u>Ibid</u>., page 39.

Tables. Figures may be compared more easily when they are presented in table form than when they are simply included in text matter. The same figures concerning the Great Lakes are shown here, for comparison, in three different ways: in text form and in two arrangements of tabulated form.

Method 1:

Lake Superior is 350 miles long and 160 miles wide. The maximum depth is 1,290 feet. The total area is 31,820 square miles, of which 20,710 are in the United States and 11,110 in Canada. Lake Superior constitutes 282.8 miles of the national boundary—and so on.

Method 2:

COMPARATIVE STATISTICS ON GREAT LAKES

Great Lakes	Length (Miles)	Breadth (Miles)	Maximum Depth (Feet)	Area (Square Miles)			National Boundary (Miles)
				U. S.	Canada	Total	
Superior.....	350	160	1,290	20,710	11,110	31,820	282.8
Michigan.....	307	118	923	22,400	......	22,400	.....
Huron........	206	101	750	9,110	13,900	23,010	260.8
Erie.........	241	57	210	4,990	4,950	9,940	251.5
Ontario......	193	53	774	3,560	3,980	7,430	174.6

Method 3:

COMPARATIVE STATISTICS ON GREAT LAKES

Statistics	Superior	Michigan	Huron	Erie	Ontario
Length (miles).............	350	307	206	241	193
Breadth (miles)............	160	118	101	57	53
Maximum depth (feet).......	1,290	923	750	210	774
Area (square miles):					
United States...........	20,710	22,400	9,110	4,990	3,560
Canada..................	11,110	......	13,900	4,950	3,980
Total...................	31,820	22,400	23,010	9,940	7,430
National boundary (miles)..	282.8	......	260.8	251.5	174.6

Presentation of figures in table form not only permits quick comparison but also saves space.

Here are some suggestions for preparing tables.

1. Read the table carefully so that you will understand its purpose. (With exceptionally technical data, of course, you may not be able to do anything but copy the material exactly as it is shown.)

2. Center the title of the table, preferably in capitals. Do not use a period after a heading. Break titles of any kind, when they must be broken, where there is a break in thought. Examples:

Poor:

NUMBER OF EMPLOYEES CARRYING
INSURANCE ON JANUARY 1

Better:

NUMBER OF EMPLOYEES
CARRYING INSURANCE ON JANUARY 1

or:

NUMBER OF EMPLOYEES CARRYING INSURANCE
ON JANUARY 1

3. Use leaders (rows of dots) to fill the space between the items at the left (called the "stub") and the first column of figures; also in the columns wherever figures have been purposely omitted.

4. Use new carbon paper when typing tables or other matter containing figures. (Used carbon paper may be kept for other typing jobs.)

5. Proofread all tables carefully, preferably with another person. It is easier and faster to read down the columns than across, but it is safer to use a ruler as a guide and to read across a line at a time. To be entirely safe, add the figures in columns showing totals, to make sure the figures you typed agree with the actual figures.

The Typing of Tables. Arranging tables for financial and other statistical reports calls for mastery of tabulation technique. Tabulation technique involves two problems—centering the material vertically on the page, and centering the material horizontally on the page. In your typing course you learned some simple rules for vertical and horizontal centering to be used in the typing of tables.

Whether the tabulation job you will have to do is simple or complex, these simple rules for planning the tabulation are followed. One successful teacher of typing gives this rule for tabulation to his students, "Plan your work—then work your plan."

Ruling Between Columns. Horizontal rules in tables can be inserted, as the table is being typed, by using the underscore key and the variable line spacer. If vertical rules are desired, it is best to hand-rule them with a ruling pen (not an ordinary pen) in india ink after the table has been removed from the typewriter rather than attempt to use any of the characters on the typewriter. Ruled lines should be rather light.

Graphs. Almost any information that can be expressed in a table can also be expressed by means of a graph; usually a table is prepared first, as a basis for the graph.

Secretaries sometimes have to plot bar graphs and line graphs. Experts usually prepare circle graphs (commonly called "pie charts"), and pictograms, which are illustrated on page 130.

Bar Graphs. A vertical bar graph made with pen and ink, together with the figures on which it was based, is shown in Figure 6.

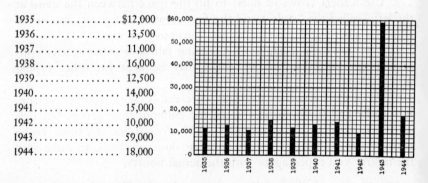

1935	$12,000
1936	13,500
1937	11,000
1938	16,000
1939	12,500
1940	14,000
1941	15,000
1942	10,000
1943	59,000
1944	18,000

Figure 6. A VERTICAL BAR GRAPH

A vertical bar graph made with pen and ink and showing two sets of figures is shown in Figure 7, together with the figures on which it was based.

	Earnings	Expenses		Earnings	Expenses
1935	$120,000	$ 70,000	1940	$ 85,000	$ 70,000
1936	165,000	95,000	1941	95,000	65,000
1937	240,000	150,000	1942	165,000	110,000
1938	205,000	140,000	1943	185,000	115,000
1939	115,000	85,000	1944	225,000	130,000

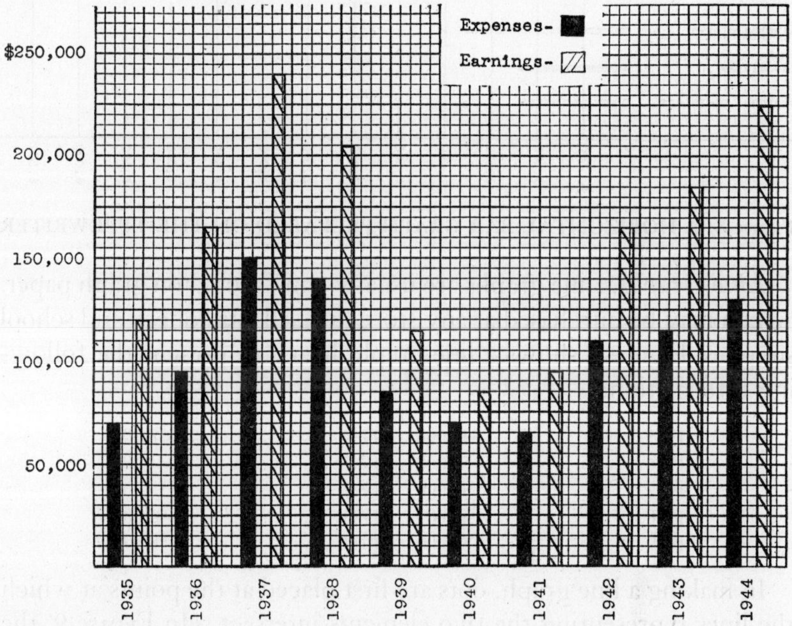

Figure 7. A VERTICAL BAR GRAPH SHOWING TWO SETS OF FIGURES

Bar graphs are often made on the typewriter. Figure 8 shows such a graph. The figures on which it was based appear at the foot of this page. The small *m* was struck once for each $100 in the various amounts. Other characters often used are small *x*, small *w* struck over small *m*, and small *m* struck over small *n*.

Two sets of information may be shown on one bar graph by using black for one set of figures and red for the other or by using a different typewriter character for the second bar.

Office manager	$6,500		Stenographers	$2,400
Accountants	5,000		Shipping clerks	1,800
Bookkeepers	3,000		File clerks	1,200
Secretaries	3,000		Telephone operators	1,200

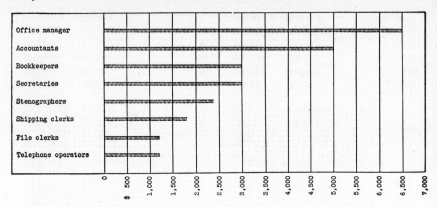

Figure 8. A HORIZONTAL BAR GRAPH PREPARED ON THE TYPEWRITER

Line Graphs. Line graphs are usually constructed on graph paper, which may be purchased at any store that sells stationery and school supplies. Figure 9 shows a line graph drawn to present the following information:

1935	$47,000	1940	$28,000
1936	56,000	1941	31,000
1937	84,000	1942	37,000
1938	63,000	1943	46,000
1939	39,000	1944	58,000

In making a line graph, dots are first placed at the points at which the lines representing the two elements intersect. (In Figure 9, the elements are years and amounts of money.) Then the dots are connected by a line. You will be given further instructions on plotting line graphs in Assignment 6 for this section in your workbook.

In making any graph, plan before you work. Be sure you know which is the least and which is the greatest figure for which you must make provision.

Flow Charts. Flow charts usually indicate the flow of operations or work in an office or through a number of offices or an entire plant. Often improvements are made after a procedure is charted by means of a flow chart and unnecessary steps are discovered. A flow chart is illustrated on page 207 of this book, in connection with the routine of the Billing Department. Secretaries should know how to make simple flow charts.

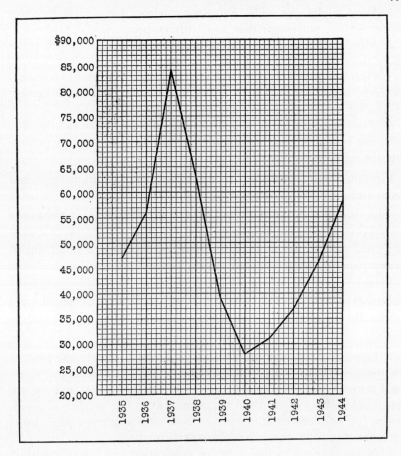

Figure 9. A LINE GRAPH

Binding. When all the material that makes up the report has been assembled in proper order (see page 173), the report is ready for binding. The style of binding depends on the thickness of the report and the handling it will receive.

Covers may be made of heavy art paper, which may be purchased at a stationery store. Ordinary Manila file folders are also suitable for covers. Loose-leaf binders are especially desirable for long reports or for those that are to receive hard wear.

Pages may be fastened together by one of several devices:

1. Wire staples, put on by a stapling machine, are suitable for short reports—those not longer than about fifteen pages.

2. Metal eyelets may be inserted through holes punched in the paper and clamped in place by a special attachment.

3. Ordinary paper fasteners, the style having a head and two separable ends, which are bent back on the under side, have the advantage of making it easy to separate the pages of the report.

4. Tape or cord may be passed through punched holes and tied in a neat, flat bow. This method of binding has the advantage of permitting the report to lie flat while open.

Gummed reinforcements may be bought to outline punched holes and prevent paper from tearing.

The title of the report should appear on the cover. If the cover material is flexible enough to go into the typewriter, the title may be typed directly on it. If not, it may be typed on a small slip of heavy paper and pasted neatly on the cover.

Manuscripts to Be Submitted for Publication. A book or magazine publisher can often tell whether a writer is a professional or a novice by his method of submitting material for possible publication.

1. Leave the top half of the first page blank. Center the title of the manuscript, with the author's name below it. In the upper right-hand corner, type the author's name and mailing address and the approximate number of words in the manuscript. (The number of words in one full line, times the number of lines on one average page, times the number of pages equals the approximate total.)

2. Never submit a carbon copy for publication, but keep one carbon for reference. If a carbon is submitted, the editor immediately assumes that the original is being submitted to another publisher.

3. Never submit the same article to more than one publisher at a time, unless it is a news release for general publication. After one publisher has rejected a manuscript, it may be sent to another.

4. If a manuscript contains twenty pages or more, it should be mailed flat in a 9-by-12 envelope. Manuscripts of fewer pages may be sent, folded once, in an envelope $7\frac{1}{2}$ by $10\frac{1}{2}$; or, folded twice, in a No. 10 envelope.

5. A manuscript may be accompanied by a brief letter of transmittal.

6. Enclose an envelope, addressed to the sender, attaching to it enough stamps to bring the manuscript back if it is rejected. Mention,

in the letter of transmittal, that this is being done. Publishers are under no obligation to return rejected manuscripts that are not accompanied by return postage.

7. A very thick manuscript—as for a book—may be placed in an empty stationery box.

8. There are only two ways to send manuscripts: by first-class mail, at regular letter-postage rates; and by express, at rates that vary according to the weight of the package and the distance it has to go. Manuscripts cannot be sent by parcel post. Book manuscripts are usually sent by express.

Answers to "Do You Know?"

1. Look up the exact title. If a report or a manuscript is technical enough to require footnotes, the absolute accuracy of all the information given is worth checking in detail. A reputation for carelessness is hard for an author to live down. You must protect the author.

2. Ask the author of the report or someone else who will know. Anyone can make a mistake; you can respect your superiors without expecting them to be infallible. Finding an obvious error like this will add to your reputation for alertness. But use the utmost tact in inquiring about it. Don't say, "I think you made a mistake here." (To renumber the footnotes yourself would be highly inadvisable.)

3. Type after the misspelled word the word *sic*, in parentheses. *Sic* is the Latin adverb meaning *thus*.

4. Suggest that she find out whether she is using the right paper and spacing. Publishers heartily dislike manuscripts that are hard to read. They prefer heavier paper and double or triple spacing to give plenty of space for editing and styling the copy.

5. Permission must be obtained from the author or the publisher, sometimes from both. One who uses copyrighted material without permission makes himself liable to legal action by the copyright owner.

SCENES FROM TWO MODERN OFFICE LIBRARIES

Above: Stacks in the library of the American Institute of Accountants. Left: The Circulation Desk and a Glimpse of the Reading Room of the library of the Public Service Corporation of New Jersey

8

THE OFFICE LIBRARY

DO YOU KNOW?

1. Your employer says, "Please make a reservation for me at the best hotel in Boston." What will you do?
2. What printed authority would you consult to find out how to pronounce the name of a foreign city?
3. How would you find out in which state and county a certain town is located?
4. What advantage will it be to you, a secretary, to become familiar with the business magazines regularly received by your employer?
5. You are working for a man who does much writing for publication. One of his favorite axioms is, "Consistency, thou art a jewel." Where would you look to find the source of this quotation?

MANY concerns—especially banks, brokerage houses, insurance companies, public utilities, engineering firms, large industrial concerns, and firms of attorneys and public accountants—maintain office libraries, usually in charge of trained librarians.

Such libraries contain general reference books and magazines as well as books and periodicals dealing with the special field of the particular business. Firms maintaining libraries are usually glad to extend the privilege of using them to executives of other companies.

When a businessman pays his secretary the high compliment of saying, "My secretary seems to know everything I ask about," he does not mean that the secretary can instantly recite any desired fact or figure from memory. What he really means is, "My secretary knows how to find facts in a hurry."

A secretary who really contributes to the effectiveness of the employer's work does not wait to be told to look up a reference or a fact but is alert to suggest, "I can look that up to make sure."

REFERENCE BOOKS FOR EVERYDAY USE

Books about the Use of Language. The secretary refers most often to books on the correct and effective use of words.

The ideal office supplies an unabridged dictionary, to which all the staff members may refer. But many businessmen, while they profess to admire accuracy in the use of words, put off, year after year, the purchase of an authoritative unabridged dictionary. Firms that deal with words as part of their stock in trade—publishers and advertising agencies, for example—do provide dependable reference books. Secretaries in such firms are expected to maintain high standards in all details of their typed output.

Courtesy G. & C. Merriam Co.

TWO INDISPENSABLE BOOKS
The unabridged, usually called the "big," dictionary, and the desk-sized abridged dictionary

The two leading unabridged dictionaries are Webster's *New International Dictionary* and Funk & Wagnalls' *New Standard Dictionary of the English Language.*

Become thoroughly familiar with your dictionary. There is more in it than you think! For a quick reference for the spelling and division of words, especially when transcribing, you will find the little book entitled *20,000 Words,* by Louis A. Leslie, invaluable and a great timesaver. And, keep in mind that changes are made in dictionaries as in other reference books; so you should use only the latest edition.

English Grammar. The secretary deals with the English language in every letter she transcribes, in every office conversation, in every telephone conversation. She is expected to know and abide by the rules of correct English usage. A standard English grammar and a handbook of writing are most effective argument settlers.

The following books will help you review and will provide a quick reference.

The English of Business, by Hagar, Wilson, Hutchinson, and Blanchard.
Crowell's Dictionary of English Grammar, by M. H. Weseen.
New Handbook of Composition, revised and enlarged edition, by Edwin C. Woolley.
The Century Handbook of Writing, by Greever and Jones.

Synonyms and Antonyms. Reference to sources of synonyms and antonyms will often help you to find the word that means exactly what the dictator wants to say when he has used a word not very well chosen. For synonyms and antonyms, refer to one or more of the following books:

A dictionary.
English Synonyms, Antonyms, and Prepositions, by James C. Fernald.
Allen's Synonyms and Antonyms, by F. Sturges Allen.
Webster's Dictionary of Synonyms.
A thesaurus.

Thesaurus. A thesaurus is a collection of words and phrases arranged according to ideas. Its object is the exact opposite of the object of a dictionary. One refers to a dictionary to find the meaning of a *word* that one has in mind. One refers to a thesaurus to find the word by which to express an *idea* one has in mind. Thus a thesaurus goes one step farther than a book of synonyms. In using a book of synonyms, one must have at least one word in mind; in using a thesaurus, one can start with a vague idea. Roget's *Thesaurus* is the classic work.

Assume, for example, that this sentence has just been dictated to you: "The buyer was short with our salesman but was finally induced to place a trial order." The dictator frowns and says, "See if you can find a clearer way of saying that. I don't like the word 'short' right there—it's not just what I want to say."

In the Index in the back of the thesaurus you find, under "short," nearly a column of words—"not long," "brittle," "concise," "uncivil," and so on—each followed by a number. The numbers refer to the numbered sections of the book.

Turning to the section bearing the number attached to "uncivil," you find the heading, "Discourtesy," followed by many words and phrases related to the idea of discourtesy. Paralleling the list, on the same page, is a column headed "Courtesy"—a most convenient arrangement.

Style Books. In your English course, much attention is given to preferred usage in the matters of capitalization, punctuation, quotations, use of figures, abbreviations, italics, and word division. It is almost impossible to carry all this miscellaneous information in one's mind; also, new problems of style are constantly presenting themselves.

The best source of such information is one of the style books prepared for the use of authors and proofreaders, but of equal value to anyone who prepares typewritten copy.

For everyday use by the secretary, the following books are authoritative:

Stenographers' Transcription Reference, by W. B. Hobson.
The Secretary's Guide to Correct Modern Usage, by C. O. S. Mawson.
Standard Handbook for Secretaries, by Lois Hutchinson.
The Private Secretary's Manual, by Bernice Turner.

For the secretary employed by a publishing firm or in advertising work, these additional books, more detailed and specifically applying to problems of printing, are often used:

A Manual of Style, The University of Chicago Press.
Style Manual of the United States Government Printing Office.

Books of Quotations. Writers, publishers, advertising men, and executives who have occasion to make public addresses often wish to use quotations. Almost no one ever remembers the exact wording of a quotation. A book of quotations gives the exact wording, the source, and the author's name. The standard books of quotations are:

Familiar Quotations, Eleventh Edition, John Bartlett.
Hoyt's Cyclopedia of Practical Quotations, J. K. Hoyt.

DIRECTORIES

Telephone Directories. The directory most often used is the telephone directory, which was described in Section 4, page 73.

Classified Directory. The classified telephone directory contains the name, address, and telephone number of business subscribers listed under a classified heading that is descriptive of the subscriber's business. This classified directory is of great convenience in the following cases:

1. When you wish to buy something.
2. When you wish to find a dealer of a trade-marked product.
3. When you have forgotten the name of a business firm. (For example, if you are looking for a certain radio repairman whose name you do not remember, look under "Radio.")
4. When you have forgotten part of a name. (A plumber named Smith is easier to find under "Plumbers" than among the many Smiths.)

City Directories. In some communities, a city directory is published, in which are listed, alphabetically, all residents, with their business and home addresses. City directories are not revised so frequently as telephone directories and may, therefore, be out of date.

Special Business Directories. Many special directories are published for use in various business activities. Most offices have copies of the directories to which employees have occasion to refer frequently; many others are available in public libraries. An advertising manager is likely to have a copy of *Standard Rate and Data*, which lists periodicals that carry advertising, with detailed information about each. A publishing company would probably have the *Publishers' Trade List Annual*, in which are listed the leading publishers, with alphabetical lists of the books each one has published.

Hotel and Travel Guides. Any organization whose salesmen or executives travel frequently is likely to have a directory of hotels. A standard hotel guide is the *Official Hotel Red Book and Directory*, in which the states and cities are listed alphabetically, as are the hotels in each city. Another directory of this kind is the *Travel America Guide and Hotel Directory*.

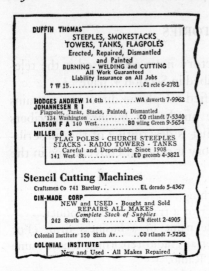

DUFFIN THOMAS
STEEPLES, SMOKESTACKS
TOWERS, TANKS, FLAGPOLES
Erected, Repaired, Dismantled
and Painted
BURNING - WELDING and CUTTING
All Work Guaranteed
Liability Insurance on All Jobs
7 W 15........................CI rcle 6-2781

HODGES ANDREW 14 6th ....WA dsworth 7-9962
JOHANNESEN R I
Flagpoles, Tanks, Stacks, Painted, Dismantled
134 Washington ....CO rtlandt 7-5340
LARSON F A 140 West..........BO wling Green 9-5654

MILLER G S
FLAG POLES - CHURCH STEEPLES
STACKS - RADIO TOWERS - TANKS
Careful and Dependable Since 1908
141 West St............ ...ED gecomb 4-3821

Stencil Cutting Machines
Craftsmen Co 741 Barclay...........EL dorado 5-4367

CIN-MADE CORP
NEW and USED - Bought and Sold
REPAIRS ALL MAKES
Complete Stock of Supplies
242 South St.. ....EN dicott 2-4905

Colonial Institute 150 Sixth Av... ..CO rtlandt 7-5258

COLONIAL INSTITUTE
New and Used - All Makes Repaired

HEBRON, *Porter Co. Pop.* 693. RR., Penna.
COMMERCIAL HOTEL. Ⓑ $1-$1.25.
HOWE, *Lagrange Co. Pop.* 700. RR., Penna.
KINGSBURY HOUSE. Ⓑ $2. C. D. Kingsbury.
HUNTINGBURG, *Dubois Co. Pop.* 3,440. RR., Southern; F.
IDEAL HOTEL, 30 rooms. Ⓐ & Ⓑ.
PHOENIX HOTEL. Ⓑ 75c up. E. F. Schwartz.
HUNTINGTON, *Huntington Co. Pop.* 13,420. RR., Erie, Wab.; Ind.
HUNTINGTON HOTEL, 60 rooms. Ⓑ $1.25 up. Jim Renner, Prop. Perry Moore, Mgr.
JEFFERSON HOTEL, 40 rooms. Ⓑ $1 up. E. Nichols:
✦LA FONTAINE HOTEL, 120 rooms. Ⓑ $2 up. Geo. J. Bippus, Mgr.
INDIANAPOLIS, *Marion Co. Pop.* 364,161. RR., Big 4; Penn.; Erie; Ill. C.; I. U.; N. Y. C. & St. L.; U. T. of I.; B. & O.; Chi., Ind. & Lv.
✦ANTLERS HOTEL, 200 rooms. Ⓑ $2 up. Albert Pick Hotels. R. I. Griffith, Mng. Dir.
✦BARTON HOTEL, 150 rooms. Ⓑ$1 up. A. L. Cummins, Mgr.
BREVORT HOTEL, 106 rooms. Ⓑ $1 up. Walter B. & Hulbert J. Smith, Props. J. M. Herbert, Mgr.
BROADWAY HOTEL, 50 rooms. Ⓑ $3 up. Al. Smith, Jr.
✦CLAYPOOL HOTEL, 600 rooms. Ⓑ *$2.50 up. Geo. G. Cunningham, Mgr.*
(*See ill. and adv. above.*)
COLONIAL HOTEL, 100 rooms. Ⓑ $1.25 up. C. B. Navin, Prop.

Above: From a Classified Telephone Directory. Right: Section of a Hotel Directory

Professional Directories. *The American Medical Directory*, the *Educational Directory*, *Who's Who in Advertising*, and the Martindale-Hubbell *Law Directory* are typical examples of the directories available for the various professions.

Directories of Public Officials. Lists of city and state officials are published by some cities and states. These lists are usually obtainable for a small charge from the city hall or the state capital if they are not available in the city library. The *Congressional Directory* gives information about the executive personnel of all the departments of the Federal Government and lists the members of Congress.

Biographical Directories. *Who's Who in America*, published every other year, gives brief biographical sketches about many thousands of notable men and women. The following information is included: birthplace, date of birth, names of parents, education, occupation, achievements, politics, membership in organizations, marriage, children. Somewhat similar directories are issued for some cities, such as *Who's Who in New York.*

Persons prominent in society are listed in the annual *Social Registers* of the larger cities. Some cities have *Blue Books,* which are similar.

Financial Information. Many business firms, with their financial ratings, financial statements, and brief histories, are listed in *Moody's Manual of Investments.* Other sources of credit information are discussed in Section 11 of this book.

FACTS AT YOUR FINGERTIPS

The World Almanac. So much information is contained in *The World Almanac and Book of Facts* (published annually by the New York *World-Telegram*) that it is impossible even to suggest the wealth of facts available in this book. It contains, for example, data on foreign affairs, important events, stock exchange prices, foreign countries, laws of the United States, the individual states, athletic events, and crops and other products. This material is thoroughly indexed for quick reference.

Miscellaneous Information. Figures on finance, trade, and world commerce are given in the *Statistical Abstract,* an annual publication, and the *World Economic Review.* Both are published by the United States Government.

Brief descriptive and statistical material on the governments of the different countries of the world is contained in the *Statesman's Yearbook.* Events and progress of the year, with special emphasis on the United States, are described in the *American Year Book.*

United States *Census* reports, which are published once every ten years by the Federal Government, give a great number of statistics on population, manufacture, agriculture, and many other subjects.

Postal and Shipping Guides. Most offices have a copy of the *United States Official Postal Guide.* Any firm that does much mail business must often refer to the postal regulations, of course. This book is indispensable for another reason—it lists every place in the United States where a United States post office is maintained. It is the authentic reference for the spelling of town names.

The *Postal Guide* is of great assistance in deciphering illegible addresses or completing fragmentary addresses. In one section of the *Guide*, all the states are listed, with an alphabetical list of the post offices in each state. In another section, all the post offices in the country appear in one alphabetical list. Another section lists the counties of each state and the post offices in each county.

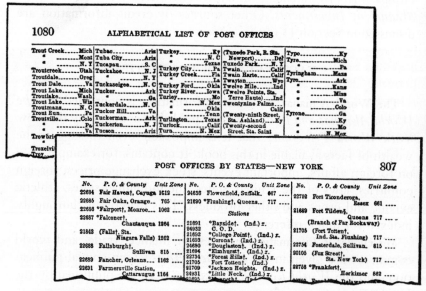

REPRESENTATIVE PAGES FROM THE UNITED STATES OFFICIAL
POSTAL GUIDE

Also invaluable in shipping and mailing departments are shipping guides. *Bullinger's Postal and Shippers Guide*, published by Bullinger's Monitor Guide, Inc., New York, is representative. These guides contain not only postal rates and regulations but also information about freight and express. In addition to post offices, they list all railroad stations, boat landings, and ports in the United States, with information for routing shipments to each.

For the correct spelling of all difficult geographic names, consult the *Sixth Report of the United States Geographic Board*.

Atlases and Maps. Nearly every office needs an atlas, especially if the company does business over a wide area. Loose-leaf atlases are especially convenient, because revised maps may easily be inserted. The large *World Atlas* published by Rand, McNally & Company contains statistics as well as maps and a good index. Maps and atlases are also available from C. S. Hammond & Company, J. B. Lippincott & Company, and other publishers.

Large detailed maps of states, counties, and cities are often used in planning sales campaigns, when salesmen's territories must be designated.

Encyclopedias. Encyclopedias contain a great deal of information, but few offices have them because of their cost. They are available in public libraries, however. The topics treated are arranged alphabetically, and an index is also provided, in which material is cross-referenced.

The *Encyclopaedia Britannica* and the *Encyclopedia Americana* are revised at intervals of several years.

The *New International Encyclopedia* is accompanied by a yearbook, published annually, which keeps the material up to date.

The one-volume *Columbia Encyclopedia*, for desk use, has a supplement that is published periodically.

Specialized encyclopedias are also available on certain subjects.

Government Publications. To obtain information about the many publications of the United States Government, write to the Superintendent of Documents, Government Printing Office, Washington, D. C., for a list of the price lists published. From this list, choose the price list covering your particular subject and then write for this price list. When it is received, order the reports or pamphlets needed.

The *United States Government Manual* is one of the most valuable reference books published by the Federal Government. It contains integrated, authoritative information on the organization and functions of the departments and agencies of the Federal Government.

Information Services. Various information services are available to the public, and the resourceful secretary makes use of them.

Public Library. The public library, with which you have become acquainted during your school work, offers much help. It will pay you to become even better acquainted with this storehouse of information and with the trained librarians who are ready and willing to assist persons in search of specific information.

If, for example, you wish certain information regarding a book—the correct title, the spelling of the author's name, the name of the publisher, the date of publication, and similar information—the reference room in the public library has various types of catalogues for this purpose. Bibliographies, or lists of books pertaining to various subjects, may also be found in the library.

The *United States Catalog* is an index to all American books in print on January 1, 1928. It is supplemented and kept up to date by the *Cumulative Book Index* (monthly and cumulations), which was enlarged in 1929 to include all books published in English, regardless of the country in which they were published. Books are listed by author, title, and subject. For each book, the price, publisher, binding, paging, size, date of publication, and Library of Congress card order number are given.

The *Publishers' Trade List Annual* contains the catalogues of most of the American publishing houses. In order to find entries in this *Annual*, however, it is necessary to know the publisher of the work in question.

The *Book Review Digest*, issued monthly, and cumulated at four-month intervals and annually, quotes excerpts from leading reviews of new books.

When you desire to ascertain the exact date of a news item important enough to have been published in a metropolitan paper, the *New York Times Index* makes it possible to locate the item. This *Index* will be found in the reference room of the public library.

The *Index* is published monthly and in a cumulative annual volume. References show the date, page, and column of the *New York Times* in which the items listed appeared. Editorials, book reviews, magazine articles, and other material published in that newspaper are also listed. When the date of an item has been located, it is then possible, of course, to refer to other newspapers and periodicals for their reports on the same event.

Daily Newspapers. In large cities, the important daily newspapers usually maintain reader services. By telephoning them, it is possible to obtain authentic information on a wide variety of topics, not only on news items.

City Bureaus of Information. Many of the larger cities maintain information bureaus specializing on information regarding the city —its government, population, transit systems, public utilities, amusements, and so on.

Trade Associations and Chambers of Commerce. Local trade associations and local chambers of commerce gather facts of particular interest to individual trades and businesses.

PERIODICALS

Magazine Articles. Articles that have appeared in the leading current magazines may be located by referring to the *Readers' Guide to Periodical Literature* in the public library. Articles are listed according to author, title, and subject.

Trade and Professional Journals. Hundreds of magazines are not sold on newsstands and are never heard of by most persons. Nevertheless, these periodicals are of keen interest and great practical value to their readers. These very specialized magazines are known as "trade journals." (Medical journals, such as the *Journal of the American Medical Association,* and periodicals published for lawyers, the clergy, and teachers are called "professional journals.")

A large baking company, for example, would probably subscribe to the *Baker's Weekly* and one or two other publications in the baking field. Manufacturers of equipment for bakeries and firms supplying materials to bakeries would probably subscribe also, and many of them would advertise in these magazines.

Next to the company's correspondence and price lists, the trade journals provide the most practical sources of information for the beginning secretary who is intent on learning about her employer's business. Casual, frequent reading, especially of the advertising, will supply a working vocabulary and a foundation for further learning.

For certain fields, articles may be located in special indexes that list material of interest to those engaged in those fields. Typical special indexes are the *Engineering Index, Index to Legal Periodicals*, and the *Industrial Arts Index*.

THE CORRECT WAY TO DO THINGS

Books of Etiquette. The secretary should have ready access to an authoritative and up-to-date reference book on etiquette. Emily Post is the accepted authority on social form; and her book, *Etiquette*, should be in every office.

Problems of business etiquette are discussed in *What Do I Do Now?* by Mildred Payne, and *Manners in Business*, by Eleanor Gregg MacGibbon.

Parliamentary Procedure. Some secretaries are called upon to attend and report committee meetings in which parliamentary procedure is used. In transcribing the minutes, the secretary is likely to need Robert's *Rules of Order*. *The Parliamentarian*, by Cora Welles Trow, is another authoritative book.

The secretary with aspirations toward executive status is likely to find it advisable to join one or more civic or business clubs. In order to take part in their business meetings, she will need to know parliamentary procedure well enough to use it with ease.

HOW TO USE REFERENCE BOOKS

To be able to use the various sources of information described in this chapter to the best advantage, the secretary must cultivate an efficient method of searching for information. Keep in mind these essentials:

1. Be sure that you know exactly what you are looking for and why. Any haziness about either aspect of the problem will only lead to loss of time. If you do not understand the nature of the problem, ask questions. And take your instructions in shorthand.

2. Make full use of the various mechanical aids each reference work offers—index, table of contents, page headings, etc. Get acquainted with the organization and individual features of the leading reference works you consult.

3. Do not dawdle over your reading. Read only the sections pertaining to the problem in hand, no matter how interesting the other material is. Later, when you may have time, you can go back and read anything that intrigues you.

4. If you work away from the office—for example, at the library or in the rooms of some technical organization—make accurate, careful shorthand notes on what you find. Any quotations must be exactly copied. Make a careful record of the source of all data, including the author's name, the title of the book, the edition, and the page.

5. If you are obliged to consult anyone for help in locating materials or information, state your problem clearly and with sufficient detail to make the object of your search clear to that person. Be courteous always. In writing for information, send a stamped self-addressed envelope.

ANSWERS TO "DO YOU KNOW?"

1. For the names of hotels, look in one of the hotel and travel guides. These guides describe the accommodations offered by various hotels, together with prices. Find out from your employer the date and the time he will arrive, whether he wishes a single or a double room, and how long he expects to stay. Write a letter or wire the hotel, giving this information as far in advance as possible, and ask the hotel to send you an immediate confirmation—by collect telegram if the time is short.

2. Some atlases give this information. So does the gazetteer—a geographical dictionary such as is found at the back of *Webster's Collegiate Dictionary*.

3. Try the *United States Postal Guide*, an atlas, or a gazetteer.

4. An immediate advantage will be the enlargement of your business vocabulary; you will no doubt learn some new technical terms that will be useful to you. Another advantage will be an increased understanding of your employer's problems. (And don't forget that his respect for your ability and intelligence will probably increase, too.)

5. Try Bartlett's *Familiar Quotations* or some other book of quotations. (You will find that the authorship of this axiom is lost in the mists of the past.)

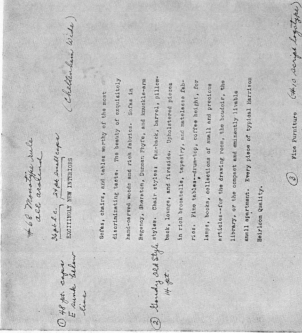

AN ADVERTISING LAYOUT AND COPY WITH TYPE MARKED

9

THE ADVERTISING DEPARTMENT

DO YOU KNOW?

1. Can you depend on a printer to correct errors in copy sent him to be set in type?

2. Is there any short-cut method for assembling the pages for fifty copies of a five-page multigraphed report?

3. Why do some companies find it worth while to publish small magazines (house organs), which they send free to their customers?

4. What returns may a company expect from the publication of an "internal house magazine"; that is, one for its own employees?

5. Why do advertising men not consistently use one type face for all kinds of advertising?

THE Advertising Department co-operates with the Sales Department in selling the company's merchandise. Although the two departments use different methods and work in different ways, their purpose is the same: to sell the company's products and to increase the company's prestige. Advertising increases the effectiveness of the work of the salesmen by strengthening their sales efforts with words and pictures and by reminding the prospective customer of the company's merchandise when salesmen cannot call on him.

Persuasion. No company can *make* anyone buy its products—it can only make him *wish* to buy. Persuasion is the tool that makes the customer wish to buy. For this reason—because the success of any business depends largely on its ability to sell what it has to offer —you should understand what persuasion really is and how to exert it. The better you understand and use it, the more valuable you will become to your employer.

Publicity Releases. Not all advertising is paid for. Well-managed promotional work results in newspaper and magazine publicity because an appeal is made to the interest of the readers of these publications.

Announcements about changes in executive personnel, new products, and new factories are often sent to newspapers, trade maga-

For release Monday morning, January 13, 194-

From Ralph S. Howard Advertising Agency
500 Fifth Avenue
New York 16, New York

January 13, 194-

Paper Manufacturer Awards Twelve Chemistry Scholarships

Scholarship awards with a total value of $15,000 were
presented yesterday by the Fortwell Paper Company, Green
Bay, Wisconsin, to twelve science students who placed highest
in the examinations conducted by the Chemistry Institute of
Chicago last September. Winners will enroll in the Institute
of Chemistry for graduate study in chemistry relating to the

A PORTION OF A PUBLICITY RELEASE

zines, important customers, and sometimes competitors. If these announcements are printed, they are printed as news, free of charge.

Sometimes such an announcement may concern a matter that the management is not at all happy to announce, but one that it wishes to have stated correctly if it is mentioned at all—for example, a factory accident that occurred in spite of the installation of all the latest approved safety devices.

Clipping Bureaus. Many business firms and public personages wish to find out just how much publicity they are receiving. One way to find out is to subscribe to a clipping bureau. The work of a clipping bureau is described as follows by the Consolidated Press Clipping Bureaus, of Chicago:

We read all the English daily papers published in the United States and many thousand weeklies. Clippings are supplied on any subject or subjects that a client may desire, and practically every field of industry is now being served with clippings. People in active public life, such as singers, politicians, churchmen, and others, also make use of a clipping service.

A clipping service also supplies dealer advertising copy to manufacturers. A manufacturer may have thousands of dealer outlets scattered all over the country. He supplies them with advertising material and expects them to advertise locally. Dealers, however, cannot be depended upon to send all local advertising copy to the manufacturer, so a clipping bureau supplies this.

Advertising Copy. "Copy," as used in the advertising and publishing field, means reading matter that is to be issued in published form. The word has no connection with carbon copies.

A "layout" is a rough sketch or design of an advertisement or of a magazine page. The layout shows the approximate size, shape, and location of illustrations and the position of paragraphs of the copy. As it is not practicable to attempt to type or write the advertising copy on the layout, the paragraphs of the copy are numbered, and only the numbers appear on the layout.

The illustration on page 160 shows the layout and copy for a magazine page.

Styling Copy. One of your responsibilities in preparing copy for quantity production, either by printing or by one of the duplicating processes, is to see that the "style" is consistent. That is, you must see that words that should be capitalized are always capitalized; that numbers are not given as figures sometimes and spelled out other times; that punctuation is correct in every case; and that words are always spelled the same way—and always correctly.

You will observe the same care in letters, of course; but in printing and duplicating this inspection is doubly important, because an error in an advertisement will be repeated thousands of times.

Copy for the Printer. It is your responsibility to see that printer's copy is complete and correct when it is sent to the printer. It may be extensively marked with copyreader's marks, but it must be right. Printers are not permitted to correct your errors. They are trained to "follow copy, even if it flies out the window."

Type changes are expensive. The insertion of so small a thing as a forgotten comma requires the resetting of an entire line of type when the copy is set on the Linotype. The insertion of a long word may require the resetting of several lines. You cannot be too careful in preparing printer's copy.

Printers sometimes grumble, "Type isn't made of rubber." This comment is made when more copy is provided than can be squeezed into the printing space available. The problem of cutting copy to fit space will usually have to be solved by your chief.

Copyreaders' and Proofreaders' Marks. In editing manuscripts use copyreaders' marks for the guidance of the printer in setting up type. Use copyreaders' marks also in correcting typewritten mate-

PROOFREADER'S MARKS

∧	Make correction indicated in margin.	⌣	Lower to proper position.
Stet	Retain crossed-out word or letter; let it stand.	////	Hair space letters.
....	Retain words under which dots appear;	*w.f.*	Wrong font; change to proper **font**.
Stet	write "Stet" in margin.	*Qu ?*	Is this right?
X	Appears battered; examine.	*l.c.*	Put in lower case (small letters).
=	Straighten lines.	*s.c.*	Put in small capitals.
∨∨∨	Unevenly spaced; correct spacing.	*Caps*	Put in capitals.
//	Line up; i.e., make lines even with other matter.	*C.&s.c.*	Put in caps and small caps.
		rom.	Change to Roman.
run in	Make no break in the reading; no ¶	*.ital.*	Change to Italic.
no ¶	No paragraph; sometimes written "run in."	≡	Under letter or word means caps.
		=	Under letter or word, small caps.
out see copy	Here is an omission; see copy.	—	Under letter or word means Italic.
¶	Make a paragraph here.	⁓	Under letter or word, bold face.
tr	Transpose words or letters as indicated.	⋀/	Insert comma.
ℐ	Take out matter indicated; dele.	;/	Insert semicolon.
ℛ̂	Take out character indicated and close up.	:/	Insert colon.
¢	Line drawn through a cap means lower case.	⊙	Insert period.
		/?/	Insert interrogation mark.
ℬ	Upside down; reverse.	(!)	Insert exclamation mark.
⌒	Close up; no space.	/=/	Insert hyphen.
#	Insert a space here.	⌄	Insert apostrophe.
⊥	Push down this space.	ᵛᵛᵛ	Insert quotation marks.
▯	Indent line one em.	ⱽ	Insert superior letter or figure.
⸦	Move this to the left.	⋀	Insert inferior letter or figure.
⸧	Move this to the right.	c/ɔ	Insert brackets.
⌐	Raise to proper position.	(/)	Insert parenthesis.
		1/m	One-em dash.
		2/m	Two-em parallel dash.

1 ¶ Copyreader(s) marks differ from proofreaders' marks.

2 The copy-reader marks corrections on the ~~copy~~ *manuscript* itself,

3 within the lines or between them. Proofreaders' marks

4 are used on proofs of type set up from manuscript.

5 *No ¶* Within the ~~type~~ lines *of type,* they show only the position

6 of the correction, the nature of it being indicated more

7 fully on the margin; the reason for this is that there

8 is not enough room between (type) lines *of* to show the de-

9 sired changes legibly. ¶ Copy marked in either of these

10 ways, according to definite rules, is entirely understand-

11 able to printers. The stenographer(s) work in reading for

12 errors [properly | is] called proofreading, however, no matter

13 whether she is using copyreaders' marks on typed material

14 or profreaders' marks on setup type.

Correction Indicated

Line
1 Make a new paragraph. Transpose a letter.
2 Take out hyphen and close up. Substitute new word.
4 Take out underscore.
5 Run in—don't make a new paragraph. Change wording.
6 Insert punctuation mark.
7 Circle any punctuation mark to indicate a period. Capitalize *T*.
8 Insert a word and transpose another.
9 New paragraph.
10 Superior figure refers to footnote, which would appear on the same typed page.
11 Slanting line indicates that capital letter is to be replaced by small letter.
12 Transpose words. Take out hyphen and close up, leaving no space. Insert comma.
13 Take out letter.
14 Insert letter. Insert hyphen.

rial that is to be recopied. When correcting proofs of set-up type, use proofreaders' marks. Some of these are the same as copyreaders' marks, but they are used in a different way, as explained in the illustration on page 165. Many of the marks shown on page 164 pertain only to proofs of type and are never used in manuscripts.

Proofs from the Printer. No matter how careful you are in preparing the copy you send to the printer, be even more careful in checking the proofs you receive from him. He will put in all your mistakes, and he may make some of his own.

Proofreaders sometimes say, "If there's an error, it's in the big type." This is by no means always true; but errors in headlines, captions, and boxes are more likely to be overlooked in proofreading than those in the main part of the text.

Transferring Corrections. The printer will deliver two or more proofs of each "job," together with the original copy and the layout. Return one proof to him, with all corrections clearly marked. Before returning it, however, transfer all corrections to another proof, which you will keep.

When the finished job is delivered, check it against the proof you kept. Check especially every word in every line in which any change was made, because new errors are sometimes made in resetting lines.

MAIL ADVERTISING

An experienced advertising man has a thorough knowledge of printing and duplicating processes, paper grades, envelope sizes, and postal rules, in addition to an uncanny knowledge of what kind of copy will cause people to buy what his company has to sell.

Planning Ahead. The following description of a mail advertising campaign will give you an idea of how thoroughly an executive must go into a plan and how thoroughly you, too, should think through your assignments if you wish to advance to a position of responsibility.

The sales manager of a factory that makes sewing machines tells the advertising manager, "Model A-13 is not moving. See what you can do with some letters."

Here are just a few of the things that the advertising man must consider before he writes a word of copy for the direct-mail advertising campaign he has been assigned to undertake.

Shall we try to sell our dealers or sell direct to housewives?

Shall we try to obtain actual orders, or to get leads for our salesmen to follow up?

Have we a mailing list of housewives, if we decide to sell direct? If not, where can we get one?

Shall we use multigraphing, stencil duplicating, letterpress printing, lithography, or rotogravure?

If we include a letter, shall we use personalized fill-ins or a general salutation?

How many pieces shall we include in the envelope?

What size of envelope do we need?

How much time have we to work on this?

How much will each item cost?

Will the mailing, as planned, conform to postal regulations?

How many extra workers must we hire to prepare the mailing?

What sales appeal shall we use?

Can we offer a special price reduction?

What illustrations?

Should all orders come to our main office? If not, do our branch warehouses have complete stocks?

All these things must be considered before the advertising man even begins to dictate the first draft of a sales letter or to plan copy and layout for printed enclosures to accompany it.

Mailing Lists. The most-used sources of mailing lists are:

1. Salesmen, who may be instructed to send, from their territories, the names and addresses of likely prospects for certain items of merchandise.

2. Specialized lists, which may be obtained from firms that make a business of compiling mailing lists for sale. Some of these lists are broken down by states according to the amount of business done annually or by some other classification. Boyd's City Dispatch and R. L. Polk & Company are among the leading companies specializing in providing lists.

How Mailing Lists Are Kept. Business firms that do much mail advertising usually compile lists over a period of years, having address plates or stencils made for each name so that mailing pieces may be addressed by machinery. These plates or stencils are filed in specially constructed drawers for easy handling.

Address plates for a list of stores, for example, might be filed alphabetically according to states; each state group, alphabetically according to cities; and all the stores in one city, alphabetically by the store names.

The address plates or stencils are often marked with small colored tabs to indicate needed data. (Red tabs might mark plates for stores that do $10,000 or more business each year; yellow tabs might be used to identify those that already use the company's products.) With some addressing machines, it is possible to put in all the address plates, address only from those with certain tabs, and still keep the plates in their proper order.

Mailing lists must be kept up to date if they are to be useful. The company's own salesmen usually report changes in their territories, and corresponding changes should be made in the mailing lists. Every time a piece of direct mail is returned from the Post Office as undeliverable, the plate from which it was addressed should be corrected or removed.

Sometimes files of 5-by-3 cards are kept, with an address on each one. The operator who can read type backward can easily work directly from the address plates in sorting and will not need cards.

There are two main types of addressing equipment: machines that use stencils, and machines that use embossed metal plates.

Addressing from Stencils. The Elliott addressing machine uses stencils made of plastic-coated paper, through which the name and address are cut with an ordinary typewriter. One of these stencils is shown on page 169. A filed stencil is readily located by referring to the name of the addressee typed across the top.

The envelope to be addressed is inserted, with one hand, into a machine like the one pictured here, and is removed with the other after it has been addressed. The stencils automatically fall back into a receiving receptacle, in their proper order.

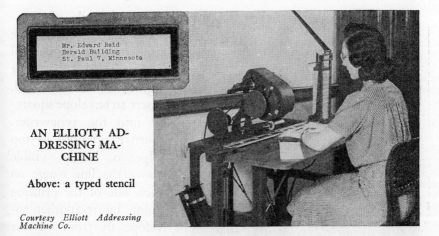

Mr. Edward Reid
Herald Building
St. Paul 7, Minnesota

AN ELLIOTT AD-
DRESSING MA-
CHINE

Above: a typed stencil

*Courtesy Elliott Addressing
Machine Co.*

Certain stencils may be automatically selected from a group by means of holes punched in the rim of the stencil. The machine can be set so that only those stencils having holes in certain positions will be used, the others passing through without printing.

Addressing from Plates. The Addressograph uses metal plates, one of which is shown on page 170.

These plates are prepared on a machine known as the Graphotype. Comparatively small users of direct mail do not purchase this machine, but have their plates made by firms that specialize in this work.

The plates, sorted correctly as needed, are filed in steel drawers and are run through the Addressograph machine as required for printing on envelopes, wrappers, or forms.

Addressographs are produced in many models, both hand and electrically operated.

Addressing on the Typewriter. When plates are not available, envelopes have to be addressed on the typewriter.

You should understand the special technique of addressing large numbers of envelopes. Lack of this knowledge is usually an indication of lack of office experience. Here is a rapid way to address No. 6¾ envelopes. The method is not so practicable for larger envelopes.

Put the pile of envelopes at your left and the list from which you will address them at your right. With the left hand, insert an envelope squarely into the typewriter. Turn it up until its top edge is barely visible above the line gauge on each side of the printing point. Insert another envelope in *front* of the lower edge of the envelope already in position— at the rear of the paper cylinder. Turn the first

AN ADDRESSO-
GRAPH MA-
CHINE

Top: Graphotype on which plates are embossed. Center: Metal address plate

Courtesy Addresso-graph-Multigraph Corp.

envelope up to the point at which you wish to write the first line of the address. This will be approximately at the point where the top edge of the second envelope reaches the top edge of the line gauge. Insert a third envelope just as you did the second one—at the back of the cylinder.

Now type the address on the first envelope, removing the envelope with your right hand, and start a stack of finished envelopes at the right of your machine. Turn the second envelope up to the writing position for the first line. If you have followed directions carefully, it is now time to insert a fourth envelope at the rear of the cylinder. Continue, addressing the second envelope, inserting new envelopes as before, and so on. This is called "chain feeding."

A little practice will enable you to achieve a fair rate of production in typing addresses. Remember that *production*, not the time you put in, determines salary increases.

Filling in Addresses. A name and an address typed in the proper place on a duplicated letter is called a "personalized" fill-in. These fill-ins should exactly match the body of the letter so that the whole letter looks as if it had been individually typed. Secretaries who do much of this work usually keep several typewriter ribbons on hand, in various shades from gray to black, so as to be able to match the body of letters that have been run on Multigraph ribbons of varying degrees of wear. Matching Multigraph and typewriter ribbons are obtainable from the manufacturer of the Multigraph.

Filling-in must usually be done at a high rate of speed, so that the entire mailing can go out at once. Nevertheless, avoid abbreviations just as you do in individually typed letters. Careless, much abbreviated fill-ins cheapen the appearance of the finished job.

Many advertising letters are prepared with some general salutation or opening, such as "To Our Customers" or "Attention All Credit Men!" in order to avoid the necessity of individual fill-ins.

Reply Envelopes. The reader of an advertisement received by mail is more likely to answer it if an envelope or a reply card is provided for him, especially one on which he will not have to pay postage. Business-reply envelopes are often used for this purpose by special arrangement with the postal authorities. The customer has only to enclose his order, seal the envelope, and mail it. The addressee pays

A BUSINESS-REPLY
ENVELOPE

the postage when the letter is received. The postage is a little higher than first-class mail, but in the long run this method of obtaining replies is cheaper than providing stamped envelopes, because postage is paid only on those actually received. Business-reply cards are also available.

Special Postal Regulations. In the Mailing Department, you learned something about postage rates and indicia. Envelopes may have the indicia printed on them so that they need not be stamped or put through a Postage Meter Machine. Letters bearing printed indicia are sorted into bundles according to states and cities, counted, and paid for in bulk at the post office.

Precanceled stamps may also be purchased for use on advertising. Postal clerks can handle envelopes bearing precanceled stamps rapidly because the envelopes need not be put through the canceling machine at the post office.

How to Work Systematically. Assume that you are working with two other persons and have the following items to be enclosed in envelopes, which have already been addressed: a multigraphed letter, two advertising folders of different sizes, a small sample of cloth attached to a card, a price list on 8½-by-11 paper, and a reply envelope smaller than the one in which the mailing is to be sent.

There is no time to waste in fumbling. Probably one worker will begin to fold and stack the letters. Another may fold the price lists and stack them, while the third arranges all the enclosures for convenience in picking them up. When some of the sheets have been folded, the third person may begin the actual insertion of the material in the envelopes. Plan the whole operation at the beginning so that the work will progress rapidly. Arrange the material so that you can use both hands—you can work faster.

Assembling Papers. There is an art to assembling, or "collating," sheets of paper—for example, several pages of a bulletin, of which perhaps a hundred sets of pages are to be stapled together. Here, too, is plenty of opportunity for wasteful fumbling; and you will not do the job the right way by accident.

The best way, usually, is to work backward. If you have a ten-page bulletin, put your pile of page 10 where you will reach it first; then page 9, page 8, and so on to the end. Pick the pages up in that order so that the last one picked up is the top page. By working this way, you collect the pages right side up and can easily see and discard any that have gone through the duplicating machine without printing.

If necessary, arrange the piles in two rows, the first row containing, from left to right, pages 10, 9, 8, 7, and 6. The order in the second row will be 1, 2, 3, 4, and 5; but you will pick these pages up from right to left so that you need not go back to the beginning of the row for the second half.

If you have a large number of pages to assemble, for a large number of sets, make a gathering box. Remove one side and one end from a box in which 8½-by-11 paper was once packed, hold the box on the left arm, and rapidly flip the pages into it as you walk along the table on which you have them arranged.

The accompanying illustration shows pages of a bulletin arranged in piles on a table, ready for assembling, one complete copy

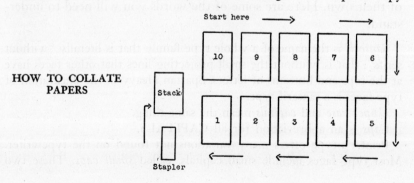

HOW TO COLLATE
PAPERS

at a time, in a gathering box. As each set is assembled, it is quickly removed from the box and stapled.

Bulletins and price sheets for salesmen must often be sent out with the utmost speed. That is why you should know how to economize on time and motion when you have repetitive work of this kind to do.

House Publications. Many business firms publish periodicals that are sent free to customers or employees, or both. These are often called "house organs."

External house publications are published for customers, dealers, and stockholders. Their chief purposes are: (1) to earn and keep the good will of the recipient, sometimes by entertaining him, and almost always by giving him advice about sales programs or new uses for the merchandise or services he buys; and (2) to remind him of the goods and services sold by the company.

Internal house publications are magazines or newspapers published by the management for employees, and usually distributed free. Internal house publications are usually published in order to increase employees' understanding of company policies and problems, thus strengthening the morale and loyalty of the personnel. Pictures and news from various branch offices and plants are usually included. Such publications range from the very informal, chatty type to the highly dignified type, depending on the purpose of the publication.

Internal house publications are sometimes sent to dealers as well as to employees.

Advertising Vocabulary. Advertising and printing have a language of their own. Here are some of the words you will need to understand.

Sanserif is the name of a whole type family that is literally "without serifs"; that is, without the small projecting lines that other faces have at the tops and bottoms of letters. Spartan Heavy in the illustration of type faces is a sanserif type.

Upper case and *capitals* mean the same thing.

Caps is an abbreviation for all CAPITALS.

Printer's type offers many variations not found on the typewriter. Most type faces include small capitals, called *small caps*. These two words are set in SMALL CAPS. These words appear in CAPS AND SMALL CAPS.

When space appears between lines of type, the lines are *leaded*. The strips of metal inserted to space out the lines are called *leads* (pronounced like the "lead" in "lead pencil").

This is set in italics. The abbreviation is *ital.*

Extra black type, **like this,** is bold face.

A *logotype* is a type plate containing two or more letters or a word or words often used by a firm in its printed matter. See page 160.

A *pica* is a measurement used by printers; there are 6 picas to an inch. A *point* is another measurement; there are 12 points to a pica, 72 to an inch. Type may be 1-point leaded (that is, the lines may be spaced 1 point apart) or more. Type itself is measured by points. This page is set in 10 point with the exception of the last paragraph.

Handbills, which are distributed by hand or left on doorsteps, are sometimes called *dodgers* or *throwaways*.

Media is the plural of *medium*, but in advertising *media* is sometimes used in the singular sense. Media advertising is magazine or newspaper advertising, as distinguished from billboard, radio, mail, or handbill advertising.

Newsprint is the comparatively coarse paper on which newspapers and most handbills are printed. *Smooth-finish* or *coated* stock is used for more elaborate advertising pieces and for many magazines.

In journalism and in advertising, the end of a piece of copy is indicated by centering, below the last line, the number 30 or the number sign (#).

A headline for an advertisement or a description accompanying an illustration is called a *caption*.

When an advertiser wishes to distribute duplicate copies of a complete ad—for example, to several newspapers—he has *mats*, or moulds, made. A mat is made by pressing the type, with cuts (illustrations), into a prepared pulp composition. The hardened mat is light and flexible and easy to send by mail. A printing plate or a *stereotype* is made by pouring molten metal into the mat.

Styles of Type. There are dozens of type faces. Although you will doubtless not be able to distinguish them at sight, still you should recognize the names of the leading faces. Caslon and Bodoni, for example, are commonly used faces. This book is printed in Janson type. Samples of several type faces are shown on the next page.

This line is set in 8-point type.
This line is set in 10-point type.
This line is set in 12-point type.
This line is set in 14-point type.

This line is set in Caslon Old Face.
This line is set in Caslon bold.
This line is set in Caslon italic.
This line is set in Bodoni Bold.
This line is set in Spartan Heavy.
This line is set in Garamont.
This line is set in Goudy Old Style.

Illustrations. Advertisers make liberal use of illustrations. Just as the printer converts typewritten copy for the reading matter of the advertisement into type from which the final printing is done, so the engraver converts the illustration copy into *engravings,* or cuts, from which the final printing is done.

The type of engraving is determined by the nature of the illustration copy. Better results are obtained when the copy is larger than the final cut is to be. The copy may be reduced or enlarged photographically during the engraving process.

If the illustration is a pen-and-ink drawing or anything that consists of lines or dots of black and white with no intermediate tones, the engraver makes a *line cut* (or a *zinc*), a zinc plate that is nailed on to a wooden block. The illustration on page 173 is a line cut.

If the illustration is a photograph or other material containing shadings, the engraver makes a *half tone,* which is also nailed on to a wooden block. During the process, the illustration is photographed through a *screen*—the finer the screen, the finer and more detailed the half tone. The most commonly used screens are 55, 65, 85, 100, 120, 133, and 150. Fine-screen half tones will print satisfactorily only on smooth-finish paper. (Line cuts will print on all kinds of paper.) The illustration on page 169 is a half tone.

A *combination* plate is made up of both a half tone and a line cut.

An overall pattern of shading or design may be superimposed on a cut by the *Ben Day* process. The illustration on page 180 has a Ben Day background.

THE ADVERTISING DEPARTMENT

When a duplicate cut is required, an *electrotype* is made of the cut. This is far cheaper than making a new cut.

ANSWERS TO "DO YOU KNOW?"

1. No. Printers are trained to follow the copy given them.

2. On a table arrange five piles of the pages, page 5 first, then page 4, and so on. Pick the pages up in this order.

3. "External house magazines" are a form of advertising; they keep the company's products in the minds of customers and often provide entertainment and extra service in the form of money-saving or timesaving ideas.

4. By publishing a magazine for employees, a company can greatly improve the morale of the organization by making employees feel themselves a part of the whole and by explaining company policies that might otherwise be resented. Improvement in morale brings an increase in output.

5. Different type faces make different impressions on the reader, though he may not be aware of the fact. Note the style of type used in a current advertisement for face powder; compare the type face with the face used for an advertisement of heavy machinery or building materials. The right type face is a definite aid in selling the product advertised.

LETTER-WRITING SUGGESTIONS

Continued from page 33

Letters of Persuasion. If you plan to advance beyond a secretarial job into an executive position, or to be able to hold the highest type of secretarial job, you must know how to write persuasively. All letters that ask for action are letters of persuasion. They range from the very easy kind—one that simply reminds someone to do something he intended to do anyway—to difficult and important letters that persuade the reader to do something that he does not want to do. (Some examples of persuasive letters will be dictated as part of your work in the assignments for this section.)

In writing any persuasive letter, you need to recognize and keep in mind the interests of the person who will receive it. What advantage is there for him in doing what you ask?

Study this letter of persuasion from the advertising manager to a salesman.

Dear Mr. Morgan: By next Friday we shall be ready to start addressing envelopes for those new Rite-Wate circulars. We have not received your list yet, so will you send it along at once by air mail? These circulars will create a great deal of interest among your dealers, and our vice-president looks for a fine increase in sales after they are sent out.

The tone is calm and unexcited, but the urgency of the situation is expressed clearly by "send it along at once by air mail."

Behind this letter is the fact that this salesman has been informed, asked, and reminded about sending the list and has continually put off sending it. The letter has no scolding tone, however.

In place of an obvious reprimand for delay, there is a mere whisper of threat in the statement, "Our vice-president looks for a fine increase in sales." Perhaps the vice-president has not even been consulted about the salesman's failure to send in his mailing list; but the suggestion is there, and the salesman may draw his own conclusions.

Now read two letters handling the same situation in less persuasive tones.

Poor Example No. 1. Dear Mr. Morgan: I hate to keep bothering you all the time, and I know this is an awful nuisance—but won't you *please* send your mailing list. I wouldn't say another thing about this, but the vice-president keeps asking me, and you know how it is.

Note, first, that this letter takes a begging tone. Nobody but beggars should beg. The writer of this letter refuses to take responsibility for his request, but passes the blame on to the vice-president. Those who will not take responsibility seldom have to worry about having it and the higher pay and more interesting work that go with it.

Poor Example No. 2. Dear Mr. Morgan: Although we have asked you at least three times to send that mailing list, we have heard nothing whatever from you. Don't you want to sell any Rite-Wate in your territory? Don't you care whether the executives in the home office consider you co-operative or not? You are certainly giving everybody here a fine impression. Send the mailing list right away if you want anything done about it.

This letter is haughty and sarcastic in tone. It is peremptory, and it reprimands instead of urging.

Avoid all these serious faults. Avoid them purposely until you are an executive with your own private office and secretary. After that, you will avoid them by habit, because you will know from experience that you must.

In writing a letter of persuasion, try to find and state some reason why the person to whom you are writing would benefit from doing what you ask. (The salesman addressed in these three letters knows that he will benefit from increased sales and commissions.) If you are asking a personal favor, the benefit may take the form of the feeling of generosity that the recipient of the letter may experience as a result of acceding to your request. Express or imply your own good will.

Consider, in every letter, the self-interest of the reader. An understanding of other people's self-interest is what makes the wheels of business turn.

Continued on page 195

PURCHASE REQUISITION

National Office Supply Company
St. Louis, Missouri

REQUISITION NUMBER 154

DATE Feb. 23, 194-

PURCHASING DEPT   PLEASE ORDER FOR DEPT. _____ Credit _____ FOR USE ON. March 5

DELIVER TO _____ Credit _____ NOTIFY R. L. Allen

ON HAND _____ ONE MONTH USAGE _____ CHARGE NO _____ DATE WANTED March 1

	QUANTITY	DESCRIPTION OF MATERIAL	PRICE
1	1 doz.	1-lb cans Duplicating ink	
2	3 cart.	Duplicating stencils	
3	1½ doz.	Black Typewriter ribbons	
4	25 rolls	Adding-machine tape	
5			

Approved R. L. Allen   Approved _____   Superintendent _____   Signed _____

PURCHASE ORDER
NO. 247

THIS ORDER NUMBER MUST APPEAR ON YOUR INVOICE AND PACKAGE

TO National Office Supply Company   February 24, 194-

St. Louis

Missouri

PLEASE ENTER OUR ORDER FOR GOODS NAMED BELOW

QUANTITY	DESCRIPTION	PRICE	PER
1 doz.	1-lb. cans Duplicating ink		
3 cartons	Duplicating stencils	1 75	ea.
1½ doz.	Typewriter ribbons, black	4 25	car
25 rolls	Adding machine tape, 3" width	49	ea.
		5 40	C

ACKNOWLEDGE ORDER AND STATE WHEN YOU WILL SHIP.
PRICE MUST NOT BE HIGHER THAN LAST CHARGED.
NO CHARGE TO BE MADE FOR BOXING OR CARTAGE.

Roberts & Jones, Inc.

BY   R. L. Allen

INVOICE

NATIONAL OFFICE SUPPLY COMPANY
ST. LOUIS, MISSOURI

DATE February 28, 194-

SOLD TO Roberts & Jones, Inc.
New York 16, N. Y.

SHIPPED TO Above

F. O. B. _____

TERMS 2/10, n/30

SHIPPED VIA Express

CUSTOMER'S ORDER 247

FOR CUSTOMER'S USE

TERMS _____
F. O. B. _____
ACCOUNT _____
APPROVAL _____
TRANSPORTATION _____
RECEIVAL _____
CALCULATIONS _____
ADJUSTMENT _____
AUDITED _____

SHIPPER'S ORDER	QUANTITY SHIPPED	DESCRIPTION	UNIT PRICE	EXTENSION		AMOUNT	
	1	doz. 1-lb. cans Duplicating ink	1.75	21	00		
	3	cart. Duplicating stencils	4.25	12	75		
	1½	doz. Typewriter ribbons, black	.49	8	82		
	25	rolls Adding-machine tape, 3" per C	5.40	1	35	43	92

A PURCHASE REQUISITION, A PURCHASE ORDER, AND THE INVOICE
RESULTING FROM THE PURCHASE

10

THE PURCHASING DEPARTMENT

DO YOU KNOW?

1. What is the relationship of the Purchasing Department to other departments in an organization?

2. What factors other than quality and price might affect the decision of a purchasing agent as to where to place his order?

3. Should the secretary to a purchasing executive try to discourage the visits of salesmen?

4. The Manufacturing Department requires a large quantity of a certain standard chemical compound. Who is the better judge of the place to buy it, the purchasing executive or the superintendent of the department where the chemical is regularly used?

5. Would news of a coal strike in Pennsylvania be of any particular interest to a purchasing agent in San Francisco whose organization uses no coal whatever?

A LARGE business organization is likely to have a purchasing executive, often called a purchasing agent, who buys everything used anywhere in the company. There are several reasons for having a purchasing agent: (1) to centralize responsibility for the spending of money for supplies and equipment; (2) to save the time that might be wasted in trying to learn who had ordered various items if orders were placed by several persons; and (3) to save money by giving purchasing authority to a trained person who keeps constantly in touch with sources of supply.

The purchasing agent must know where to seek what he needs to buy, when to buy it, and what prices to pay. In order to buy intelligently and economically, he must know a great deal about the materials used in his organization and what is done with them. He can keep operating and manufacturing costs to a minimum by wise planning and by buying needed materials and equipment when opportunities arise unexpectedly.

Among the purchasing agent's chief sources of information are the following:

1. Salesmen who call on him
2. Catalogues, pamphlets, and price lists
3. Trade papers
4. Government bureaus and technical associations
5. Newspapers having financial sections

From these and other sources, the purchasing agent keeps in touch with the market. He must know whether present prices are high or low by comparison, whether the price trend is up or down, whether labor disputes or changes in weather are likely to affect his sources of supply.

The purchasing agent must know something about transportation, because shipping expense often constitutes a large part of the cost of what he buys. He has to have, or be able to obtain, information as to the approximate quantity of a particular item that will be needed during a certain period of time so that he can avoid overbuying and still take advantage of quantity prices. He keeps in touch with other departments of his company, particularly the Production Department, for which he orders raw materials, and the Traffic Department, which helps him save money on shipping costs.

Requisitions. A Purchasing Department receives purchase requisitions from other departments and obtains the items needed by means of purchase orders. Refer to the illustrations on pages 180 and 183 while reading this section.

A requisition is a written notice that some item is needed. Two kinds of requisitions are in general use: (1) stock requisitions, or orders for materials or supplies that are already on hand and are to be taken from stock; and (2) purchase requisitions, which are orders for materials that must be purchased outside the organization. The person who makes out a purchase requisition may recommend the source from which the material or equipment is to be bought.

Purchase Orders. The purchasing agent orders the items specified on the requisition by issuing a purchase order. Purchase orders are numbered consecutively and are usually issued in multiple copies. The original of the purchase order is usually sent to the supplier. Copies are sent to the department from which the order came; to the Receiving Department, for checking against the merchandise on delivery; and to the Accounting Department, for checking against

```
Supply Requisition
Form No. 153
                                    Date   November 6, 194-
WAREHOUSE
STOCKROOM ✓

Deliver to   Jessie Diamond          Credit          Department
```

Quantity	Description	Remarks
1 ream	Half sheet letterheads, sulphite	✓
1 ream	8½ x 11 Embossed letterheads, rag bond	✓
500	No. 10 Rag bond envelopes	*no rag stocked sulphite sent* ✓
2	Dust cloths	✓
4 boxes	Paper clips	✓
1 pr	Scissors	*none here - ask Mr. Wells*
6	Shorthand notebooks	✓

Signed _Jessie Diamond_

A REQUISITION FOR SUPPLIES, WITH NOTATIONS BY STOCK CLERK

the bill when it arrives. The Purchasing Department also retains a copy for its permanent file. Many Purchasing Departments also require another copy of each order for their own follow-up files. All copies of each purchase order bear the same order number.

When an order is placed with a new source of supply, terms and prices are usually stated in the purchase order. Many purchases, however, are made on the basis of contracts, and many more are made from firms with which the purchaser has done business for years. In these cases, the terms and price are seldom stated. Purchase orders for merchandise to be imported from foreign countries always show full details of price and terms, however.

Order Letters. In small organizations, formal purchase requisitions are often dispensed with and purchases are ordered by letter. An order letter, however, must contain all the details that a requisition would enumerate; thus:

1. A complete description of the article being ordered. This should include such important items as color, size, catalogue number, and

weight. The more complete your description, the greater the probability that you will receive the exact article ordered.

2. The price, if it is known.

3. Method of payment. Mention whether the payment is being enclosed or whether the merchandise is to be sent C.O.D. or on account.

4. Method of shipment. Is the merchandise to be sent by parcel post, express, freight, or messenger?

5. Special conditions of shipment. Give the delivery date if it is important to receive delivery on a certain date, and any other special delivery conditions.

The Secretary's Work. The duties of the secretary to a purchasing agent usually include:

1. Receiving callers, chiefly salesmen. Salesmen's visits are important to a purchasing agent.
2. Dictation, transcription, and the writing of routine letters and form letters.
3. The typing of purchase orders.
4. The operation of several different kinds of files.
5. Keeping miscellaneous departmental records.

The secretary to a purchasing agent must be familiar with many highly technical terms and abbreviations. The sooner she becomes familiar with their meaning, the sooner she will become indispensable. Accuracy, of course, is of the greatest importance in typing orders representing purchases that may total hundreds of thousands of dollars.

The secretary to a purchasing agent usually keeps several kinds of records and operates several filing systems. If the purchasing agent buys according to a budget set up in advance, the secretary may be required to keep records of the cost of purchases. In many firms, however, the Accounting Department keeps these records.

The secretary usually keeps a file showing the prices paid for various items in the past. The filing of catalogues, price lists, and advertising pamphlets is sometimes complicated by their varying sizes and the variety of their contents. A very large Purchasing Department may have to maintain a subject filing system similar to that used in libraries.

Copies of purchase orders may be filed in several ways: by number, by date, by department, by the name of the supplying firm. The permanent file of purchase orders is often kept numerically, by the serial numbers of the orders. A tickler file, used in following up orders that have been placed but not yet filled, is usually kept by date, so that copies of unfilled orders will automatically come up for attention after a certain interval has elapsed.

ANSWERS TO "DO YOU KNOW?"

1. The Purchasing Department is a service department. It does not make profits for the company, but it helps other departments to do so. Wise purchasing prevents unnecessary expenditures of money and insures that a sufficient quantity of all merchandise sold by the company is on hand when needed.

2. A purchasing agent's decision would probably be based on such factors as the supplier's reputation for keeping promises, his distance from the point of delivery (because this would make a difference in shipping costs), his financial stability, and labor relations in his organization (because strikes delay delivery).

3. Cartoons and jokes have long given the erroneous impression that salesmen are never welcome anywhere. Salesmen constitute the purchasing executive's most important source of information.

4. The purchasing executive is likely to know much more about prices and other important facts than anyone else in the organization, because it is his business to know these things.

5. A shortage of coal needed by manufacturers of items for which the purchasing executive had placed orders would probably slow up deliveries.

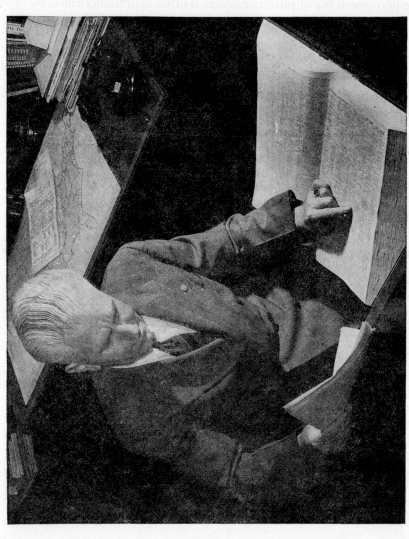

Courtesy Dun & Bradstreet, Inc.

THE CREDIT MAN INVESTIGATES THE CREDIT STANDING OF A CUSTOMER

11

THE CREDIT DEPARTMENT

DO YOU KNOW?

1. An order is received from a customer whose name you do not recognize. What source of information would you consult first to find out whether the customer is in the habit of paying his bills promptly?

2. In shipping merchandise to a wholesaler who is not able to buy on open account because of financial difficulties, would your company prefer to receive from the wholesaler a trade acceptance or a promissory note for the amount due?

3. A customer owes your company money on open account and is not able to pay all of it now. What arrangement can your Credit Department make that will give your company additional security and will enable the debtor to pay in installments?

4. Why is the drawing of a sight draft by a creditor likely to antagonize the debtor?

5. If a sight draft may antagonize a debtor, why do creditors run the risk of losing a customer by taking this way of collecting money?

A CREDIT man has several important responsibilities:

1. He decides, on the basis of information available, how much credit, if any, to grant to new customers who ask for it.

2. If a customer tries to buy more merchandise than he is likely to be able to pay for, the credit man restrains him tactfully, thus keeping the customer from taking on too heavy a financial burden and also protecting his own company from probable loss.

3. He helps to increase sales by encouraging customers to use their available credit through larger and more frequent purchases.

4. He co-operates with customers in arranging convenient payments for large orders and in financing seasonal purchases when necessary.

Granting Credit. Quiet feuds often exist between the salesmen and the personnel of the Credit Department because that department occasionally has to restrain salesmen from accepting orders that the purchaser would not be able to pay for. Salesmen are by nature optimistic, but a credit man cannot afford to be. The credit man can, and does, actually help to increase sales, however. When a customer of sound financial standing is buying less than the company would like to sell him, the credit man backs up the salesman's efforts with a subtly flattering, though sincere, offer to grant more credit.

In most firms, all incoming orders must be approved by the Credit Department before they can be filled. A purchase order received from a customer will be found on Work Sheet 90 of your workbook. This purchase order has been marked "OK" by the Credit Department and is ready to go to the Sales Department for further attention.

Sources of Credit Information. The credit man has many sources of information as to the financial position and payment record of his customers. For established and active accounts, he refers to his own company ledgers to learn the customer's record as to promptness of payment. He also makes frequent comparisons with the information available from other credit-reporting sources. It would be hazardous to his capital and profits to rely solely on his own experience with an account.

With new accounts, it is necessary for him to set up a mental picture of the character, capital, and capacity of a customer. First he ascertains whether or not the order came from an established business. This he does by consulting Dun & Bradstreet's *Reference Book* or some other directory of business. If the order is substantial —say, over $100—he will order a credit report through one of the mercantile agencies or credit bureaus. Many suppliers obtain reports on all first orders to determine whether the new customer's account is worth developing.

Credit Agencies. Hundreds of agencies, bureaus, and associations render national, regional, or specialized credit-reporting services, the largest and oldest being Dun & Bradstreet. Among the others of special scope are The Lyons Agency, Proudfoot, Jewelers Board of Trade, and the National Association of Credit Men. Some trade associations and local chambers of commerce maintain what is known as "an interchange," in which they pool their payment experiences.

Dun & Bradstreet's *Reference Book* lists commercial enterprises by state and local communities (cities, towns, and villages) and identifies them by trade symbols and credit rating symbols. The rating symbol is a guide to the merchant's financial strength and payment record. For example, B 1 indicates that the merchant has an estimated capital of between $200,000 and $300,000, and is of first or high credit.

In large cities, firms that do a great deal of credit business—for example, retail stores—sometimes have a direct telautograph or teletype connection with the credit bureau.

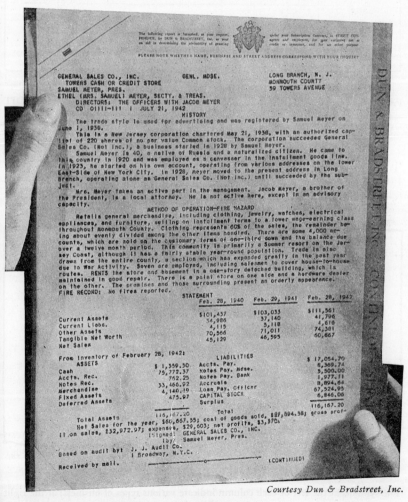

Courtesy Dun & Bradstreet, Inc.

PART OF A CONFIDENTIAL REPORT FROM DUN & BRADSTREET

CREDIT INTERCHANGE BUREAU OF THE STATIONERS AND PUBLISHERS BOARD OF TRADE, Inc.

REPORT ON: Smith & Jones   Date 4-22-4..

METHOD OF PAYMENT		TERMS	
1. Discounts.	8. In attorney's hands.	A—Net 30 days.	I—3% 10, net 30 or
2. Pays when due.	9. Slow and unsatisfactory.	B—2% 10—30 net.	3% 10th Prox.
3. Slow but considered good.	10. Deducts unearned discounts.	C—2% net.	
4. Settles by note.	11. Trade acceptance.	D—3% 10—30 or 60 net.	
5. Cash in advance.	12. Unjust claims.	E—3% 10, 2% 30, net 60.	G—Designates
6. Secured or guaranteed.	13. Anticipates.	F—Dating.	Greeting Card Member.
7. Collected through attorney.	15. Pays on Account.	H—2% 10th Prox.	

Member's Key No.	How Long Sold	Date of Last Sale	Highest Recent Credit	Total Owing Including Notes	Amount Overdue	Days Past Due	Terms of Sale A—1	Method of Payment 1 to 15	How Slow	Payment Trend X—Unchanged Y—Slower Z—Improving
378*			$	$	$					
347	3-37	4-42	75	11			B	2		
378	4-42	1 sale	300	300			H no	pay	exp	
433	9-41	11-41	117			2/1	EOM	1		
751	yrs	4-42	224	12			C	1		
610	7 mos	9-41	25				H	1		
424	1926	2-41	12				B	1		
915	yrs	8-41	38				A	3	30	

Courtesy Stationers and Publishers Board of Trade

PART OF A CONFIDENTIAL REPORT FROM A CO-OPERATIVE CREDIT BUREAU

Co-operative credit bureaus sometimes correspond with delinquent accounts in behalf of bureau members. If the account is so far in arrears that a threat of suit is advisable, this threat sounds better coming from an impersonal credit bureau than from the indi-

Courtesy Dun & Bradstreet, Inc.

PART OF A CREDIT RATING BOOK

The symbols at the left of each column indicate various types of business; at the right are the ratings

vidual creditor, who later may wish to do business with the debtor without any shadow of past threats to mar the record. The following form letter was used by a co-operative credit bureau:

We have been requested by the above-named member to write you with respect to the payment of your long overdue account, as evidenced by the attached statement.

If you contend that the amount due is not correct, or that there is an extenuating circumstance that warrants your delaying payment, the matter should be taken up at once for adjustment or reconciliation. Otherwise, a check should be promptly mailed to our member.

Members report the paying habits of their customers regularly to this office. Their experiences are incorporated in reports supplied to all interested members. Therefore, your response to this request will determine the manner in which our member will report with respect to your account.

The Board of Trade is composed of manufacturers and publishers whose names appear on the reverse side of this letter. Its purpose is to be of mutual assistance to its members and their customers. Naturally, we do not wish to see your relationship with our member become strained, due perhaps to some temporary condition or misunderstanding.

Very truly yours,

Form Letters. A great many routine letters go out from the credit department. These letters range from mild reminders and humorous pleas for payment to stronger requests, and occasionally even to threats of suit. Form letters are widely used in order to save time in dictating. (The use of form letters was described on pages 51-53.)

Collecting Money Due. Often a debtor wishes to pay his debt but requires time to obtain funds. The credit man may persuade the debtor to sign a series of time notes, the total of which will cover the entire amount of the indebtedness. As a result, the debtor will have a satisfactory agreement with his creditor and can pay his bill in installments, while the creditor will have the additional security represented by the notes, which are written and usually negotiable evidences of debt. Notes are described in detail in Section 13.

Commercial Drafts. The creditor has a useful collection tool in an instrument called a commercial draft, or bill of exchange. (Do not confuse this with a bank draft, which is a bank's check, used mainly as an accommodation to depositors who desire to transfer money from one city to another.)

The commercial draft is a demand for money and is initiated by the creditor. The parties to a draft are the *drawer*, who writes the request or order demanding payment; the *drawee*, who is asked to pay the money; and the *payee*, in whose favor the draft is made and who is to receive the money. The drawer usually names his own bank as the payee, as in the accompanying illustration of a time draft. The bank acts in the capacity of agent for the drawer.

Drafts are used for two general purposes: (1) to collect money immediately when a sale is made to a customer whose credit standing is doubtful or is not known, and (2) to collect old debts or to convert the creditor's accounts receivable into cash when he needs money.

Sight and Time Draft. Both sight and time drafts are in general use. A draft bearing the words "at sight" is a sight draft; it is payable immediately on presentation to the drawee. Sight drafts are often used in collecting for current transactions. (See also page 246.)

A time draft is one that specifies payment a certain length of time "after sight" or "after date." "Thirty days after sight," for ex-

NO PROTEST TEAR THIS OFF BEFORE PRESENTING

$500.00 Newport News, Virginia, March 4, 19-

at sight Pay to

the order of Fred Howe

Five hundred and no/100 Dollars

Value received and charge the same to account of

To John Root

No 116 Rutland, Vermont

Fred Howe

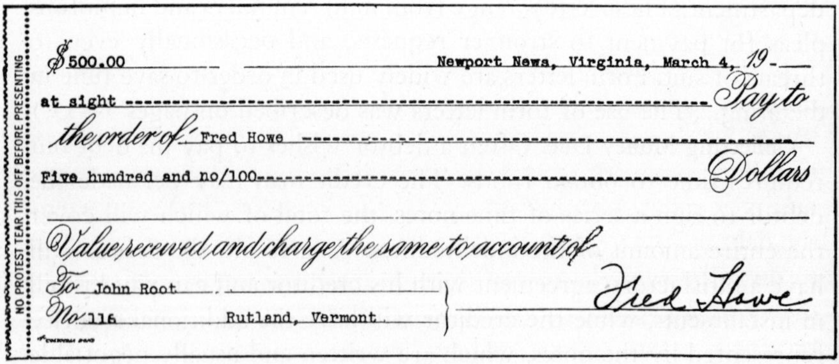

A SIGHT DRAFT

```
$ 347.27                          New York, N. Y., June 30,  19 -
Sixty days after date----------------------------------Pay to
the order of Traders Bank Trust Company----------------------
REGISTERED                                                    Dollars
  7861      ★ ★ ★ 3 4 7 DOL'S 2 7 CTS

Value received and charge the same to account of

To Robert Ryan, Inc.---------
   419 West 34 St., New York---  } STANDWELL PRODUCTS CORPORATION
No. 342                         James L. Stuart  Treasurer
```

A TIME DRAFT

ample, is thirty days after the date of acceptance written on the
draft by the drawee. "Thirty days after date," however, is thirty
days after the date on which the draft was drawn, regardless of
the date on which the drawee accepts it.

In accepting a draft, the debtor writes across its face the word
"Accepted," the date, and his signature. Acceptance gives the draft
the effect of a promissory note. Once the drawee has accepted a
draft, he is obligated to pay it. He has converted his verbal or im-
plied promise to pay into a written promise.

Banks will discount (that is, buy) accepted drafts under the same
conditions as promissory notes; but they use extreme care in doing
so, because the existence of a draft usually indicates that the drawee's credit is not established or that he pays his debts slowly.

In the collection of debts, the draft is usually considered the last
resort of the creditor preliminary to placing the account in the
hands of a collection agency or an attorney. The drawing of a draft
to induce payment of a debt is usually looked upon as a drastic
means of collection and is likely to antagonize the debtor. Although
the debtor (drawee) is not obligated to accept the draft, if he fails
to do so he runs the risk of impairing his credit standing with his
own banking connections. If he refuses to accept the draft, it is
returned to the drawer with that notation. The drawer will then
have to use some other method of collecting.

Trade Acceptances. If a customer wishes to buy merchandise for resale but cannot pay for it at once, he may sign a trade acceptance, planning to pay for the merchandise with the money he will receive from selling it. A trade acceptance differs from a commercial draft in three ways:

1. It results from the purchase of merchandise from the drawer.
2. It is never given in payment of old accounts or of loans.
3. It is accompanied by a bill for the goods sold.

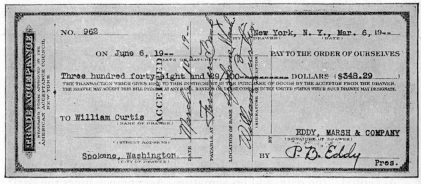

A TRADE ACCEPTANCE

A trade acceptance cannot be renewed or extended. It is always part of a current transaction from which profit may be expected, and it is preferred by banks over ordinary drafts or notes.

The customer, who is the drawee, completes the acceptance by signing it. It is then returned to the drawer, who holds it until it matures. If the credit of the customer is good, the drawer may discount the acceptance at his bank in order to obtain cash for it at once. When the acceptance matures, it is presented directly to the drawee or to his bank.

Answers to "Do You Know?"

1. Consult your own company's credit records first. If you have had business dealings with the customer in the past, you will be able to learn whether he has paid his bills on schedule.

2. A trade acceptance.

3. Your Credit Department can ask the debtor to sign a series of time notes.

4. The debtor may find it inconvenient to pay the draft, but his credit standing with his own bank will be injured if he refuses to do so.

5. A creditor uses a draft as a last resort, when he is more interested in collecting an old debt than he is in receiving future business from the slow-paying customer.

LETTER-WRITING SUGGESTIONS

Continued from page 179

Collection Letters. The writing of collection letters requires considerable business experience, knowledge of the firm's policy and the history of its slow-paying accounts, and familiarity with the laws relating to financial papers and debt collections. Secretaries seldom compose collection letters. If you will study the collection letters assigned for dictation in the Credit Department during this course, you will have a general idea of what constitutes an effective letter of this kind.

Letters of Adjustment. The writing of letters to adjust customers' complaints is not usually delegated to secretaries but is entrusted to correspondents with considerable knowledge of company policies and special training in tactful expression.

An answer to a complaint sometimes must be a refusal. Sometimes the answer expresses a partial acceptance of responsibility; for example, if a customer demands a refund and is given a partial refund. If even part of his request can be granted, a good adjustment letter gives him the good news first, before the refusal, as:

We are glad to credit your account with $10, half the original purchase price of the dress about which you wrote on August 3. (Note that this sentence does *not* read, "the dress about which you complained.") You need not return the dress, of course.

The wrong way to say the same thing is:

Although we cannot refund the full purchase price for the dress about which you complained (or "which you claim has come apart at the seams"), we will let you have half the price credited to your account.

Take a positive attitude; avoid negative words such as "complaint," "sorry," "mistake," "wrong." You may say, "We are glad you wrote to us about this," or "Thank you for telling us about this occurrence." But a most unfortunate phrasing, sometimes actually used, is: "We are glad to hear about the trouble you had with the wallpaper."

Negative Suggestion. Whole chapters in business correspondence texts are written on the subject of avoiding negative suggestion. You should read some of them before you undertake the writing of really important letters. Here are some examples of negative suggestion, with positive restatements of the same thoughts:

1. *Negative*: You neglected to state which size you wished to order. (*Do not criticize a customer.*)

Positive: We shall be glad to fill this order as soon as you let us know what size you need.

2. *Negative*: Your complaint about telephone service failure has been referred to the writer. (Forget the word "complaint." Forget "the writer," too. This expression is too stilted for use in your letters.)

Positive: Thank you for reporting the temporary discontinuance of your telephone service last Tuesday. This was due to . . .

3. *Negative*: We deeply regret our inability to fill your order and realize what a disappointment this will be to you. We can, however, supply you with . . . (If the customer did not feel bad about this before, he surely will now.)

Positive: The supply of No. B-3221 was completely exhausted before your order reached us; but we can recommend for your installation the new model, B-52, which has all the advantages of the one formerly sold, plus several improvements.

4. *Negative*: Apparently you made a mistake in specifying the item number.

Positive: Our current catalogue does not include any number 2-X-4223, but we wonder whether 12-X-423 is not just the article you wish to order.

Keeping Secrets. An important thing to remember when writing routine letters is not to give away information that your employer may not want broadcast. Unless you know his wishes and business connections very well, it is unwise to say that you are writing in his stead because he is out of town, or to tell why he is away or exactly when he is coming back.

Here are some things it is better *not* to say unless you know your employer's interests thoroughly:

1. Mr. Blank will answer your letter as soon as he comes back next Monday. (Maybe he will be too busy on Monday.)

2. Mr. Blank left on Tuesday to attend a conference of jobbers in New Orleans. (Not all the businessmen who write pleasant letters to one another are really friendly. Information of this kind may give a competitor or an outsider just the lead he needs in order to guess at your company's future plans.)

3. Mr. Blank is seriously ill and will not return to the office for at least a month. (A competitor, hearing of this, may think, "Ah, this is just the time to jump in with our campaign, while Blank is out of the picture.")

You must use your own intelligence in deciding how much to tell, even in a routine letter such as can be written by any secretary. Although you must guard your employer's secrets, and even some facts that are not really secrets but are simply nobody's business, you should not, of course, give the appearance of being secretive or suspicious.

Continued on page 291

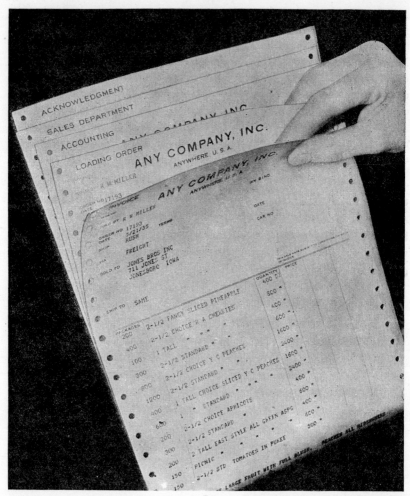

Courtesy American Telephone and Telegraph Co.

A BILL TYPED IN QUINTUPLICATE

The invoice is mailed to the customer when the order is shipped. The loading order is sent to the Shipping Department and packed with the shipment for checking by the customer. The accounting copy is posted to the customer's account and then filed. The fourth copy, after checking by the Sales Department, is usually sent to the salesman. The acknowledgment is mailed to the customer as soon as the order is billed, although the order may not be shipped for weeks or even months. A somewhat different billing system is described on pages 205-208

12

THE BILLING DEPARTMENT

DO YOU KNOW?

1. A certain manufacturer customarily prepays shipping costs on the goods he sells and then charges the shipping costs to the purchaser. Although the manufacturer allows liberal trade discounts on his merchandise, he refuses to allow any discount on the shipping charges. Why?

2. A newcomer to your office asks, "Do you do your invoicing at the end of the year?" Obviously, this person has used the wrong word. What common business term is he confusing with invoice?

3. What is meant by the "extensions" on a bill?

4. All the invoices used in your office have serial numbers printed on them. You have been told that if you spoil an invoice, you must keep a record of the serial number. Why?

5. Why do many business firms allow a discount on purchases for cash?

THE Billing Department—sometimes called the Order Department, depending on the way the organization is set up—is an important part of the business, because it links most of the other operations: manufacturing, selling, shipping, and collecting. Billing must progress rapidly, because a delay may hold up other departments or even alienate a customer.

Definition of Terms. The terms *bill* and *invoice* are used interchangeably for all practical purposes, although the meanings of the two words are not exactly the same. (An invoice is really a list of goods and need not show prices.)

A bill, or invoice, represents an abbreviated business letter written to the buyer by the seller so that each of them will have a brief but complete and accurate record of a transaction that has taken place. The charge slip that the retail store clerk fills out when you buy merchandise to be charged to your account is the same as an invoice.

Retail customers sometimes use the word "bill" when they mean *statement*: "The milk bill from the Lewis Dairy was $8.90 this

STANDWELL PRODUCTS CORPORATION
PRODUCERS AND .DISTRIBUTORS
270 MADISON AVENUE, NEW YORK

SOLD TO

International Supply Company, Inc.
463 North LaSalle Street
Chicago, Illinois

SHIPPED TO

INVOICE No. 6107

| DEPT. NO. | YOUR ORDER NO. 84632 | DEPT. NO. | YOUR ORDER NO. |
| DATE | June 30, 194- | TERMS: NET CASH 30 DAYS | VIA Fast Frt Collect |

QUANTITY	ITEMS	PRICE	AMOUNT	TRANSPORTATION	TOTAL
4	#2950 Typewriter Desks	70.25	281.00		
4	#6415 Typist's Posture Chairs	27.25	109.00		
2	#1520 Filing Cabinets	51.00	102.00		
3	#6304 Side Chairs	24.25	72.75		
2	#2012 Office Cupboards	44.50	89.00		653.
					MM

A TYPEWRITTEN BILL

month." In business parlance, however, a statement denotes a reminder to the customer of how much money he still owes on his account. A statement shows the balance from the preceding month, if any, plus the amounts of this month's purchases. From this figure are subtracted payments made on account and credits for goods returned. If an error has been made in billing, the adjustment is made on the statement.

Two kinds of statements are illustrated. One gives the balance due at the beginning of the month and lists the charges and credits entered during the month, identified only by dates, together with the balance due. The other form is the type of itemized statement used by most retail stores. It gives the same information as the first type of statement but, in addition, describes briefly all the items entered, for easy identification by the customer.

Information Included on Billhead. A billhead or invoice contains a great deal of information in a very compact form. Some of the data usually included are the date, the order number, the invoice number, the name and address of the customer, the name and address of the firm to which shipment is to be made (often identical with

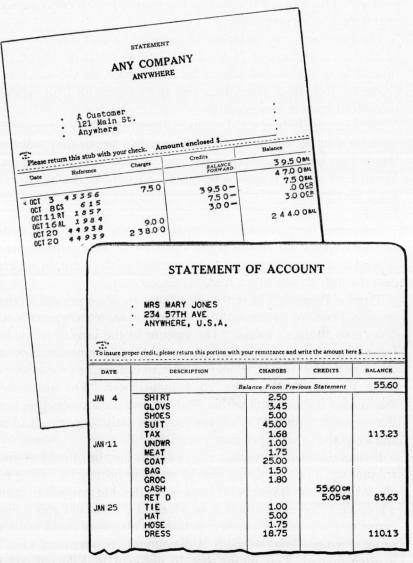

STATEMENT

ANY COMPANY
ANYWHERE

A Customer
121 Main St.
Anywhere

Please return this stub with your check.   Amount enclosed $

Date	Reference	Charges	Credits		Balance
			BALANCE FORWARD		39.5 0 BAL
		7.50	39.50−		47.0 0 BAL
			7.50−		7.5 0 BAL
OCT 3	43356		3.00−		.0 0 CR
OCT 8 CS	615				3.0 0 CR
OCT 11 RT	1857				
OCT 16 AL	1984	9.00			2 4 4.0 0 BAL
OCT 20	44938				
OCT 20	44939	2 38.00			

STATEMENT OF ACCOUNT

MRS MARY JONES
234 57TH AVE
ANYWHERE, U.S.A.

To insure proper credit, please return this portion with your remittance and write the amount here $..............

DATE	DESCRIPTION	CHARGES	CREDITS	BALANCE
	Balance From Previous Statement			55.60
JAN 4	SHIRT	2.50		
	GLOVS	3.45		
	SHOES	5.00		
	SUIT	45.00		
	TAX	1.68		113.23
JAN 11	UNDWR	1.00		
	MEAT	1.75		
	COAT	25.00		
	BAG	1.50		
	GROC	1.80		
	CASH		55.60 CR	
	RET D		5.05 CR	83.63
JAN 25	TIE	1.00		
	HAT	5.00		
	HOSE	1.75		
	DRESS	18.75		110.13

Top: A STATEMENT LISTING AMOUNTS ONLY. Bottom: AN ITEMIZED STATEMENT OF ACCOUNT

the customer), instructions as to the method of shipping, terms of purchase, and the itemized list of the merchandise ordered.

The order number is taken from the customer's order form, if he used one. This number is typed on the invoice for his convenience in referring to his own records.

The purchaser may order merchandise to be sent direct to one of his own customers or to one of his branch stores or offices, although he wants the bill sent to himself. Notice, on the set of invoices for Roberts & Jones, Inc., that space is provided for typing this information if it is needed.

Invoices usually bear serial numbers. Sometimes these are printed, the same number appearing on each copy in a set; or they may be stamped on with a numbering machine; or they may be typed on. When a set of bills is spoiled or wasted, a record of the number is kept, because a break in the number sequence might cause confusion.

Sometimes the customer gives explicit shipping instructions, such as "Air Express" or "Fast Freight Collect"; or the purchaser may depend on the sender to choose the method of shipment, in which case the instructions often read, "Cheapest way."

Terms of Payment. The terms of payment are often printed on the invoice. Terms of payment differ in various business organizations. "Net cash 30 days" means, "The amount of the invoice is due in full within 30 days of the invoice date." Some companies allow a discount if a bill is paid at once in cash, to encourage prompt payment. Terms of "2/10, n/30," for example, mean, "The amount of this invoice is due in full within 30 days after the invoice date; but if you pay it within 10 days, you may pay only 98 per cent of it and keep the other 2 per cent yourself."

Besides this cash discount, trade discounts may be offered. A distributor sets a price for each item he sells, but he may be willing to allow a discount on orders for large quantities. He may sell to both wholesale and retail customers, in which case he would give a discount to a wholesale customer, so that the customer could make a profit when reselling the goods. A discount of "two tens and a five" is often quoted. This means that 10 per cent is deducted; then another 10 per cent of the amount remaining after the first 10 per cent has been subtracted; then 5 per cent of the amount remaining after both discounts have been subtracted. (Note that this is not the same as deducting 25 per cent from the original amount.)

Be sure you understand the customary discounts and terms of payment allowed by the company for which you may work. Terms of payment differ widely in various businesses.

No discount is allowed on prepaid shipping charges. These charges represent money actually paid out by the shipper, and the purchaser reimburses him for it in full.

Credit Memorandum. A credit memorandum is issued to correct an error in billing or when goods are returned for credit. It is prepared in the same way as a bill. It lists the items returned, their prices, the transportation costs billed to the customer, and other details. The total is entered on the customer's account but is credited to him instead of being charged against him.

Usually at least two copies of a credit memorandum are required —one for the customer's records and one for the seller's records.

Credit memorandums and invoices are arranged in the same way and look alike; but credit memorandums are usually printed on a different color of paper or in a different ink, and the words "Credit Memorandum" appear across the top of the form.

CREDIT MEMORANDUM

STANDWELL PRODUCTS CORPORATION
PRODUCERS AND DISTRIBUTORS
270 MADISON AVENUE, NEW YORK

August 5, 194-

International Supply Company, Inc.
463 North LaSalle Street
Chicago, Illinois

Order No. 84632

Your account has been credited as follows:

DATE	QUANTITY	ITEMS	UNIT PRICE	EXTENSION	TOTAL
June 30	2	#2950 Typewriter Desks	70 25	140 50	
30	2	#6415 Typist's Posture Chairs	27 25	54 50	195 00

A CREDIT MEMORANDUM

INTERNATIONAL SUPPLY COMPANY
INCORPORATED

Affiliated with
International Supply Company, Ltd.
London, England
International Supply Assn. Ltd.
Toronto, Canada

463 North LaSalle Street,
CHICAGO, ILLINOIS

New York
Chicago
San Francisco
New Orleans

June 25, 194-

Standwell Products Corporation
270 Madison Avenue
New York, New York

Gentlemen:

Please ship us immediately the following items listed
in your latest general catalogue:

4	#2950	Typewriter Desks	70.25	281.00
4	#6415	Typist's Posture Chairs	27.25	109.00
2	#1520	Filing Cabinets	51.00	102.00
3	#6304	Side Chairs	24.25	72.75
2	#2012	Office Cupboards	44.50	89.00
				653.75

This is our order number 84632. Please be sure that
this number is placed on the invoice and on other papers
referring to this order.

Yours very truly,

INTERNATIONAL SUPPLY COMPANY

John F. Quinn

JFQ:da

THIS IS AN ORDER
from

INTERNATIONAL SUPPLY COMPANY, Inc.
463 North LaSalle Street . . . Chicago, Illinois

Purchase Order No. 84632
Date June 25, 194-

To Standwell Products Corporation
270 Madison Avenue
New York, New York

Ship When Immediately

QUANTITY	DESCRIPTION	PRICE	AMOUNT	TOTAL
4	#2950 Typewriter Desks	70.25	281.00	
4	#6415 Typist's Posture Chairs	27.25	109.00	
2	#1520 Filing Cabinets	51.00	102.00	
3	#6304 Side Chairs	24.25	72.75	
2	#2012 Office Cupboards	44.50	89.00	653.75

By *John F. Quinn*

TWO METHODS OF ORDERING—BY LETTER, BY PURCHASE ORDER
Marked with prices and extensions, these orders are ready for billing

What Happens to a Customer's Order. Briefly, this is what happens after a sale is made.

Either a salesman of the company or a customer places an order with the company. The order from the customer may be a formal purchase order, or a letter describing what is wanted and how much of it, or even a telephone call. The order, if sent in by the salesman, may be on a company order blank.

An order received by mail is usually routed in some such way as the following:

1. Received by the Mailing Department. The order is received with other incoming mail. It is dated with a date stamp (sometimes also with a time stamp), to show when it was received.

2. Delivered to the Credit Department. Unless the order is accompanied by cash—and most orders, except in mail-order businesses, are not—it is delivered at once to the Credit Department, where the customer's financial responsibility is checked. If the records of this department show that the customer may be depended upon to pay for what he wants to buy, the order is stamped "OK."

3. Passed on to the Order (or Billing) Department. The order is then "edited"—that is, the items on it are checked for clarity. If the editing clerk cannot judge exactly what is wanted and how much of it, he may consult the sales records for that particular customer, to learn what has been purchased before.

4. Given to the pricing clerk. Another clerk receives the corrected order and checks the prices shown on it against actual, current selling prices.

5. Given to the extension clerk. A clerk (perhaps the same one who priced the order) extends these prices on the order itself. That is, if the order calls for 15 tables at $17.50 each, he multiplies 15 by $17.50; the result, $262.50, is the "extension." If there are two or more of these extensions, this clerk also adds them, to find out the total.

These computations are sometimes made on one of the various calculating machines; then the figures are written on the order by hand. Some calculating machines, however, have typewriter keyboards. The whole operation of computing and typing the order can be done on these machines.

Copies of the Order. In a typical business organization, the typing is done on a fanfold billing machine, into which bills already interleaved with carbon paper are fed continuously. As each bill is finished, it is torn off along perforations. Each copy in a set is a different color, so that it will be recognized immediately by everyone who has occasion to handle bills. All copies in one set bear the same serial number. The copies are distributed as follows:

1. The *original* goes to the customer by mail. If the order is from a new customer, he also receives a pleasant letter of acknowledgment from the Sales Department.

2. The *packing list* goes to the Shipping Department. There are perforations around the section on which the address appears, so that this part can be torn off and pasted on the package as a shipping label. The part of the bill that remains after the label is torn off is enclosed in the package so that the recipient can check the package contents against the bill.

3. The *posting memo* goes to the Shipping Department also, attached to the packing list. The shipping clerk marks on the posting memo the amount of the shipping charges, if they are prepaid by the sender. All the copies for one day are accumulated. The next morning, all the posting memos are delivered to the Accounting Department, where prepaid shipping charges are charged against the individual accounts.

4. The *stock record copy* goes to a recording clerk, who records on visible index cards the items sold, so that this card record is a perpetual inventory of stock on hand. When the stock of an item is running low, more of the merchandise is ordered or manufactured. Sales reports are also based on these cards. The stock record copy finally goes into a file, according to its serial number.

5. The *salesman's copy* goes to the Sales Department for a routine examination; if there is something unusual about the order, a letter may be written about it. If the order is the result of correspondence that the Sales Department has carried on, a notation will be made to this effect so that no more form letters will go out. The salesman's copy is then sent to the salesman in whose territory it originated, so that he will know just what is going on. Orders often come direct to the home office without going through the hands of the salesman whose previous efforts were responsible for the order.

The entire procedure in handling an order may be summarized in the following flow chart.

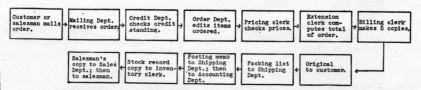

| Customer or salesman mails order. | → | Mailing Dept. receives order. | → | Credit Dept. checks credit standing. | → | Order Dept. edits items ordered. | → | Pricing clerk checks prices. | → | Extension clerk computes total of order. | → | Billing clerk makes 5 copies. |

| Salesman's copy to Sales Dept.; then to salesman. | ← | Stock record copy to inventory clerk. | ← | Posting memo to Shipping Dept.; then to Accounting Dept. | ← | Packing list to Shipping Dept. | ← | Original to customer. |

A FLOW CHART SHOWING THE COURSE OF AN ORDER

Multiple Copies. Various ways of making multiple copies of bills have been devised. One of these is by means of the fanfold bill. The bills are printed on very long strips of paper instead of on single sheets. Perforations between the bills make it possible to tear them apart neatly. These long strips feed through a "truck" attachment on the typewriter or billing machine, permitting the carbon sheets to be used over and over again.

Sometimes copies of bills come in sets, interleaved with carbon sheets, which are used only once and then discarded.

Another method of producing the many copies needed of each bill is by duplicating them on one of the various duplicating machines. In large organizations, where many bills are made and several copies of each one are required, the duplicating method is becoming increasingly popular. The typist simply types one master copy, and the duplicating-machine operator makes as many copies as are needed, on billheads of the proper kind.

Timesavers. In addition to the various machines made especially for billing purposes, and pictured on page 208, an automatic typewriter called the Auto-typist is sometimes used. A billing typewriter can be attached to the push-button Auto-typist. Material that is used regularly is prepared on perforated rolls and the parts needed are selected by a stenographer-operator, who sets the machine into automatic motion by pressing the desired buttons. This machine can be used to type name, address, shipping instructions, terms, and descriptions of items manufactured. The operator fills in special items by typing in the usual way.

If separate forms and carbons must be used for bills, they should be assembled and stacked during slack times so that they will be ready for rush periods. Each set should be laid crosswise on the one beneath it. If carbon sheets are to be used again, and are the

VARIOUS TYPES OF BILLING MACHINES

The machine at the upper left is a computing biller with continuous feed attachment; the other three are fanfold billers with electric carriages

same size as the paper, they are sometimes difficult to separate when the job is finished. They are easier to handle if they are a little larger than the printed bill forms.

Answers to "Do You Know?"

1. Shipping charges represent money paid out by the shipper, for which he should be reimbursed. He makes no profit on shipping.

2. The word is *inventory*.

3. The quantity of an item multiplied by the price of the item is the extension. On a bill for six toy engines at $2 each, the extension is $12.

4. If a numbered invoice is spoiled and thrown away without a record of the number, confusion may result later. A person who is checking for an error in figures is especially likely to assume that a missing paper may hold the key to his problem.

5. Immediate payment by a purchaser saves the seller expense in bookkeeping, repeated billing, and collecting. Also, the seller obtains the immediate use of his money and saves the interest he would have to pay if he were forced to borrow an equivalent amount until the bill was paid.

Courtesy Underwood Elliott Fisher Company

MACHINE BOOKKEEPING

The accounting procedure in an office is mechanized when an accounting machine is installed. This illustration shows various accounting records and the machine that performs the accounting operations

13

THE OFFICE OF THE TREASURER

DO YOU KNOW?

1. Why should you never sign a check on which the name of the payee or the amount is left blank?
2. What is the advantage of using voucher checks in paying bills?
3. What excuse is there for overdrawing a checking account?
4. Why is it necessary to check your bank statement against your checkbook stubs?
5. Can interest ever be collected on a note if the words "with interest" do not appear on it?

THE treasurer is the financial officer of the company. He has control of the funds of the company and attends to its financial details. In all but the very large companies the treasurer is usually responsible for the accounting records and the financial reports. In large corporations, however, these responsibilities are taken over by another executive known as the comptroller.

The comptroller makes recommendations concerning costs, expenses, and the economical management of the company. He prescribes the accounting methods and is responsible for the accuracy of all financial statements and reports. He also has charge of internal audits and helps to prepare budgets of financial requirements.

In modern business, very little actual money changes hands. An Accounting Department may keep the books for a concern that does many thousand dollars' worth of business during a year, and the employees who work in that department may never handle any actual money except the few dollars kept as petty cash and used for the purchase of minor items, such as stamps.

The most common substitute for money is the check, which is discussed on pages 217-229. Other forms of substitutes are notes, money orders, and drafts. (See pages 230-232 and Section 11.)

Bank Accounts. The funds against which checks are drawn are kept in commercial banks. (The savings bank is an entirely different type of bank and is not discussed here because it is not commonly used in business. If a company has surplus funds, they are usually invested in quickly convertible bonds and stocks.)

Checking accounts do not draw interest, and most commercial banks make a small charge when the daily bank balance falls below a stated minimum amount. They also charge for various services rendered depositors, such as for collecting certain out-of-town checks and notes, for protest fees on dishonored checks, or for rental of a safe-deposit box.

Making Deposits. One of the most common financial duties of the secretary is the making of deposits in the bank. Most business concerns deposit each day.

Each depositor has a passbook in which the deposit is entered, and you are expected to present this book to the bank each time you make a deposit.

Deposits may consist of money (both coins and bills), checks, postal money orders, express money orders, and bond coupons. These items must be arranged in an orderly fashion and listed on a printed form, known as a *deposit slip*, which is supplied by the bank. A passbook and deposit slips are shown on page 213.

Coins (also known as *specie*) should be sorted according to denomination and enclosed in coin wrappers, which the bank also supplies. Special wrappers are made for each denomination and hold an exact number of coins; thus:

50 pennies	$ .50	40 quarters	$10.00
40 nickels	2.00	20 half dollars	10.00
50 dimes	5.00		

By a little practice you will be able to insert the coins and fold the end of a wrapper over neatly, making a compact package. Write the name of the company on each wrapper. In case you do not have enough coins of any one denomination to fill a wrapper, enclose the coins in envelopes, a separate envelope for each denomination, and write the denomination and the amount on each envelope you will deposit.

COINS WRAPPED

Paper money (or currency) should be grouped, with the various denominations clipped together. Bills should also be placed face up—with the portraits on top.

Checks and money orders must be properly indorsed before they can be deposited. Indorsements are discussed on pages 221-223.

The bank will tell you how it prefers to have coupons presented for deposit.

Counterfeit Money. Despite the efforts of the Federal authorities, a good deal of counterfeit money gets into circulation. You should therefore be on the lookout constantly to "spot" such money.

The accompanying diagram shows the position of important features of paper currency. By studying a genuine bill, noticing all its details and how clearly they are printed, you will learn how "good money" looks. Then, should you see a counterfeit bill, you will recognize crudities and defects. All bills of the same denomination bear the same portrait.

$1 bills—Washington	$100 bills—Franklin
2 bills—Jefferson	500 bills—McKinley
5 bills—Lincoln	1,000 bills—Cleveland
10 bills—Hamilton	5,000 bills—Madison
20 bills—Jackson	10,000 bills—Chase
50 bills—Grant	

You would not accept a $1 bill altered to represent $10 if you knew that a $10 bill should have a portrait of Hamilton on it.

The United States Secret Service has issued these guides for recognizing counterfeit money.

How to Detect Counterfeit Bills

1. *Know your money.* Study the bills you receive, so as to become familiar with the workmanship, especially in the portraits.
2. *Compare* a suspected bill with a genuine of the same type and denomination.

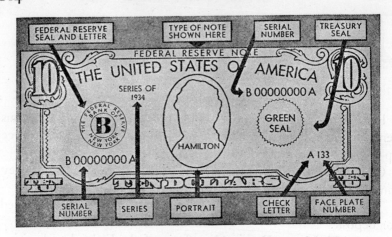

KNOW YOUR MONEY

Portrait: *Counterfeit*—Dull, smudgy, or unnaturally white, scratchy; oval background is dark, lines irregular and broken. Portrait merges into the background.

Genuine—Stands out distinctly from the oval background. Eyes appear lifelike. Background is a fine screen of regular lines.

Colored seal: *Counterfeit*—Saw-tooth points around rim are usually uneven, broken off.

Genuine—Saw-tooth points even and sharp.

Serial numbers: *Counterfeit*—Poorly printed, badly spaced, uneven.

Genuine—Figures firmly and evenly printed, well spaced.

Paper: *Counterfeit*—Generally has no silk threads, but these may be imitated by small red and blue ink lines.

Genuine—Printed on distinctive paper in which small red and blue silk threads are scattered. The silk threads are not always noticeable on badly soiled or worn bills.

3. *Rubbing* a bill on a piece of paper will *not* prove whether it is genuine; ink can be rubbed from good as well as bad bills.

4. *Consult* an experienced money-handler or police officer to make sure, if you are still in doubt, whether a bill is genuine or counterfeit.

5. *Remember,* not all strangers are counterfeiters, but all counterfeiters are likely to be strangers.

How to Detect Counterfeit Coins

1. *Know your money.* Study the coins you receive so as to become more familiar with the expert workmanship of the U. S. mints.

2. *Ring* coins on a hard surface. Genuine coins have a clear, bell-like ring; counterfeit coins, a dull sound.

3. *Feel* all coins. Most counterfeit coins have a greasy feeling.

4. *Compare* the reeding (the corrugated outer edge). The ridges on a genuine

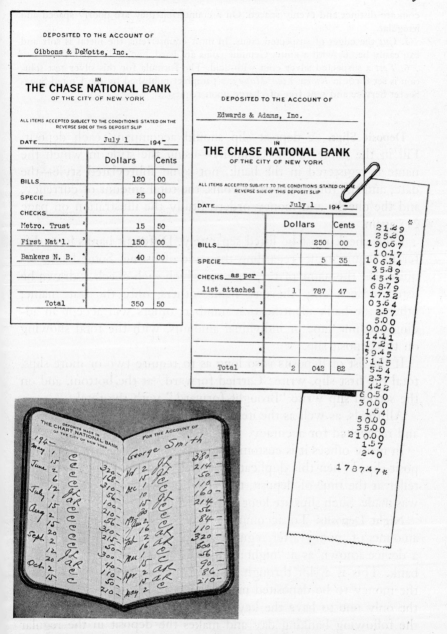

A PASSBOOK AND DEPOSIT SLIPS WITH ADDING MACHINE TAPE

coin are distinct and evenly spaced. On a counterfeit they are poorly spaced and
irregular.

5. *Cut* the edges of suspected coins. In most counterfeits, the metal is soft and
can easily be cut with a knife. Genuine coins are hard, not easily cut.

6. *Test* a suspected silver coin with acid. The formula for this silver test solu-
tion is set forth in *Know Your Money*, a pamphlet published by the United States
Secret Service and sent free of charge upon request.

Deposit Slips. A deposit slip should accompany each deposit.
Fill in the name of the company—using the style in which the
name is registered in the bank, not some abbreviated style—the
date; and the total amount of coins, the total amount of currency,
and the checks and money orders. Study the illustration on page
215 again.

Each check must be listed separately. Different banks have different requirements regarding the style of listing. Some banks require that the name of the bank on which each check is drawn be
listed; others, only the city name; others, only the state name;
others, the bank identification number; others will accept an ad-
ding-machine tape of individual amounts, with the total showing
on the deposit slip.

If the list of deposits is so long as to require two or more slips,
total the first slip, write "Carried forward" at the bottom, and on
the second slip write "Brought forward," with the total.

All totals, as well as the items of the deposit, should be checked
and rechecked for accuracy.

In many offices it is customary to make a duplicate of every deposit slip. When this duplicate is initialed by the bank's receiving
teller at the time of deposit, the slip becomes proof that a deposit
was made. Such slips are kept in a special file.

Night Deposits. To accommodate depositors who take in large
amounts of money after regular banking hours, many banks have
a device known as a "night depository" built in the wall of the
bank. This is a slot through which a locked canvas bag holding
the money to be deposited may be thrust. The depositor, who is
the only one to have the key to the bag, returns to the bank on
the following banking day and makes the deposit in the regular
way. A depositor may also simply enclose his deposit in an envelope

with the deposit slip made out in duplicate. The bank will enter the deposit and mail the duplicate slip to the depositor.

Checks. The most common means of transmitting money is by check. In drawing a check, the signer is simply directing his bank to pay a certain amount to the order of a certain person. Secretaries often are expected to prepare their employers' personal checks for signature as well as company checks.

Printed checks are usually provided by the bank and distributed to the depositor in book form. They are usually printed on "safety paper." If anyone tries to erase on this paper, or to use ink eradicator, the word "Void" appears. Many checks are printed over a fine network or pattern of colored lines, so that if an erasure is attempted, the color is removed and the white paper shows through as a warning that a change has been made.

Checkbooks. Checkbooks are manufactured in various styles. For business use, a common style contains three or more checks to the page, each check being separated by perforations from other checks and from the stub that remains in the book after the check is torn out. A personal checkbook usually contains only one check to the page.

All checks, with their corresponding stubs, should be numbered in sequence from 1 up or beginning with the next number following the last number in the preceding book. This numbering may be done by pen or by numbering machine. Business concerns, however, usually ask the bank to imprint the number as well as the company name on each check.

Photo by Ewing Galloway

NIGHT DEPOSITORY OF A BANK

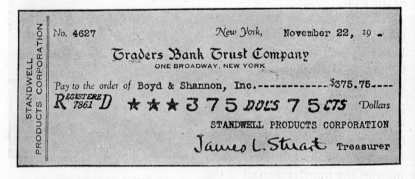

No. 4321 $ 8 95
Feb 2 19--
To Ind Elec Co
For Jan Bill

	Dollars	Cents
Bal. bru't For'd.	6 5 2	1 8
Amt. deposited..	3 5	5 0
Total	6 8 7	6 8
Amt. this cheque	8	9 5
Bal. car'd For'd.	6 7 8	7 3

No. 4321   Indianapolis, Ind. Feb 2, 19--

INDIANA NATIONAL BANK 24-101

Pay to the order of *Indiana Electric Company*

Eight and 95/100 ————————————— Dollars

$ 8 95/--   *George P. Barrett*

A PERSONAL CHECK, SHOWING STUB

The Stub. The stub should *always* be filled in before the check is written. If the check is written first, the stub may easily be forgotten; thus no record of the check appears.

The stub contains space for the following information in addition to the number: the balance remaining after the preceding check was drawn, the date, the amount, the name of the person or company to which the check was drawn, a brief description of the purpose for which the check was issued, and the balance remaining after the amount of the check was deducted. This new balance is carried forward to the next check stub.

Writing Checks. The following rules should be observed in writing checks:

No. 4627   *New York,* November 22, 19--

STANDWELL PRODUCTS CORPORATION

Traders Bank Trust Company
ONE BROADWAY, NEW YORK

Pay to the order of Boyd & Shannon, Inc.------------$375.75----

R*EGISTERED* 7861 D ★★★ 3 7 5 *DOLS* 7 5 *CTS* *Dollars*

STANDWELL PRODUCTS CORPORATION

James L. Stuart Treasurer

A COMPANY CHECK WRITTEN ON A CHECK WRITER

1. Type all checks or write them in ink—never in pencil.

2. Leave no empty spaces on lines that are to be filled in. Start writing at the extreme left of each space and draw or type a line through any space not filled.

3. If you make a mistake, do not attempt to erase or alter the check. Mark both the check and the stub "Void" and draw another check. (The voided check should be filed for auditing purposes, to prove that it was not issued.)

4. Write the amount of the check, in figures, in the space provided, using one of these forms:

$$\$56.10 \qquad \text{or} \qquad \$56\frac{10}{} \qquad \text{or} \qquad \$56\frac{10}{100}$$

Write the spelled-out amount thus:

$$\text{Fifty-six and } \frac{10}{100} \quad \ldots\ldots\ldots\ldots\ldots\ldots\ldots\ldots\ldots\ldots\text{Dollars}$$

5. Amounts less than $1 are written in figures thus:

$$\frac{\$.87}{100} \qquad \text{or} \qquad ^{87}/_{100}$$

In words: "Eighty-seven cents only," with the word "Dollars" that is printed at the end of the line crossed out.

6. Make checks payable to a person or to a company rather than just to "Cash" or to "Bearer," because any holder can obtain payment on a check drawn payable to "Cash" or "Bearer."

7. A check should never be signed until it is completed in all details. If the amount, for example, is left blank and the check is signed, the person to whom it is drawn can fill in any amount he wishes and the signer will have to pay the amount. If both the name and the amount are left blank, anyone can fill in his name and any amount.

In most offices, especially in those offices in which large numbers of checks are issued, the amounts—both the figures and the spelled-out form—are filled in on check writers, or check protectors. These machines are designed to insure against fraud. They usually press the characters into the paper so that erasure is impossible. The rest of the check is filled in on the typewriter, and of course the check is signed as usual. The lower check pictured on page 218 was written on a check protector. See also page 220.

Courtesy the Todd Company

A CHECK PROTECTOR IN USE

Postdated Checks. Occasionally a businessman who is short of funds will pay a pressing bill with a check dated ahead to a time when he expects to have enough money in his account to cover it. This is called *postdating* a check. The practice is undesirable and reflects discredit on the maker of such a check because it indicates that his financial standing is unsound. A check is assumed to be a negotiable instrument for immediate payment, but a postdated check is an order on the bank to pay at some future date. For this purpose, a promissory note (see page 231) might be more advisable.

Overdrafts. When a check for a larger amount than the signer has on deposit in the bank is paid by that bank, he is said to have *overdrawn* his account. This is a serious matter. Most banks are not permitted to honor overdrafts. If a check overdrawing an account is received by the bank, it will return it, marked "Insufficient Funds," to the person who deposited it and will probably charge a fee against the account on which it is drawn. In some states a person who receives such a check can bring criminal suit against the person who drew it.

Overdrafts usually result from carelessness. Any of these four things may be the cause:

1. Failure to keep a continuous and correct record of checks drawn and deposits made, on the stubs.

2. Mistakes in arithmetic. (A common mistake is to add a deposit twice.)

3. Failure to check the stubs once a month against the bank balance. This matter will be more fully explained in the discussion of checking the bank statement.

4. Drawing immediately on a deposited check from a distant city before the check has had time to "clear" (to be collected by the depositor's bank). The bank can tell you how long you must wait before drawing on such checks.

Bank officials, however, realize that even the most careful persons will make mistakes in their bank accounts once in a while. Bank officials therefore follow the rule of notifying a depositor by telephone if a check that would overdraw his account has been presented for payment. In this way, the depositor is given the opportunity of correcting his mistake by making an immediate deposit large enough to cover the check in question. The deposit must be made before bank closing time on the day the check is presented; otherwise, the check may be returned dishonored.

Stopping Payment. If it is discovered that a check has been lost, stolen, or made out incorrectly, payment can be stopped by notifying the bank at once. Banks supply special stop-payment request forms providing spaces for all the details needed—the current date, the date and number of the check, the name of the person to whom it was drawn, the amount, and the reason for stopping payment. In an emergency, the request may be made by telephone, but the oral request must be supplemented at once by the written form.

Indorsements. In the discussion of making deposits in the bank, it was stated that all checks offered for deposit must be properly indorsed.

An indorsement is a form for transferring a check legally from one person or organization to another by writing (in business usually by rubber-stamping) the appropriate wording across the back of the check near the left end.

There are several types of indorsement, the choice of which depends on the circumstances of the transfer.

1. The simplest of all indorsements is the *blank indorsement.* The person or organization to whom the check is drawn simply writes that name on the back of the check. The check then becomes payable to anyone at any time, and it may change hands any number of times without further indorsement. This type of indorsement is thus inadvisable to use unless you are in the bank and wish to cash or deposit

the check immediately. It should never be used on checks mailed or given to a messenger.

2. In the *full indorsement*, the indorser specifies the person, company, or bank to whom payment is to be made; thus:

a. Pay to the order of
　　First National Bank of Chicago
　　　Robert R. Jones

b. Pay to the order of
　　　Mary Sims
　　Robert R. Jones

Form *a* is the customary form of indorsement used in depositing checks by mail. Even if the mail is lost, no finder could cash the check. Also, if Form *b* is lost, no bank would cash the check until it is first indorsed by Mary Sims.

3. A *restrictive indorsement* is used when it is desired to transfer the check to a person or a business concern for some specific purpose; thus:

a. Pay to John Hill only
　　Roberts & Jones, Inc.

b. For deposit only
　　Roberts & Jones, Inc.

A check so indorsed is nontransferable—it is of use only to the individual person or concern designated.

In order, from top to bottom:

1. A blank indorsement—makes check payable to any holder

2. A restrictive indorsement—must be deposited, not cashed

3. A full indorsement—check cannot be cashed or transferred until indorsed by Richard Roe

4. A restrictive indorsement—check may be paid only to Richard Roe

5. A qualified indorsement—identifies the holder without guaranteeing payment

6. A full indorsement—made by a rubber stamp

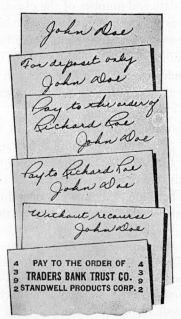

TYPES OF INDORSEMENTS

Other Details of Indorsements. Irrespective of the type of indorsement used, strict rules govern the various details of indorsement.

1. Indorsements should always be written in ink (or stamped with a rubber stamp).

2. An indorsement should be close to the edge of the check or close to the indorsement just above it, so that nothing can be written above the indorsement.

3. The indorsement must agree exactly in spelling and form with the name on the face of the check. If the name is incorrectly written on the face, indorse the check first as written; then below write the correct form of the name.

Cashing Checks. Sometimes a person not known to the management may wish to pay for a purchase or a service by check. The secretary should not take the responsibility of accepting such checks without specific instructions regarding the firm's policy in these matters.

It is customary to ask such persons to produce identification. A Social Security card, club membership cards bearing his signature, a hospital-insurance card, or letters addressed to him that he has with him may be accepted as identification.

Also, a person who presents for payment a check that is not his own must prove that he is entitled to receive the money. He should be required to identify himself conclusively; then he should indorse the check in the presence of the person who is to cash it.

If a check has already been indorsed when it is presented, the person to whom it is presented for cashing should insist that it be indorsed again and should compare the handwriting of the two indorsements to see that both were written by the same person.

Most business concerns ask a signer or an indorser of a check to write his address below his signature in case the check turns out to be a forgery or an overdraft.

Vast numbers of Government checks are issued to Social Security benefactors and to families of servicemen. The Government therefore urges all persons who receive Government checks to observe the following recommendations:

1. Have some member of the family at home when the checks are due to be delivered.

2. Be sure your name is clearly printed on your mailbox.

3. Try to cash your checks in the same place each month. This will make identification easier. Merchants are being cautioned to ask for identification.

4. Do not indorse your check until you are in the presence of the person you will ask to cash it.

Canceled Checks and the Bank Statement. At the end of the month, most banks send each depositor a statement of his account, together with all his checks that have passed through the bank and been charged against his account. The word "Paid" is either perforated through or stamped on these checks. Canceled checks should be kept, for they are the drawer's receipts for the bills they have paid.

The bank statement contains the balance at the beginning of the month, the deposits made during the month, the checks paid, any additional charges made by the bank, and the balance at the end of the month.

Almost never does this final balance agree with the balance shown on the checkbook at the end of the month, for the following reasons:

1. Checks issued the last few days of the month have not had time to reach the bank and be cleared. Such checks are known as *outstanding checks*.

2. Deposits made on the last day of the month may not show on the statement.

3. Any checks that were deposited but *dishonored* (not paid) by the bank will not have been deducted from the checkbook balance.

4. Any service charges made by the bank will show on the statement for the first time.

Reconciling the Statement. It is most important that the bank statement be compared with the checkbook at once and the differences between the two records accounted for. This process is called *reconciling the bank statement*, or *making a bank reconciliation*.

This comparison work should be done systematically. The following procedure covers all the necessary steps.

1. Compare the amount of each canceled check with the amounts listed on the statement. As returned, the checks are not always in numerical order; they may be in the order in which they were presented to the bank for payment.

2. Arrange the canceled checks in numerical order.

3. Compare the canceled checks with their corresponding stubs in the checkbook, noting whether the amounts agree. When a check agrees with its stub, place a check mark on the stub.

4. Compare the deposits shown in your checkbook with those shown in the statement.

5. Go over the stubs again and list the amounts of all on which you have not placed check marks. The total of these is the total of the outstanding checks.

6. Subtract from your checkbook balance at the end of the month the special charges made by the bank. These are identified on the statement by certain letters, as *SC*, meaning "Service Charge," or *EX*, meaning "Exchange."

BANK RECONCILIATION STATEMENT

October 1, 194—

Balance on Bank Statement		$485.90
Plus September 30 Deposit		37.95
		$523.85
Less Checks Outstanding:		
No. 121	$ 3.56	
No. 143	11.45	
No. 163	9.04	
Total Checks Outstanding		24.05
Corrected Bank Balance		$499.80
Checkbook Balance		$511.80
Less:		
Bank Service Charges	$ 2.50	
Dishonored Check	9.50	
Total Deductions		12.00
Corrected Checkbook Balance		$499.80

Some of your checking may reveal errors in addition and subtraction, in carrying wrong amounts forward, or in failing to record a deposit. More serious than these are errors in writing checks for wrong amounts or failure to fill out a stub. The errors in arithmetic can be easily corrected; but the only wise plan, if you find a serious error, is to tell your employer frankly what happened and ask instructions as to how to handle the matter.

Occasionally you will find that the bank has made an error, in which case take the statement, the canceled checks, and the stubs to the bank for further checking and advice.

You still have two final duties in reconciling the statement: (1) to type a bank reconciliation statement (a typical one is shown here); and (2) to make the necessary additions and subtractions in your checkbook balance.

Special Kinds of Checks. Up to this point, only the usual type of check has been discussed. Several special types of checks, however, are used for various purposes.

Occasions arise in business where a person or a concern wishes a guarantee that a check is "good" before it will be accepted. Three types of checks are used for such situations: a certified check, a cashier's check, or a bank draft.

Certified Checks. A certified check is simply a regular check guaranteed by the bank on which it is drawn. It is drawn just like any check and taken to the bank. The bank charges the amount against the depositor's account at once and writes "Certified" on

A CERTIFIED CHECK

the face of the check. This certification indicates to the recipient of the check that ample funds are available for the payment of the check.

Cashier's Checks. A cashier's check, on the other hand, is drawn by the cashier of the bank on his own bank. Naturally, a person or a concern will accept a check drawn by a bank in preference to one drawn by a person or a concern unknown to him. A cashier's check is obtained by giving the bank cash or your own check. It may be made payable to the person buying it or to the person who is to receive it. If it is payable to the person buying it, that person indorses it over to the one who is to receive the money.

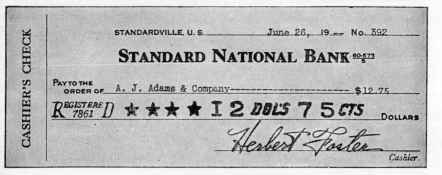

A CASHIER'S CHECK

Bank Draft. A bank draft is really a bank check. It is an order by one bank to another in which the first bank has an account—usually in a distant city—to pay an amount to some specific person or concern. A bank draft is purchased from the sender's bank.

For example, H. E. Waller, who has an account in the Standard National Bank of New York, wishes to pay a sum of money to Ebers & Smith, in San Francisco. Mr. Waller buys a draft from his New York bank, payable to Ebers & Smith by a specified bank in San Francisco. The bank draft is really an order from the Standard National Bank in New York to the First National Bank in San Francisco to pay a specified amount of money to Ebers & Smith. Mr. Waller has already deposited this money with his bank in New York.

A bank draft is entirely different from a commercial draft, which was described in Section 11.

STANDARD NATIONAL BANK 60-575/5

NEW YORK 16, N. Y. June 4, 19-- No. 821

PAY TO THE ORDER OF F. W. Long $200.00

REGISTERED 7861 ★★★ 200 DOLS 00 CTS DOLLARS

To the First National Bank
SAN FRANCISCO

Herbert Foster
CASHIER

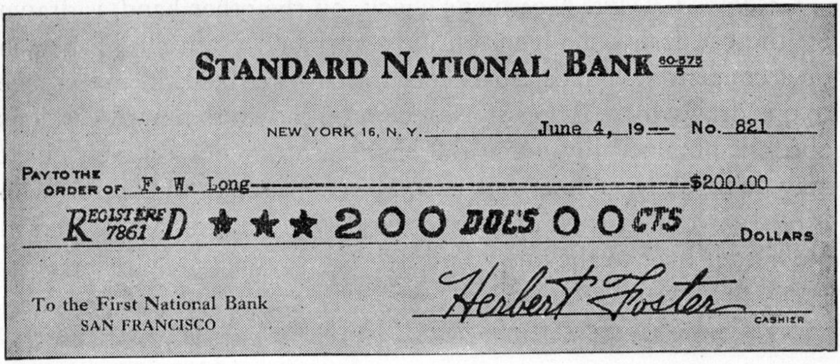

A BANK DRAFT

Voucher Checks. Some companies use a form of check that indicates the purpose for which the payment is being made, as for payment of taxes, pay-roll payments, and so on. This form of check is known as a voucher check. The space for the information may be on the face of the check itself, as in the accompanying illustration; it may be on a stub; or it may be on a detachable part of the check. Also, an ordinary check may be made into a voucher check simply by writing the purpose of the payment on the face of the check; for example, "For March rent." (See page 229.)

STANDARDVILLE MANUFACTURING COMPANY

AUDIT NO. 46
Sales DEPT. NO. 2
DATE OF VO. 5-1-19--
APPROVED James Smith
APPROVED John Watson
AUDITED Frank P. Adams
STANDARDVILLE, U. S.

Your invoice 4-9-19-- 1 typewriter desk

IN SETTLEMENT OF THE ABOVE ACCOUNT

PAY TO THE ORDER OF
City Office Equipment Company
285 Madison Avenue
New York, N. Y.

Eighteen and 19/100 DOLLARS $18.19

STANDARD STATE BANK
60-575/5 STANDARDVILLE, U. S.

Henry Geiger Pres.

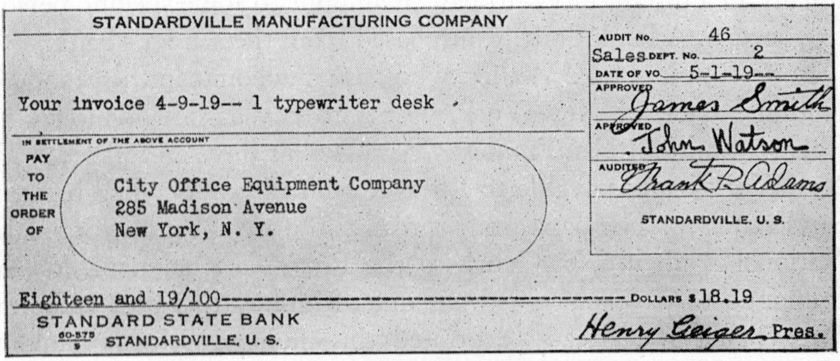

A VOUCHER CHECK

STANDARDVILLE, U. S. _____ August 21, 19— No. 1998 _____

STANDARD TRUST COMPANY ^{co-575}

PAY TO THE ORDER OF Stationery Service Company--------------------$14.75

REGISTERED 7861 ★ ★ ★ ★ I 4 DOLS 7 5 CTS DOLLARS

Harry C. Hatch

For invoice Aug. 10, 19--

A COMMON CHECK USED AS A VOUCHER CHECK

Do not be confused by the word "voucher." It simply means that the check contains a little more information than other checks contain. Voucher checks are handled in the same way as ordinary checks.

Receipts. One of the commonest forms that the secretary handles is the receipt. A receipt is a written acknowledgment of the delivery of money, merchandise, documents, registered mail, or of anything else of which a record is to be kept. The article need not have value. The recipient of a telegram or of a package is often asked to sign a receipt. Always read such a receipt form before signing it, to be sure that you are not signing for something that you have not received or for something that has been damaged.

October 3, 19 –

RECEIVED from John F. McAllister

Sixty-five 30/100 ------------------------------Dollars

in full payment of account to date

$65 30/100

Andrew Cromwell

A RECEIPT

Printed receipt blanks are widely used, but a receipt may take the form of a letter, a memorandum, or a canceled voucher check. All receipts should be dated. (Any business paper, even an unimportant office memorandum, should carry the date.)

Money Orders. There are three types of money order—postal, express, and telegraph. Each offers a safe means of sending money. (Cash, of course, should never be sent by mail.)

Business concerns seldom *send* postal and express money orders, but issue checks in making payments. Concerns, however, often *receive* such money orders from customers and others who do not have checking accounts.

Postal Money Order. A person who wishes to send a postal money order simply applies for it at a regular post office, makes out an application form, and pays a small fee for the service, the fee varying with the amount of the money order. The largest amount that can be sent in one money order is $100.

The recipient of a postal money order may either cash it at his post office upon proper identification or—the usual business practice—deposit it as he would a check. Like a check, it must be indorsed first. A postal money order can be transferred by indorsement but once.

Express Money Order. The express money order resembles the postal money order. It may be purchased at express offices, drug stores, and at other agencies. No application form is needed. Like the postal money order, the express money order may be deposited

Courtesy American Express Company

AN EXPRESS MONEY ORDER

in a bank. Unlike the postal money order, however, it may be transferred and indorsed more than once.

Telegraph Money Order. The telegraph money order was discussed in Section 4.

Promissory Notes. Many times a customer is not in a position to pay for goods or services at the time that payment is due, but he has every reason to believe that he will be able to do so in one, two, three, or more months. In such case he may ask permission to give a promissory note, which is a written promise to pay the specified amount at a certain time, at a certain place—frequently a bank or the maker's office—and often at a certain rate of interest.

If the customer's credit standing is good, the request will doubtless be granted, and a form prepared for him to sign. A supply of blank forms, which may be purchased at any stationery store, is usually kept on hand.

Notes are described variously according to various features. When the time of payment is specified, as in the illustration, the note is called a *time note*. If no time is specified, the note is payable on demand and is called a *demand note*. Notes that read "Pay to the order of," as in the illustration, or "Pay to Bearer" are *negotiable notes;* but the first mentioned must be indorsed by the person or concern to which it is made payable before it is transferable. Notes that read "Pay to Bearer" need no indorsement.

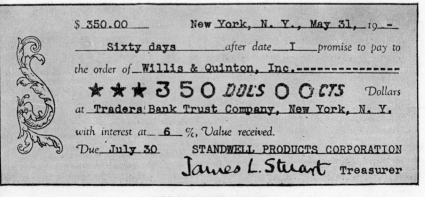

$350.00   New York, N. Y., May 31, 19 -

Sixty days _____ after date__I__promise to pay to the order of__Willis & Quinton, Inc.------------------

★★★350 *DOLS* 0 0 *CTS*   *Dollars*

at__Traders Bank Trust Company, New York, N. Y.

with interest at__6__%, *Value received.*

*Due*__July 30__   STANDWELL PRODUCTS CORPORATION

James L. Stuart   Treasurer

A PROMISSORY NOTE

A *collateral note* is similar to an ordinary promissory note except that it contains a statement that certain valuable collateral (stocks, bonds, mortgages, and so on) has been deposited with the payee as security that the note will be paid. This collateral must be returned when the note is paid.

As notes are valuable documents, they should be filed in a safe or a vault until the time for collection—the *maturity* date—approaches.

Several days before the due date, it is customary to notify the maker of a note that the note will fall due on a certain date and to remind him to make provision for meeting the payment. Your company then indorses the note and leaves it at your bank for collection.

When the money has been collected, your company receives a notice that the collection has been made and that the amount has been credited to the company's account.

This entire procedure, in reverse, is applied to cases where it is necessary for your company to issue a note to pay some account that it owes.

Sometimes the person or the company to whom a note is made out decides to sell the note to a bank or a finance company before it comes due, so as to have immediate use of the money. This is called *discounting* the note. The bank or finance company deducts a certain fee for this service. The big problem in discounting a note is to determine how much the note is worth at the time it is sold. Such computations seldom fall to the lot of a secretary to do.

Petty Cash. Most offices keep a small sum of money—$10 or more—for miscellaneous expenditures for small items or for change. For each expenditure, a petty cash voucher or a receipt should be signed by the person receiving the money. The total of these vouchers, plus the remaining money, must always equal the original sum. The vouchers are redeemed periodically by the cashier, who draws a check to

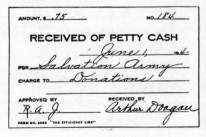

A PETTY CASH VOUCHER

"Petty Cash" for the exact amount of the vouchers to be redeemed and replaces the cash expended with the cash obtained from the check.

Pay Rolls. Office workers are usually paid on a straight salary basis—weekly, semimonthly, or monthly. Factory workers are paid on an hourly basis, a record

A RECORDER
FOR PAY
ROLL AND
JOB-TIME
RECORDS

Above: Employee's Attendance Card

Courtesy International Business Machines Corp.

of each employee's time being kept on a time card, usually by means of a clock. A card for each employee is kept in a rack beside the clock. When an employee arrives or leaves, he inserts his card into a slot in the time clock, which prints the hour and minute of his arrival or departure. Some time clocks, after a certain hour, print in red to indicate tardiness. Tardiness is discouraged in many organizations by penalizing the late employee 15 minutes for any tardiness up to that length of time.

Pay for overtime is usually one and one-half as much an hour as the regular hourly pay. (This is called "time and a half.")

The Federal Government and most of the states have laws regulating minimum wages for certain jobs and maximum hours that employees may work.

Salaries and wages are sometimes paid by check; sometimes in cash. When paid in cash, it is necessary to calculate the exact number and denomination of bills and coins required in order to fill all the pay envelopes. This is done by preparing a currency memorandum. The object is to request the fewest bills and coins possible. A pay envelope of $18.77, for example, would require one $10 bill, one $5 bill, three $1 bills, a half dollar, a 25-cent piece, and two pennies.

Pay Roll Deductions. Employees do not receive the full amount of their salaries on pay day, however. Certain amounts are withheld by Federal law for: (1) Social Security payments, and (2) income tax payments. In addition, by agreement with the employee, still other amounts may be deducted for sick benefits, for the purchase of bonds, for various employees' funds, and so on.

EMPLOYEE'S STATEMENT OF EARNINGS AND DEDUCTIONS

YOUR COMPANY
ANYWHERE, U.S.A.

№ 995

NAME:— Catharine Rottier

DETACH AND RETAIN

REGULAR WAGES		OVERTIME WAGES		OTHER	TOTAL WAGES	DEDUCTIONS		NET PAY	DAY AND MONTH END. 194—	CHECK NO.
HOURS	AMOUNT	HOURS	AMOUNT			F.O.A.B.	Ins.			
40	30.00	--	--	--	30.00	.30	.15	29.55	9/7	1148

SHAW-WALKER—KOPI-SPOT. 2785-1

PAY ROLL CHECK

YOUR COMPANY
ANYWHERE, U.S.A.

№ 995

PAY TO THE ORDER OF Catharine Rottier September 7, 194—

VOID IF DRAWN FOR MORE THAN $100

REGISTERED 7861 D ★ ★ ★ ★ 29 DOLS 5 5 CTS $ 29.55

PAY ROLL ACCOUNT
ANY COMPANY

Robert L. Allen
Treasurer

PAYABLE AT YOUR BANK
12-34 / 5 ANYWHERE, U.S.A.

Courtesy Shaw-Walker Co.

A VOUCHER PAY CHECK

Social Security Deductions. The purpose of the Social Security deduction, which began in 1937, is to provide old-age and retirement benefits for wage and salary earners when they reach the age of sixty-five. The employer pays an amount equal to the amount paid by the worker.

These deductions apply only on earnings up to $3,000. On salaries over $3,000, the deduction is on the first $3,000 only. A deduction of 1 per cent was made for the years 1937 through 1947.

Note that the Social Security deduction is not a tax, but a form of compulsory insurance. The deductions are credited to each employee's own account, the number of which appears on his Social Security card. This card may be obtained by applying to the nearest Social Security office, which is usually located in the post office building. Be sure to obtain your card before applying for a job, in order to avoid delay and inconvenience to your employer.

Income Tax Returns. Each employee earning more than a certain amount each year is required to pay a Federal tax on his net income. Since 1943, this tax has been collected through the employer, who on each pay day withholds a certain percentage of the employee's pay and remits the total thus collected to the Federal Government. Many states also levy income taxes.

Financial Statements. The purpose of keeping a complete record of business transactions is to supply the proprietor or the manager of a business with information that will be of use in the management of his business. Bookkeeping records are simply a history of what has happened, and the information they contain is valuable in planning future operations and policies.

It is necessary to determine at regular intervals the condition of a business and to determine what has brought about any changes in that condition since it was last determined. This is done by a process technically known in bookkeeping as the *preparation of statements* and *closing the ledger.*

Two statements are usually prepared in addition to a number of detailed analytical schedules. The financial statement commonly called the *Balance Sheet,* or *Statement of Assets, Liabilities, and Capital,* is simply a list of the assets, the liabilities, and the capital of a business in approved form and exhibits the condition of the

```
                        GEORGE WATSON & SONS
                   BALANCE SHEET, DECEMBER 31, 19--
─────────────────────────────────────────────────────────────

                         A S S E T S

CURRENT ASSETS:
  Cash . . . . . . . . . . . . . . . . . . . $ 3,645.19
  Notes Receivable . . . . . . . . . . . .     3,960.10
  Accounts Receivable:
    Customers . . . . . . . . . .  $52,608.18
    Less Reserve for Losses . . .    1,052.16
               Net . . . . . . . . $51,556.02
    Others . . . . . . . . . . . .   3,624.13
                                               55,180.15
  Accrued Interest Receivable . . . . . . . .     431.25
  Merchandise Inventory . . . . . . . . . . .  41,978.87
          Total Current Assets . . . . . . . . . . . . $105,195.56

PROPERTY:
  Land . . . . . . . . . . . . . . . . . . . $12,000.00
  Buildings . . . . . . . . . . . . . . . . .  18,600.00
  Furniture and Fixtures . . . . . . . . . .    2,500.00
  Auto Trucks . . . . . . . . . . . . . . . .   3,500.00
      Total . . . . . . . . . . . . . . . . $36,600.00
  Less Reserve for Depreciation . . . . . . .   7,320.00
          Net Property . . . . . . . . . . . . . . . . .  29,280.00

DEFERRED CHARGES:
  Prepaid Insurance . . . . . . . . . . . . . $   250.16
  Advances to Employees . . . . . . . . . . .     145.56
          Total Deferred Charges . . . . . . . . . . . .     395.72
                    TOTAL . . . . . . . . . . . . . . . $134,871.28


                     L I A B I L I T I E S

CURRENT LIABILITIES:
  Notes Payable . . . . . . . . . . . . . . . $16,000.00
  Accounts Payable . . . . . . . . . . . . .   25,461.18
  Accrued Taxes . . . . . . . . . . . . . . .   1,475.11
          Total Current Liabilities . . . . . . . . . . $ 42,936.29
RESERVE FOR CONTINGENCIES . . . . . . . . . . . . . . . .   6,000.00
CAPITAL STOCK . . . . . . . . . . . . . . . . . . . . . .  55,000.00
SURPLUS . . . . . . . . . . . . . . . . . . . . . . . . .  30,934.99
                    TOTAL . . . . . . . . . . . . . . . $134,871.28
```

A BALANCE SHEET

business. The *Statement of Profit and Loss* is another statement
that exhibits in approved form for convenience and analysis the
various sources and amounts of the income or profit that the busi-

BERTRAM MANUFACTURING COMPANY

STATEMENT OF INCOME AND PROFIT AND LOSS
FOR THE YEAR ENDED DECEMBER 31, 19--

GROSS SALES			$380,674.75
Less Returns and Allowances			4,568.20
NET SALES			$376,106.55
COST OF GOODS SOLD:			
Inventory, January 1, 19--	$251,675.43		
Purchases	327,119.80		
Freight and Drayage	2,654.00		
Total	$581,449.23		
Less Inventory, December 31, 19-- . . .	252,436.93		
Total Cost of Goods Sold		329,012.30	
GROSS PROFIT		$ 47,094.25	
GENERAL AND SELLING EXPENSES:			
Salaries	$ 12,420.00		
Commissions	1,647.20		
Traveling Expenses	1,241.16		
Office Salaries	2,460.00		
Office Rent	960.00		
Office Supplies	1,020.16		
Telephone and Telegraph	1,060.15		
Advertising	345.00		
Depreciation of Furniture and Fixtures	245.16		
Miscellaneous	176.82		
Total		21,575.65	
PROFIT FROM OPERATIONS		$ 25,518.60	
DEDUCTIONS FROM INCOME:			
Cash Discounts on Sales	$ 2,974.17		
Uncollectible Accounts	2,427.84		
Discounts on Trade Acceptances	254.47		
Interest on Accounts Payable	94.88		
Total		5,751.36	
NET GAIN		$ 19,767.24	
ADDITIONS TO INCOME:			
Selling Commissions	$ 658.17		
Interest Earned	116.88		
Total		775.05	
SURPLUS FOR PERIOD		$ 20,542.29	

A PROFIT AND LOSS STATEMENT

ness has earned and the expenses that have been incurred in order
to earn this profit or income. The results are transferred to the
ledger accounts by the process known as *closing the ledger*.

The preparation of statements and the closing the ledger require a more or less comprehensive knowledge of bookkeeping and accounting. Therefore, no attempt is made to treat this phase of the subject. You will, however, often be called on to type various financial statements.

Very definite rules govern the setup of accounting statements—the scheme of indentions, the position of dollar signs, the margins of subtotals and totals, and so on—although the setup may vary in different offices. A representative form of balance sheet and of profit and loss statement appear on pages 236 and 237. The safest plan in typing a statement is to follow the style of the last similar report. The accountant who compiled the statement should be consulted before any changes are made.

Accounting Machines. More and more, accounting is done by machine rather than by the traditional pen-and-ink method. An accounting machine is equipped with an adding-subtracting device, a wide carriage, a dating attachment, and a mechanism that moves the carriage automatically into the positions for printing. As a rule, by operating certain keys, the operator can place the machine carriage in the debit position, the credit position, and so on.

Accounting machines may be either hand or electrically operated, may have either ten-key or selective adding-subtracting keyboards, and may be equipped with typewriters.

Electrically run tabulating machines have been designed to record and classify accounting and other statistical information by means of a code system. First, a hole-punching machine is used to record the desired information on cards of a special size and material. Each perforation on one of these cards represents a unit of information.

When a total of all cards having certain units of information in common is desired, the unsorted cards are placed in a sorting machine that is adjusted to pick out automatically the cards according to the unit or units desired. Then the picked group of cards is run through a tabulating machine, which tabulates as many as five columns at once and prints the result. See illustration on page 241.

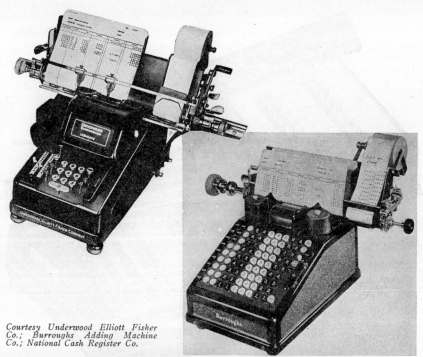

Courtesy Underwood Elliott Fisher Co.; Burroughs Adding Machine Co.; National Cash Register Co.

BOOKKEEPING MACHINES

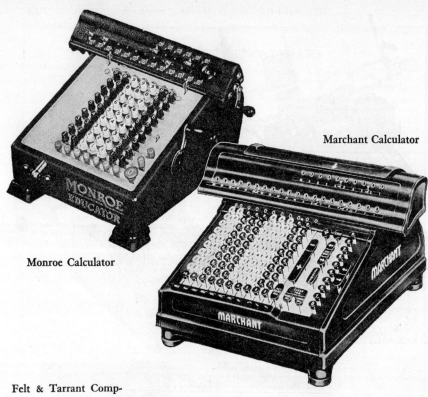

Marchant Calculator

Monroe Calculator

Felt & Tarrant Comptometer

Burroughs Calculator

Courtesy Burroughs Adding Machine Co.; Felt & Tarrant Mfg. Co.; Monroe Calculating Machine Co.; Marchant Calculating Machine Co.

CALCULATORS

REMITTANCE STATEMENT

TRANSMITTAL
ADVICE NO.
G47279   FEB 11 19

APPROVED FOR
PAYMENT

MERCER TOOL AND SUPPLY CO
15835 E 52ND STREET
BUFFALO   N Y

DATE MO.	DAY	YOUR NUMBER	OUR NUMBER	GROSS AMOUNT	DISCOUNT	CODE	NET AMOUNT
1	15	A15382	46284	25 75	52	D	25 23
1	15	A15390	46301	48 05	96	D	47 09
1	17	A15477	46395	41 24	82	D	40 42
1	18	A15523	46472	637 21	12 74	D	624 47
1	20	A15744	47010	78 32	1 57	D	76 75
1	21	A15915	48853	504 73	10 09	D	494 64
1	24	A16163	49224	385 64	7 71	D	377 93
1	24	A16180	49280	23 41	47	D	22 94
1	24	A16264	49326	68 63	1 37	D	67 26
1	25	A17516	50147	52 75	1 06	D	51 69
1	25	C3353	50172		54 01	YC	54 01C
				125 00	1 96	D	4 69
						D	149 08
						D	3790
						YC	37 62C
							79 53
							200 799T

SALES ACCOUNTING

A STATEMENT PREPARED ON AN AUTOMATIC TABULATING MACHINE

The inset shows a card with perforations made by a card-punching machine. When these punched cards are run through the sorter, the holes permit electrical contacts, which control the sorting

ANSWERS TO "DO YOU KNOW?"

1. Anyone who finds a "blank" signed check on which the name of the payee or the amount is missing can fill in his own name or an amount and cash the check. Even though such an act is dishonest, the maker of the check will have to stand the loss.

2. A voucher check that has been canceled and returned to the maker constitutes a record of payment for whatever item is noted on it.

3. There is no good excuse for overdrawing a checking account. Overdrafts result from carelessness and in some states are illegal.

4. The balance shown on the statement is often larger than the actual balance on which checks may be drawn because some checks have not cleared through the bank.

5. Yes. Interest can be collected for the time the note runs after it has matured.

Courtesy United Air Lines

Courtesy Railway Express Agency, Inc.

Photo by Ewing Galloway→

Courtesy Northern Pacific Railway

VARIOUS METHODS OF SHIPPING

14

THE TRAFFIC DEPARTMENT

DO YOU KNOW?

1. Freight charges are assessed partly according to the weight of the commodity shipped. Does the amount of space the commodity takes up in a freight car have any bearing on the shipping rate?
2. How many copies of a bill of lading are usually made?
3. Under what circumstances would you make an order bill of lading?
4. What advantage has express over parcel post as a means of shipping?
5. Can parcel-post packages be sent "special delivery"?

Note: If, in reading the following pages, you encounter some shipping term that you do not understand, refer to the Glossary on pages 252-253.

THE FUNCTION of the Traffic Department in moving goods has been described as follows by the Academy of Advanced Traffic, in New York:

The world of today is a world of continually moving materials, manufactured articles, foods, supplies. By railroad, steamship, motor truck, airplane, and pipeline, the nation's goods are carried from point to point in a never-ending stream. A very complex transport mechanism underlies this movement of commodities—a mechanism that involves interstate commerce; regulation by the Interstate Commerce Commission; thousands of tariffs containing rates; proceedings before the Commission; hearings; solemn decisions. Out of all this seeming complexity, a rather exact body of scientific knowledge has been built—the science of traffic management.

Which method of transportation is best for a given shipment? Which the fastest? How shall the shipment be routed? Should a combination of routes be used? Is the charge for the movement reasonable? If not, what can be done? Is there a cheaper way? A more efficient way? A safer way? Over and over, the traffic specialist answers these and hundreds of other questions that occur in the day-to-day work of traffic administration.

243

Indeed, it is difficult for the nonspecialist to realize the many factors that must be taken into consideration if economy and efficiency are to be maintained consistently in shipping.

Methods of Shipping. Three methods are used for shipping goods: (1) freight, (2) express, and (3) parcel post. Each method has a definite advantage, as well as some disadvantages. The detailed information that the shipper must have regarding each service in order to choose the most suitable service for a particular shipment is contained in shipping guides. *Leonard's Guide* and the *Shipper's Guide* are widely used for this purpose.

FREIGHT SHIPMENTS

The great bulk of the commodities handled in commerce are shipped by freight. The means of transporting freight are rail, water, highway, and air. The term "shipping by freight," however, generally refers to the transportation of property in railroad freight cars. More time is required to ship by freight than by express or parcel post, but the saving in shipping cost is considerable. Freight rates are much lower than express or parcel-post rates.

Courtesy Great Northern Railway

PART OF A FREIGHT TRAIN

Freight is shipped in cars especially adapted to the requirements of the load. Shown here are cars for oil, perishable foods, automobiles, and miscellaneous bulky goods. The conductor and the rear brakeman ride in the caboose, the last car of the train

Freight Rates. Freight moves under two types of rates—class rates and commodity rates. Rates are changed from time to time.

Class rates apply to goods that are classified in accordance with recognized transportation characteristics, such as value, liability to damage, and the amount of space the goods will take up in a freight car. The principal railroad classification is published in the *Consolidated Freight Classification*, which applies to nearly all sections of the country.

Commodity rates are special rates applying to goods conforming to more specific descriptions. These rates ordinarily apply between specific given points; they are designed to meet particular traffic transportation conditions and problems and are based on the quantity of the particular kind of goods shipped to the city involved.

L.C.L. Shipments. Freight rates are usually quoted in cents per 100 pounds or per net ton. Shipments too small to fill a freight car are made at the l.c.l. (less than carload) rate. Shipments large enough to require an entire freight car are referred to as carload shipments. As the unit cost of transporting goods is much lower for carload lots than for less-than-carload lots, carload rates are usually materially lower.

Pool Cars. Sometimes the goods that are shipped from one consignor to one consignee consist of a consolidation into a carload lot of shipments from different consignors or of shipments for distribution to various consignees at the point of destination. Such a shipment is called a *pool car*.

Freight-Forwarding Companies. When shippers have several small consignments that would ordinarily require l.c.l. service, they sometimes employ freight-forwarding companies to collect these small shipments, consolidate them into carloads with consignments from other companies, and distribute them at the point of destination.

Delivery. Freight shipments are usually delivered by the shipper to the train or the wharf and are picked up at the other end by the consignee. Some transportation companies, however, are adopting store-door delivery—delivery to the consignee's warehouse or place of business. This is a convenience for both shipper and consignee.

Motor Freight. Trucks give door-to-door delivery on freight shipments requiring relatively short hauls—that is, hauls of a few hundred miles. Bills of lading (described below) used for truck shipments are similar to those used for rail freight.

Shipping by Water. For shipments to foreign countries by boat, the United States Government requires that a paper identifying the goods and indicating their value be filled out. Such a document is called a *manifest*. During such national emergencies as a war, water shipping, particularly ocean, is subject to special Government regulation.

Air Freight. Air freight has been used to some extent, and its use will increase rapidly. Air freight has been largely confined to plane loads, but the air lines plan to increase the scope of air freight to include the transportation of less-than-planeload lots. This service will be similar to l.c.l. rail freight shipments.

Bills of Lading. A secretary's work often includes the typing of bills of lading. The bill of lading is the contract between the shipper and the transport agency. There are two kinds—the straight bill of lading, and the order bill of lading.

Straight Bill of Lading. The straight bill of lading, the form more commonly used, is ordinarily made out in triplicate. Copies are used as follows:

1. The original is forwarded to the consignee and surrendered by him to the carrier's agent at destination, in order to identify the consignee so that he can claim the shipment.
2. The second copy is the shipping order. It is retained in the office of the carrier's agent.
3. The third copy is the memorandum copy, which is retained in the file of the shipper for record purposes.

Order Bill of Lading. The order bill of lading is commonly used to cover C.O.D. shipments, where a bank or other agency is to collect for the shipment before it is released. Goods cannot be surrendered at destination until the order bill of lading has been properly indorsed and surrendered to the carrier's agent. Three copies of an order bill of lading are made. The consignee's copy is sent by the shipper, with a sight draft, to the consignee's bank, which collects for the shipment and gives the consignee the re-

3 THIS MEMORANDUM is an acknowledgment that a Bill of Lading has been issued and is not the Original Bill of Lading, nor a copy or duplicate, covering the property named herein, and is intended solely for filing or record.

Uniform Domestic Order Bill of Lading, Adopted by Carriers in Official, Southern, Western and Illinois Classification Territories, March 15, 1922, as amended August 1, 1930.

Printed in U.S.A.

NYCS PTD-4

Shipper's No.............
Agent's No.............

THE NEW YORK CENTRAL RAILROAD COMPANY

RECEIVED, subject to the classifications and tariffs in effect on the date of the receipt by the carrier of the property described in the Original Bill of Lading, at *New York* *July 15*, 193=

from *Armstrong & Co.*

2 THIS SHIPPING ORDER must be legibly filled in, in Ink, in Indelible Pencil, or in Carbon, and retained by the Agent

Uniform Domestic Order Bill of Lading, Adopted by Carriers in Official, Southern, Western and Illinois Classification Territories, March 15, 1922, as amended August 1, 1930.

Printed in U.S.A.

NYCS PTD-4

Shipper's No.............
Agent's No.............

THE NEW YORK CENTRAL RAILROAD COMPANY

1 UNIFORM ORDER BILL OF LADING
ORIGINAL

Uniform Domestic Order Bill of Lading, Adopted by Carriers in Official, Southern, Western and Illinois Classification Territories, March 15, 1922, as amended August 1, 1930.

Printed in U.S.A.

NYCS PTD-4

Shipper's No.............
Agent's No.............

THE NEW YORK CENTRAL RAILROAD COMPANY

RECEIVED, subject to the classifications and tariffs in effect on the date of the issue of this Bill of Lading,

at *New York* *July 15*, 193=

from *Armstrong & Co.*

the property described below, in apparent good order, except as noted (contents and condition of contents of packages unknown), marked, consigned and destined as indicated below which said company (the word company being understood throughout this contract as meaning any person or corporation in possession of the property under the contract) agrees to carry to its usual place of delivery at said destination, if on its own road or its own water line, otherwise to deliver to another carrier on the route to said destination. It is mutually agreed, as to each carrier of all or any of said property over all or any portion of said route to destination, and as to each party at any time interested in all or any of said property, that every service to be performed hereunder shall be subject to all the conditions not prohibited by law, whether printed or written, herein contained, including the conditions on back hereof, which are hereby agreed to by the shipper and accepted for himself and his assigns.

The surrender of this Original ORDER Bill of Lading properly indorsed shall be required before the delivery of the property. Inspection of property covered by this bill of lading will not be permitted unless provided by law or unless permission is indorsed on this original bill of lading or given in writing by the shipper.

Consigned to ORDER of *Armstrong & Co.*

Destination *St. Paul* State of *Minn.* County of

Notify *J. C. Baker & Son* *800 North St.*

At *St. Paul* State of *Minn.* County of

Route *N. Y. C. & C. B. Z.*

Delivering Carrier Car Initial Car No.

No. Packages	DESCRIPTION OF ARTICLES, SPECIAL MARKS AND EXCEPTIONS	*WEIGHT (Subject to Correction)	CLASS OR RATE	CHECK COLUMN	
10	Sacks Coffee	1000			Subject to Section 7 of conditions, if this shipment is to be delivered to the consignee without recourse on the consignor, the consignor shall sign the following statement:
					The carrier shall not make delivery of this shipment without payment of freight and all other lawful charges.
					(Signature of Consignor)
					If charges are to be prepaid, write or stamp here, "To be Prepaid."
					Received $ to apply in prepayment of the charges on the property described hereon
					Agent or Cashier
					Per
					(The signature here acknowledges only the amount prepaid.)
					Charges Advanced $

*If the shipment moves between two ports by a carrier by water, the law requires that the bill of lading shall state whether it is "carrier's or shipper's weight."
NOTE—Where the rate is dependent on value, shippers are required to state specifically in writing the agreed or declared value of the property.
The agreed or declared value of the property is hereby specifically stated by the shipper to be not exceeding

per

Armstrong & Co. Shipper *A. B. Davis* Agent

Per Per

Permanent post-office address of shipper

AN ORDER BILL OF LADING

$210.00   New York, N. Y., July 15, 19—

at sight--- *Pay to*

the order of Armstrong & Co.-------------------------------

Two hundred ten and no/100------------------------------ *Dollars*

Value received and charge the same to account of

To   J. C. Baker & Son

No. 116   St. Paul, Minn.

J. C. Baker, Jr.

COLUMBIA BOND

A SIGHT DRAFT ACCOMPANYING ORDER BILL OF LADING

ceipted bill of lading. He surrenders this to the freight company in claiming the shipment.

Waybills. A waybill is a document prepared by the transportation company covering shipment from origin to destination. It contains data about a shipment, guides its routing and helps to effect proper delivery and to compute the proper charges for service rendered. It is a part of the accounting procedure of the transportation company, and no copy is given to the consignor or to the consignee.

EXPRESS

Speed in Shipping. When articles, goods, luggage, and other things are sent by express they are usually called for at the sender's place

AN EXPRESS RE-CEIPT

UNIFORM EXPRESS RECEIPT—NON-NEGOTIABLE

The Company will not pay over $50, in case of loss, or 50 cents per pound, actual weight, for any shipment in excess of 100 pounds, unless a greater value is declared and charges for such greater value paid.

RAILWAY EXPRESS AGENCY (INCORPORATED)

(3000)
(Printed in U.S.A.)

Issued at *New York, N. Y.*   *June 25*   19—

Received from *M M Smith*

Address *144 South St.*

No. Pieces	Article	Description	Weight
1	Cat typewriter		42

Value herein declared by Shipper to be *Forty-eight*   DOLLARS $ 48   CHARGES

Consigned to *Southern Agricultural School*

At *185 Lee St*   2.44

Greenville   *Miss*

Which the Company agrees to carry upon the terms and conditions printed on the back hereof, to which the shipper agrees, and as evidence thereof, accepts and signs this receipt.

NO. PIECES
1

M. M. Smith   *A. H. James*
Shipper   For the Company

HOUR
1.30

Courtesy Railway Express Agency

of business or home, are transported on passenger trains or airplanes, and at destination are delivered direct to the recipient.

This transportation method, now over a century old, is carried on by the Railway Express Agency, which is owned by the railroads of the United States. Trains, planes, steamships, and motor trucks are used to expedite the movement of express shipments.

Pickup and Delivery. The express company, which has 23,000 offices, calls on request, at the consignor's door, in principal cities and towns, and gives a receipt for each shipment. It then transports the shipment rapidly to the specified destination, where delivery to the address indicated is made and a receipt is taken from the consignee. Instructions regarding the packing of shipments should be obtained from the express company.

Articles That Can Be Shipped. Almost any kind of commodity, large or small, perishable or nonperishable, live or inanimate, can be sent by express, when properly packed or crated.

It is well to consult the local express agent on such matters, and to be sure that the address on a shipment is complete, legible, and accurate. Both the sender's and the receiver's name and address (including street and number) should be given in the address.

Express Rates. Costs for express transportation vary according to the distance, weight, and nature of the goods shipped. There are three classifications: merchandise, first class; articles of food and drink, second class; and printed matter, third class.

The Official Express Classification is used to determine in what rate class the shipment falls and other specifications. Rates are calculated on the basis of the Official Directory of Express Stations, giving the "block" location of the destination point and the express charge, according to actual weight in pounds. In wartime a special emergency charge and Federal tax are added.

Express shipments may be sent with charges prepaid, paid in part, or "collect," to be paid for on delivery. With a few exceptions, insurance is provided up to $50 for any shipments of 100 pounds, or not exceeding 50 cents a pound for any shipment in excess of 100 pounds. Higher insurance protection can be obtained at time of forwarding at 10 cents per $100 or fraction thereof in excess of the value above stated.

Express shipments can also be sent C.O.D., which means that the amount the shipper specified will be collected before delivery and the proceeds remitted to the sender.

Personal Services. The Railway Express Agency will perform many services. It will collect notes, obtain signatures to legal documents, deposit bank funds, purchase goods, pay taxes, and so on.

Air Express. Air express, operated on 45,000 miles of air lines, is the swiftest shipping method in the country. It is used extensively in meeting pressing situations and emergencies in business and industry; and for highly seasonal commodities. Merchants use it to replenish depleted lines and to place style goods on sale quickly.

Because of the high speed at which air express is sent, air-express rates are higher than rail express, but they have been greatly reduced in recent years. Extra cost is often offset by the resulting saving in time.

The nation's air lines, through an arrangement with the Air Express Division of the Railway Express Agency, provide for immediate, door-to-door pickup and delivery service on air-express shipments. The service is co-ordinated with rail service, so that cities not directly on airplane routes may take advantage of air-express speed through combination air-rail schedules.

PARCEL POST

"Parcel post" is the familiar term for fourth-class mail. Almost any kind of merchandise may be sent by parcel post provided it is wrapped properly in packages of the correct size and weight. It is a comparatively fast method of shipping.

Rates. The cost of shipment by parcel post depends on the weight of the parcel and the distance it is to be sent. Every post office in the United States or its possessions is located in one of the eight parcel-post zones, the zone being determined by the distance between the sending and the receiving office. The accompanying table shows the rates for packages of varying weights from the zone in which the shipper is located to any other post office in each of the eight parcel-post zones.

A Partial Table of Parcel-Post Rates

Weight in pounds	Local	1-2 Up to 150 miles	3 150 to 300 miles	4 300 to 600 miles	5 600 to 1,000 miles	6 1,000 to 1,400 miles	7 1,400 to 1,800 miles	8 Over 1,800 miles
					ZONES			
1	$0.08	$0.09	$0.10	$0.11	$0.12	$0.13	$0.15	$0.16
2	.09	.11	.12	.15	.18	.20	.24	.27
3	.09	.12	.14	.18	.23	.27	.33	.38
4	.10	.13	.16	.22	.28	.34	.42	.49
5	.10	.14	.18	.25	.34	.41	.52	.61
10	.13	.19	.28	.43	.61	.77	.98	1.17
20	.18	.30	.48	.79	1.15	1.49	1.91	2.31
30	.23	.41	.69	1.15	1.70	2.21	2.83	3.44
40	.28	.53	.90	1.51	2.25	2.94	3.76	4.57
50	.33	.64	1.10	1.87	2.79	3.66	4.69	5.71
60	.38	.75	1.31	2.24	3.34	4.38	5.61	6.84
70	.43	.87	1.51	2.60	3.88	5.10	6.54	7.97

Packages must not weigh more than 70 pounds and must not measure more than 100 inches when the length and girth are added together.

Written matter must not be included; but a letter or other message may be attached to the outside of the package, provided first-class postage appears on the envelope.

Parcel-post packages may be sealed only if they bear a statement giving postal authorities permission to open the package if necessary.

THE GREGG PUBLISHING COMPANY
270 MADISON AVENUE, NEW YORK, N. Y.

POSTMASTER: CONTENTS MERCHANDISE—THIS PACKAGE MAY BE OPENED FOR POSTAL INSPECTION IF NECESSARY. PLEASE NOTIFY US IF THIS PACKAGE IS NOT CLAIMED IN FIVE DAYS. RETURN POSTAGE GUARANTEED.

No. 32911

S. T. PRICE & COMPANY
1507 BROADWAY
NEW YORK 19, N. Y.

A PARCEL-POST LABEL TO BE USED ON SEALED PACKAGE

Special Parcel-Post Services. Payment of a *special-delivery* charge will expedite shipment to the post office of the addressee and delivery to him by special messenger. This charge is small, ranging from 17 cents on packages weighing up to 2 pounds; over 2 pounds, but not over 10 pounds, 25 cents; over 10 pounds, 35 cents.

A service known as *special handling* speeds delivery of a parcel-post package to the post office of the addressee but does not entail delivery by special messenger. The fee is 10 cents on packages weighing up to 2 pounds, 15 cents on packages weighing up to 10 pounds, and 20 cents on those weighing more than 10 pounds.

Do not request both special handling and special delivery on the same package, for special delivery includes all the benefits of special handling, plus delivery by messenger. Special delivery is of little value in small towns.

Parcels may be sent C.O.D. The postman who delivers the package collects the price of the goods shipped, plus the cost of mailing and the C.O.D. charge, if the shipper desires. The C.O.D. charge begins at 15 cents for amounts up to $2.50. On a shipment worth $200 (the maximum that can be collected by C.O.D. parcel post), the fee is 60 cents.

All the fees for these special services are, of course, in addition to postage at the fourth-class rate.

GLOSSARY OF COMMON SHIPPING TERMS

Airport. An area for airplane take-offs and landings.

B/L. Bill of lading.

Cargo. Goods, merchandise, or mail taken on board a ship or plane.

Carrier. A transportation company. *Common carrier.* A railroad, steamship line, air line, or interstate trucking line.

C.i.f. Cost, insurance, and freight.

C.O.D. Collect on delivery for value of merchandise plus shipping charges.

Collect. Transportation charges paid by consignee. (See also *C.O.D.*)

Commodity. An article of commerce; anything movable that is bought and sold.

Consignee. The one to whom goods are shipped.

Consignment. The goods shipped. *Sold on consignment.* An arrangement whereby unsold goods may be returned.

Consignor. The shipper.

Cwt. Hundredweight. *Per cwt.* Per 100 pounds.

Depot. A storage place for freight shipments.

F.o.b. Free on board. Free delivery from plant to train or other carrier.

Gross weight. Weight of package or shipment after packing. *Tare weight.* Weight of materials or container used in packing goods. *Net weight.* Weight of goods without container.

K.D. Knocked down; taken apart for convenience in shipping. (*S.U.* means "set up," the opposite of "knocked down.")

L.C.L. Less than carload lot.

L.P.L. Less than planeload lot.

Manifest. List of goods on board a steamer or plane.

N.O.I.B.N. Not otherwise indexed by name (in schedules of freight rates).

Pier. A steamship terminal.

Pits. Places in plane where cargo is stowed.

Prepaid. Transportation charges paid by shipper.

R.R. Railroad.

Ry. Railway.

Route. The course a shipment takes from one point to another.

Tariff. Schedule of rates or charges for shipping goods.

Answers to "Do You Know?"

1. Yes. Density, or the amount of space required, is considered in setting freight rates.

2. Three copies: one for the shipper, one for the consignee, and one for the carrier.

3. An order bill of lading is made when a freight shipment is sent collect; that is, when the goods as well as the shipping charges are to be paid for by the consignee on delivery.

4. Express packages are called for by a representative of the express company. Parcel-post packages must be delivered to the post office.

5. Yes. The charge (in addition to regular fourth-class postage) on a package weighing up to 2 pounds is 15 cents.

MORTGAGE

THIS MORTGAGE, made the seventh day of June, nineteen-
hundred and forty-four (1944), between David J. Lawrence and
Sarah Gray Lawrence, of Memphis, Shelby County, Tennessee,
the mortgagors, and Annie A. Freeman, of Newark, Licking
County, Ohio, the mortgagee.

WITNESSETH, that to secure the payment of an indebtedness in the sum of five thousand dollars ($5,000), lawful
money of the United States, to be paid on the first day of
June, nineteen hundred and forty-nine (1949), with interest
thereon to be computed from the seventh of June, nineteen
hundred and forty-four (1944), at the rate of six per centum
per annum, and to be paid on the first day of December, nineteen hundred and forty-four (1944), and on the first day of
June, nineteen hundred and forty-five (1945), and on the first
day of each succeeding December and June until and including
the first day of June, nineteen hundred and forty-nine (1949);
according to a certain bond of obligation bearing even date
herewith, the mortgagor hereby mortgages to the mortgagee all
that certain piece and parcel of land known as Lot Number
Twelve (12), of Riverview Park, otherwise known and described
as 1239 Lookout Terrace, in the City of Memphis, Shelby County,
Tennessee, together with the appurtenances thereto belonging
or appertaining. And the mortgagor covenants with the mortgagee as follows:

1. That the mortgagor will pay the indebtedness as
hereinbefore provided.

A TYPEWRITTEN MORTGAGE WITH STAPLED BACKING SHEET

15

THE LEGAL DEPARTMENT

DO YOU KNOW?

1. Your company has perfected a new process of manufacturing a certain product. How may the company protect the process?

2. In a letter dictated to you, a boy nineteen years old is referred to as an infant. Should you bring this matter to your chief's attention?

3. You have just made a typing error on the last printed mortgage form in your office. Should you erase it, delay the typing while you go to a stationery store for more forms, or type the entire form?

4. If an employee of your company signs a note in his own name, is the company responsible for its payment?

5. If an executive is to be away for a long time and wishes to appoint an agent to act for him in legal matters, what does he do?

THE Legal Department of a concern, headed by an attorney, takes care of all the legal matters that arise in the company's business. Some of these matters include:

Workmen's compensation.

Employer's liability for industrial accidents.

Bad debts after the Credit Department has failed in its efforts to effect collection.

Taxes.

The borrowing of large sums of money.

Buying, selling, and renting property.

Contracts for the construction of buildings.

Purchase contracts with private concerns and with the Government.

Copyrights and patents.

Giving legal advice to employees.

Defending the company in legal actions brought against it and representing the company in bringing suit.

Examining the content of material to be published, especially advertising copy, to see that all statements are legal and according to accepted business ethics.

Checking rules and regulations and all other publicity regarding contests held by the company.

Specialized Nature of Legal Work. Many of the usual secretarial procedures cannot be used by the lawyer's secretary. Almost never, for example, may she make changes in her transcripts in an effort to improve the dictator's wording. The language of the law is highly technical, and the change of a word or even of a mark of punctuation may alter the meaning. Too, most secretaries are encouraged to practice the art of erasing skillfully, but a lawyer's secretary must not erase at all in some kinds of work. An especially neat erasure in the figures in a will, for example, would be particularly objectionable if the will were contested.

Citations. A lawyer's dictation often contains citations. A citation is the caption, or title, given to a case that has been decided by a court and printed in court records.

Mortimer v. Waldeck, 135 Wis. 243 is an example of such a title. It means that Mortimer (known as the *plaintiff*) sued Waldeck (known as the *defendant*) and that the record of the case is contained in Volume 135 of the court records of Wisconsin, on page 243.

The records compiled in each state are called "state reports." There are also "sectional reports," such as the *Northwestern Reporter*.

Typing Legal Papers. Legal documents are typed on a size of paper known as "legal cap," which is longer than regular letterhead size, measuring 13 or 14 inches in length.

Printed forms for many of the more common legal papers may be purchased at stationery stores. These forms contain blank spaces in which the appropriate material is typed. Many printed forms are spaced so that the regular typewriter spacing fits, but on others it is necessary to use the variable line spacer in typing fill-ins.

Papers that are completely typewritten are usually double spaced. Legal documents are usually stapled to a backing sheet or cover.

Corrections and Changes. In a legal paper, erasures and interlineations are presumed to have been made after the execution (signing) of the legal paper unless the contrary can be proved. No erasing at all is permitted in sums of money stated in figures, and not more than one letter should be erased in the written-out form of a sum of money, such as "Four Hundred Dollars."

If an error is made in a document before it is signed, the entire page should be retyped. If an error is found after the paper has been signed, the correction must be initialed by all parties concerned. If pages must be added, they should be lettered, and signed by all the parties concerned. Two pages added after page 5, for example, would become 5a and 5b.

Paging. As legal documents are usually fastened to a backing sheet that folds over the top of the pages, the pages are numbered at the bottom. The page numbers are usually centered about half an inch above the bottom of the sheet.

DAVID J. LAWRENCE
and
SARAH GRAY LAWRENCE

To

ANNIE A. FREEMAN

M O R T G A G E

Dated: June 7, 1944

Amount: $5,000.

Principal Due   June 1, 1949

Interest Payable: Dec. 1 and
                   June 1, semiannually

. . . .

Recorded:

Left: AN INDORSEMENT

The indorsement, or identification of contents, appears on the backing sheet. Legal papers are folded so that the indorsement shows on the outside

Below: METHOD OF FOLDING A LEGAL PAPER

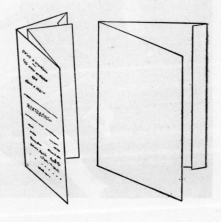

Signatures. Use the underscore for typing lines on which words are to be penwritten. Do not use a line of periods because the pen point will catch in the depressions.

A signature must not stand alone on the last page of a legal paper. At least one line of typing should appear above the signature, and several lines are preferred.

A married woman may sign her name in either of two ways; as, "Mary Smith Walker" or as "Mary Esther Walker." The first form, using her first name, her maiden name, and her husband's last name, is preferred.

Everyone, man or woman, should adopt one form of signature and use that form on all legal and financial papers.

Figures. Sums of money are usually spelled out and also shown in figures; as, "the sum of Four Hundred Fifty Dollars ($450.00)." Notice that the parenthetical amount follows the word "Dollars."

Copying Legal Papers. Type "(COPY)" at the top of the first page of every legal paper that is copied from another paper. Punctuation and spelling must be copied exactly as in the original, even if it is wrong. The word *sic*, in parentheses, should be typed after a misspelled or incorrectly used word to indicate that the error exists and is being copied intentionally. (See also page 137.)

THE LINE-A-TIME COPYHOLDER IN OPERATION

Each depression of the lever at the right moves the copy one line upward. A copyholder of this nature is a great aid to the typist in copying line for line legal forms, statistical reports, and other material of special importance

Courtesy Remington Rand, Inc.

State of New Jersey)
)SS
County of Hudson   )

On the nineteenth day of October, one thousand nine hundred and ...., before the subscriber personally appeared John Richards and George Anderson, to me personally known to be the persons described in and who executed the foregoing instrument, and they severally acknowledged to me that they executed the same.

Ernest Watson

Notary Public for Hudson County, New Jersey

AN ACKNOWLEDGMENT

Acknowledgment. An acknowledgment is the act by which a party who has executed a legal instrument declares, or acknowledges, before a notary public or other competent officer that the instrument is his act or deed. An experienced legal stenographer is expected to affix the acknowledgment without dictation. The usual wording is shown in the above illustration.

An acknowledgment should not be typed on a sheet of paper separate from the legal paper to which it applies. If there is not

State of New Jersey)
)SS
County of Hudson   )

George Anderson, being duly sworn, says that he is the owner of ten Business Brand No. 5 typewriters, with the serial numbers 2410756, 2410757, 2410758, 2410759, 2410760, 2410761, 2410762, 2410763, 2410764, 2410765.

George Anderson

Subscribed and sworn to before me this 18th day of October, 19--.

Ernest Watson
Notary Public for
Hudson County, New Jersey

AN AFFIDAVIT

enough room at the bottom of the last sheet of the legal document for the entire acknowledgment, a few lines of the legal document itself should be carried over to another sheet and the acknowledgment typed below it.

Affidavit. An affidavit is a statement attesting to the truth of the statements made in a legal paper. (See page 259.)

Signing as a Witness. Your employer may ask you to witness the signing of a legal paper. In such a case, you affix your signature as an individual, not as an employee. To protect yourself, read carefully the statement you are asked to sign (not the entire document), in order to make sure that you are signing only as a witness. If you should be asked to sign as a witness when you have not actually seen the signatures being written on the paper, you should refuse.

LEGAL PAPERS USED IN BUSINESS

Every secretary should have some familiarity with at least the rudiments of business law. It is assumed that you will take or have taken a course in the subject. A few of the most common legal papers are described here as a review.

Contract. A contract is an agreement between two or more parties. Four elements are essential:

1. The parties must be legally competent to enter into the contract.
2. There must be mutual agreement, or a "meeting of the minds."
3. There must be legal consideration (compensation).
4. The thing to be done (or not to be done) must not be contrary to law.
5. All important contracts should be reduced to writing. Certain contracts must be in writing in order to be enforceable.

A contract should be clearly and definitely worded so that no misunderstanding can arise. Important contracts are often sworn to before a notary public. Both persons and corporations may enter into contracts.

Lease. A lease is a contract by which a landlord transfers the use of buildings or land or both to a tenant for specified purposes and for a specified length of time, in return for the payment of rent. A lease protects the landlord against loss of rent in case his tenant should cease to use the property before the lease expires, and also against liability for damages caused by the tenant. It protects the tenant against illegal eviction and sudden increases in rent.

```
          This agreement made in duplicate and entered into on this,
the 19th day of October, one thousand nine hundred and ........., by
and between John Richards of the City of Jersey City, County of Hudson,
and State of New Jersey, party of the first part, and George Anderson
of the City of Elizabeth, County of Union, and State of New Jersey,
party of the second part:
          WITNESSETH: That the said party of the first part, for and
in consideration of ten Business Brand No. 5 typewriters, sold to him
this day by the said party of the second part, and by him agreed to
be delivered to the party of the first part at Jersey City, New Jersey,
free of all charges for delivery and other expenses whatsoever, on or
before the first day of November next, shall pay to the party of the
```

```
          IN WITNESS WHEREOF, the parties named herein have hereunto
set their hands and seals the day and year first above mentioned.
In the presence of
Ernest Watson

                              John Richards (L.S.)
                              George Anderson (L.S.)
```

A TYPEWRITTEN CONTRACT

In large cities, the rental of nearly all apartments, houses, offices, and other residential and business properties is covered by leases. Read a lease very carefully before signing it, so that all the restrictions are clearly understood. If any changes or exceptions are to be arranged, make sure that they are incorporated in the lease *before* you sign it. A representative lease appears among the model forms in your workbook.

Bill of Sale. A bill of sale is a form of contract that transfers ownership of personal property from one person to another. The bill of sale describes the property and guarantees that the seller owns it and has a right to sell it. See model form in your workbook.

Deed. A deed is a contract that transfers the ownership of real estate. It describes the property, specifies the parties involved in the transaction, and tells whether or not there are any liens or other encumbrances on the property.

A deed should be recorded in the office of the county clerk or recorder in the county where the real estate is located. This record becomes a notice to the public that the transfer of ownership has been made.

Mortgage. A property owner who wishes to borrow money may use his property as security for the loan. The document that is evidence of this security is a mortgage. In addition, the mortgagor (that is, the borrower) gives a bond or a note in which he agrees to be personally liable for the debt. A mortgage gives the lender, or mortgagee, the right to have the property sold if the debt is not paid. Mortgages must be in writing. When the amount due is paid, the mortgage is "satisfied," or canceled.

A *real estate mortgage* is given in return for a loan when real estate is offered as security. A *chattel mortgage* gives personal property as security.

Examples: Whittingham wished to borrow $300 to pay an important bill. He borrowed the money from Baker, giving a mortgage on a plot of ground as security. If he fails to pay, Baker can foreclose and sell the lot in an effort to realize the amount of his loan.

Leonard buys some showcases from the Boyd Electric Company, paying part of the agreed-upon price in cash and giving a mortgage on the showcases for the rest of the sum. Because this is personal or movable property, he gives a *chattel mortgage*.

Representative real estate and chattel mortgages appear among the model forms in your workbook.

Release. In a release, one person gives up a right or a claim that he holds against another person. A release is itself a contract and may be used to terminate another contract.

Example: Carver, a carpenter, contracted to build a small house for Anderson before September 1, for $3,000. Before the work was begun, Carver was offered a more profitable building job, and Anderson was obliged to move to another city. They agreed to drop the building plan, signed a release before a notary public, and thus discharged the contract without performing it.

Guaranty and Surety. A guaranty is a promise to answer for the debt, default, or obligation of another.

Example: The Mountain Area Utilities Company requires that anyone who has an electric meter installed shall either deposit $5 in advance or obtain the signature, on a contract, of another person who must be a property owner, and who thus becomes the guarantor that ensuing bills will be paid.

A surety is an agreement whereby a third party binds himself as an original promisor, together with the principal debtor, for the payment of a debt or the performance of a duty to the creditor.

Certificate of Incorporation. Three or more persons may legally unite to form a corporation, which is really an artificial being with most of the legal rights and obligations of a person. The persons who wish to form the corporation create it by signing a *certificate of incorporation*, which is filed with the secretary of state in the state under the laws of which the corporation is formed. Any corporation that is formed for business purposes, in order to make a profit, and has capital stock is a private stock corporation.

Example: Jones, Watterson, and Bentley create a private stock corporation, which they call the Electric Supply Company, Inc., by signing a certificate of incorporation setting forth, among other things, the amount and the kind of stock issued, the names and addresses of the directors, and the purposes of the corporation.

Certificate of Doing Business under an Assumed Name. If a person wishes to do business under a name that is not his own but does not wish to incorporate, he must file with the county clerk a certificate of doing business under an assumed name, showing his full name and address and the name he wishes to use for the business.

Example: Joseph V. Callahan wishes to open a small eating place, to be called "Joe's Diner." He files a certificate of doing business under an assumed name. There is no stigma attached to this, as the name of the certificate may suggest.

Capital Stock in a Corporation. In order to obtain money with which to run its business, a corporation sells membership by means of shares of stock. The holders of the stock hope to profit from their investment, through dividends declared from profits or from earned surplus.

Holders of preferred stock receive dividends at fixed rates before holders of common stock have a right to share in the earnings of the corporation. Holders of preferred stock usually cannot vote on corporation policies.

Holders of common stock have voting power, thus controlling the affairs of the corporation. In times of prosperity, holders of common stock sometimes receive larger dividends than do preferred stockholders.

Proxy. When a stockholder cannot attend a meeting in order to vote, he may authorize someone else to vote for him. This person is his proxy. The signed authorization he gives this person is also a proxy.

Know all Men by these Presents,

That, I...........GEORGE CONE, of 1038 Broadway, Bayonne, New Jersey...........

do hereby constitute and appoint-------------JOHN ROE------------,
Attorney and Agent for me in my name, place and stead, to vote as my proxy at any election of stock-

holders of the SMITH PRODUCTS CORPORATION,..

according to the number of votes I should be entitled to cast if then personally present.

In Witness Whereof, I have hereunto set my hand and seal this..................1st..................day

of..................May,..................one thousand nine hundred and forty-------------.

Sealed and delivered in the presence of

G. E. Ellison   *George Cone*

A PROXY

Power of Attorney. If a person does not wish to manage his own business affairs, he may appoint an agent to do this for him, giving the agent a document called a power of attorney. A power of attorney states definitely what an agent is authorized to do and for how long a period of time his authority is to continue. See model form in your workbook.

Summons. A summons is a legal document that requires the defendant in a legal action to appear at a specified time and place to answer the complaint brought against him by the plaintiff—that is, the person who instituted the action.

Subpoena. A subpoena is not the same as a summons. A summons opens a litigation, but a subpoena is used after litigation has begun and is used to notify witnesses that they must appear at the trial and give testimony. There are severe penalties for failure to comply with a subpoena.

Example: Michael Appey wishes to bring suit against Norman Welch. Appey, the plaintiff, has his attorney issue a *summons* informing Welch of the suit and giving him a certain time in which to reply.

Later, when a date has been set for the trial, the plaintiff's attorney issues subpoenas that demand the attendance of certain persons who can give testimony favorable to the plaintiff, Appey. At the same time, Welch's attorney subpoenas witnesses qualified to testify in favor of the case of the defendant, Welch. (*Subpoena* is a verb as well as a noun.)

Patents. The exclusive right to make, use, and sell an invention is called a patent. The official document that confers this right is called "letters patent." If, for example, your company invents a new manufacturing process or a new product, it may protect its interest and prevent unauthorized use of the invention by having it patented.

A patent, which is granted by the Federal Government and is issued by the Patent Office at Washington, D.C., protects an invention for seventeen years.

Registration of Trade-Marks and Trade Names. Company trade-marks and trade names, if they have been adopted for goods used and sold in more than one state and if they are distinctive and novel, are often registered in the United States Patent Office. Such registration insures to the company the exclusive right to its trade-marks and trade names for twenty years. This registration may be renewed at the end of that time.

Copyrights. A copyright is the exclusive right, granted by the Federal Government, to reproduce, publish, and sell a literary or artistic work. Artists' designs, musicians' scores, and the work of writers are among the things on which copyrights may be obtained. A manufacturer of food products, for example, may protect his interests in a new recipe book by copyrighting the book. A copyright protects the material for twenty-eight years from being used by someone else without permission and may be renewed for another period of that length.

Frequently Used Legal Terms

Affiant. One who makes oath to a statement.

Alias. An assumed name.

Allegation. That which is alleged or asserted.

Bailee. A person who receives the custody of goods in trust for a specific purpose other than as owner.

Chancery. A court of equity, or law based on natural principles of justice.

Chattel. Any item of movable or immovable property except real estate, or the freehold, or things that are parcel of it. *Chattels personal* may be goods, furniture, etc. *Chattels real* may be rights in land, such as leases, mortgages, etc.

Codicil. A supplement to a will.

Defendant. One who is sued.

Demurrer. A pleading by a party to an action that, assuming the truth of the matter alleged by the opposite party, sets up that it is insufficient in law to sustain his claim.

Deponent. One who makes an affidavit or testifies in writing under oath.

Dower. The interest that the law gives to a widow in the realty of her deceased husband.

Equity. A body of laws based on natural principles of justice; the value of property in excess of liens against it.

Escheat. Reversion of property to the state in default of a person who can inherit it.

Garnishee (v.). To attach salary, wages, or other income to pay a debt.

Hereditaments. Any property that can be inherited.

Infant. In common law, a person under twenty-one years of age. By statute in many states, however, a woman ceases to be an infant at eighteen years of age.

Interlocutory. Incident to a suit still pending.

Intestate. Not having made a will; also one who dies without having made a lawful will.

Litigation. An action or suit.

Plaintiff. A person who brings a suit or complaint.

Praecipe. A writ commanding a person to do something or to appear and show cause why he should not.

Probate. To prove legally and officially, as a will; also, having jurisdiction over wills.

Replevin. An action to recover the possession of chattels unlawfully taken.

Subpoena. A writ commanding attendance in court at a certain time and place.

Tort. A civil wrong independent of a contract for which a civil suit can be brought.

Voidable: Capable of being adjudged invalid or of no force.

Waiver. A voluntary relinquishment of some right.

Writ. An instrument in writing, under seal, issued by the proper authority, commanding a person to do or not to do something.

LEGAL PHRASES OF LATIN ORIGIN

A posteriori	From effect to cause.	*Habeas corpus*	A writ to produce a person in court.
A priori	From cause to effect.		
Ad valorem	According to the value.	*In re*	Concerning.
		Modus operandi	Manner of operating.
Caveat emptor	Let the buyer beware.		
		Per annum	Annually.
De facto	Actually.	*Per capita*	For each person.
De jure	By lawful title.	*Per se*	By itself.
Et al.	And others.	*Per diem*	By the day.
Ex officio	By virtue of an office.	*Prima facie*	At first view.
		Pro forma	As a matter of form.
Ex post facto	Having a retroactive application.	*Pro rata*	Proportionately.
		Pro tem	Temporarily.
		Status quo	The state in which.

ANSWERS TO "DO YOU KNOW?"

1. By applying at the United States Patent Office for a patent.

2. The young man will be legally an infant until he reaches the age of twenty-one.

3. It is never wise to erase on any legal document. A legal paper typed from beginning to end is just as binding as a printed form on which the necessary information has been typed in.

4. No. The employee alone is liable.

5. He has a power of attorney prepared.

THE RECEPTIONIST GREETS A CALLER

16

OFFICE OF THE GENERAL SALES MANAGER

DO YOU KNOW?

1. The man you work for is planning a trip that will take about a month. He will visit several cities in which he is not known. What arrangements can he make for carrying funds?

2. One morning the following letters addressed to the sales manager are received. What disposition should his secretary, who opens his mail, make of them? (a) A letter saying that goods ordered had not been received. (b) A letter from a former employee requesting a reference. (c) A catalogue from an office supply house. (d) A complaint regarding a salesman. (e) A letter from a creditor asking for an extension on a note.

3. If a caller tells you he has an appointment with your chief, the sales manager, and you have no record of the appointment on your sheet, would you admit the caller at once?

4. In making a hotel reservation for a businessman, is it sufficient to inform the hotel of the day of arrival?

5. If your chief has a conference scheduled, what preparations can you make for it?

BUSINESS may be divided into four major functions—manufacturing, finance, sales, and personnel management. The sales activities of a business are under the direction of a general sales manager. His major responsibility is to get other persons to sell the products of his company, not to sell them himself.

The accompanying chart shows that the general sales manager has charge of three major divisions—sales operation, sales develop-

A DEPARTMENTAL ORGANIZATION CHART

ment, and sales planning. The chart also shows that the head of each of these three divisions has charge of subdivisions.

Familiarize yourself with this organization chart so that you will know where the responsibility lies for the promotion and operation of specific activities within this department.

The secretary to the general sales manager of a company has considerable authority as well as heavy responsibilities. She continues, of course, basic secretarial duties—takes dictation, prepares transcripts so accurate and well arranged that they could be used as models for beginning stenographers, checks details in all her own work, and keeps track of her own duties to see that nothing is being overlooked.

In addition, she writes many letters without dictation, keeps a record of her chief's appointments and reminds him of various things he has to do, keeps records and follow-up systems for him, receives his callers and most of his phone calls, and tries to learn to read his mind so as to be able to anticipate his wishes.

A secretary must take orders, and sometimes she must also give them. She is responsible for the carrying out of the instructions that she gives to other persons, but she must be tactful and avoid a domineering attitude toward subordinate employees.

HANDLING PEOPLE

Your Attitude Toward Others. Any group of persons can work better together if they are not tormented by petty jealousies, bickering, and office politics. In your personal life, it is a simple matter to avoid persons whose company you do not enjoy; but you cannot do this easily in an office. Therefore, your relationships with others are worthy of careful and frequent thought. You will be more comfortable, and the work will go more smoothly, if personal prejudices do not enter into your business affairs.

Within your own organization you must consider how you will treat both superiors and subordinates. You need not be subservient to your superiors, and you must not treat subordinates with condescension.

Use tact to protect your chief from persons who want to know too much about his affairs. If tact fails, be unobtrusively firm. When someone is obviously trying to see your transcript of a confidential letter, for example, simply cover it as casually as possible —but cover it.

No one can tell you, before you go to work, how much you may safely tell about your chief's affairs, even to his fellow executives. Remember that you owe him your loyalty. If you doubt the advisability of answering certain questions asked by other persons, refer the questioners to the chief himself if possible. In most offices, there is a certain amount of jealousy among the executives, just as there is among the typists, file clerks, and stenographers. If you should happen to tell too much, just to show that you know what is going on, you might do your chief some harm.

As we have said, no flat rules can be laid down about how much you can tell when someone asks you a question. You will learn that as you go along.

Speaking and Writing. Your tone of voice should *always* be courteous, whether you are arranging an appointment for your chief with the chairman of the board or asking the office boy why your outgoing mail has not been picked up. Your speaking voice is easy to control—you know just how it sounds.

The tone of what you write, however, is not so easy for you to judge, although it is equally important. You might say pleasantly to a delivery man, "Put the filing cabinet here." When you write, however, your reader cannot hear your voice; he can only see your words, and words chosen without due thought for the reader may seem curt or even rude, especially in a direct command. Direct commands are better avoided.

Building Morale with Words. The wording of instructions to employees sometimes has a marked effect on employee morale. If the majority of employees in a firm are satisfied that they are being treated fairly, morale is said to be good. If there is much dissatisfaction and wrangling, morale is not good. The credit or blame for the state of employee morale usually rests with the company executives and does not concern you, as a secretary, except in so far as you can help your own chief to retain, for his company, the loyalty of the employees.

You are likely to be in closer contact with employees in the lower salary brackets than your chief can be. It is sometimes possible for a trusted, experienced secretary to hint to her chief that certain rules are causing dissatisfaction out of proportion to their importance, or that a bulletin to employees might be better received if the wording were changed a little.

Your comments, if you decide that it is advisable to make any, should all be constructive. Your purpose is to improve morale, not to tattle on other employees.

Workers who continually complain about company policies and rules are not likely to advance to positions of responsibility and higher pay, partly because they become known as troublemakers and partly because they do not contribute anything constructive to the organization. Those who are able to take the point of view of the management and understand the underlying reasons for existing policies and systems have a much better chance of advancing and thus influencing these policies and systems.

Receiving Callers. A secretary's work includes receiving callers, while a receptionist's work is devoted mainly to this important activity. The advice that follows was prepared for the guidance of the receptionist of a large business concern. Because much of it applies to the secretary, it is reprinted in full.

What a Receptionist Ought to Know

You hold the contact position. You are "the firm" to everyone who comes up to your desk. The callers may or may not see the people they ask for—but they do see you!

So what? Be human—be courteous and considerate—and, if you can, place yourself in the mental attitude of the person you are receiving.

And then, cultivate a little mental ambidexterity—the word is worth looking up—and place yourself, also, in the mental attitude of the executive the caller wants to see.

Get the name right. Get the pronunciation right, too. Ask to have the name repeated if necessary so that you will be sure to announce it correctly.

And then explain the situation to the caller. But, right here, remember you are working for the firm and not for him. If you are told to say that Mr. So-and-so is "out" when you know right where he is, remember that is his business—not yours. Don't say it with the disdainful implication that the caller is not welcome.

Or if the man asked for is away because of personal or business reasons, simply state the fact—don't give out information—for the very good reason that it is his prerogative to select those to whom his business or personal affairs should be known.

For the same reason, don't tell when an out-of-town executive expects to return—or where he is—unless he has already notified you to give his callers the information.

Make a practice of obtaining a caller's full name. There are too many J. B. Woods in this country for the executive to remember whether it is John Woods whom he would like to see or persistent Jerome Blascom Woods making a time-wasting routine call.

Find out what company the caller represents or is connected with. This is not "asking him his business." It's merely the customary thing to do and saves you that embarrassing moment when the executive makes you get it anyway.

If the executive tells you he expects certain callers but may be in conference although he would like to see them if possible, try to make them feel at ease and check into the situation frequently enough so that no more time is lost than is necessary.

You know the qualities of a good hostess. To a certain extent, you are your firm's social secretary. Try to act that way—you can always be gracious without being personal. And this doesn't mean undue familiarity either.

Know something about what your company makes or sells or does. Enough to answer the simple questions. This doesn't include any broadcasting as to how "business is." Even if the plant is working nights or is all but shut down, it is not your province to say so.

And be careful when you leave your desk for any reason. Be sure your "relief" understands just who is waiting and why. Don't leave business cards in sight where an alert eye can find out who the other fellow is.

Remember you are the "lookout" for a very earnest group of busy men. Their time is precious in both the cost and effort sense. Conserve it, by getting them the right information.

For the same reasons, make sure that when you admit the caller you give him clear directions for finding the office or desk he is supposed to go to.

Observe the same methods and precautions over the phone. You may be only a voice over the phone—but you are the voice of the firm.

And read these suggestions over again every once in a while. Not only will you be a better Receptionist but you can never tell—a Receptionist today may be Somebody Great tomorrow!

Callers Correctly Handled. Here are some examples of callers who were correctly handled.

Mr. Dickinson visits your office regularly and is always welcome. Greet him: "Good morning, Mr. Dickinson. Mr. Ward is expecting you. Will you go right in, please?"

Mr. Haliburton, whom you recognize, approaches your desk. Say to him, "Good morning, Mr. Haliburton." You have already checked over your chief's appointment sheet for the day; so you know that he is expected. Telephone to your chief: "Mr. Haliburton is here for his ten o'clock appointment. It is 9:55 now." If Mr. Ward says, "Send him in," do so.

When a stranger enters, say, "Good morning," to identify yourself as the person he should talk to about his call. He should either tell you his name and business connection or hand you his card bearing this information. Announce him thus: "Mr. Edward Riley, of Portable Machines Corporation, would like to see Mr. Ward." (*Never* say, "There's a Mr. Riley out here." This is discourteous.)

Note that it is advisable to announce a caller impersonally even when you are speaking directly to the person he wishes to see. If you say, "Mr. Ward, Mr. Sanders is here," and Mr. Ward does not wish to see the caller but does not wish to offend him either, you will place both yourself and Mr. Ward in an embarrassing position.

It is sometimes necessary to refuse admittance to a caller. You may say, "I'm sorry, Mr. Ward is just leaving the office," or "Mr. Ward is going to be busy all afternoon. May I arrange an appointment for another day?"

Legitimate callers should be announced, whether they have appointments or not. The decision about admitting them rests with the person who is being called upon.

Some callers are hard to deal with. An insistent salesman may try by various means to get past your desk; he may be very friendly, or he may attempt to deceive you by pretending to be very important. Persons having legitimate business will tell you what their business is if you insist courteously that you must know it. Those who will not tell you their names or errands should not be admitted or even announced. If you keep your temper and answer courteously at all times, neither a bank president nor a shoelace vendor will have any legitimate grounds for complaint about the way you receive callers.

Persons who are not familiar with business may refuse to identify themselves simply because they do not realize that they are expected to do so. Job seekers may try to pass you, if they do not realize that your function is to help all callers. Make this clear, and you will have no difficulty.

Some secretaries do not telephone to announce callers, but simply walk into the chief's office to make the announcement.

Callers Incorrectly Handled. Here are some examples of callers who were not correctly handled.

Alice P. liked to talk to office visitors while they were waiting. She did not like to have her conversation interrupted by other callers and often simply ignored them while she laughed and talked with those whom she knew. A severe reprimand for this was a painful but an improving experience. She is a good receptionist now.

Betty M. catalogued callers in the order of their apparent importance and treated them accordingly. She was effusive to those who looked influential and prosperous, condescending to some others, and almost rude to messengers and peddlers. She guessed wrong on one of the company's stockholders, an elderly man who did not seem very alert, and refused to allow him to see one of the executives. Now she is back at the job where she started. She feels that she has been treated badly, and she is impairing the morale of her department by constantly complaining and criticizing.

Catherine R. was so eager to seem efficient that she often failed to ask enough questions to enable her to guide the caller to the proper department. She was pleasant and courteous, but she wasted the time of too many persons in getting mixups untangled. After a more experienced girl explained her real function in the organization, Catherine became more careful.

Doris T. was afraid of strangers. If a caller refused to tell her his name and business, she was too timid to insist on obtaining the information. She permitted many persons to see the general manager instead of lesser dignitaries. She is happier back in the Filing Department, where she does not come in contact with the outside world.

HANDLING THE MAIL AND KEEPING RECORDS

Opening Mail. Some executives prefer to open their own mail. If your chief wishes you to open the mail for him and does not specify any particular system for arranging it, sort it in neat piles as follows:

1. *Rush*: Telegrams, interoffice memoranda requiring immediate attention, letters received by air mail or special delivery. Put his list of appointments for the day on the top of this pile.

2. *Personal attention*: Letters for which he will dictate replies or instructions to you, including his personal mail.

3. *No hurry*: Advertising letters, printed matter, magazines. (Do not throw away advertising letters just because they are advertising. The product or service advertised may be exactly what your chief has been trying to locate.)

4. Mail that you yourself can answer.

Get from the files the correspondence that your chief will need in handling his mail, and attach relevant correspondence or memoranda to the incoming mail to save his time. Keep pile No. 4 for yourself. Place the other three, each in its own folder, on the chief's desk.

When he is out of town, he will probably want you to acknowledge incoming letters. You will send some of these to him for his attention and hold others for his return. Do not forward printed matter, such as catalogues and books, without special instructions. The postage will be expensive, and a person who is traveling can easily collect too many burdensome stacks of papers to carry around.

Secretarial Records. In addition to the records that have already been discussed in connection with various aspects of secretarial work, most secretaries find it necessary to keep certain other records peculiar to their job. When you step into a secretarial position that is already established, you will find many routines already in effect. Probably it is wise to continue with them until you know the work thoroughly, so as to make the change in secretaries just as easy as possible for your chief. By the time he is used to you and no longer likely to compare your regime unfavorably with your predecessor's, you may have found some ways of doing your work that you think are improvements. Think them out carefully and introduce them unobtrusively.

If you are assigned as secretary to a man who has not had a secretary before, you may have to introduce entirely new routines and methods of record keeping. This is a real opportunity and calls for a thorough review of all your secretarial training so that you may get off to a good start.

From the beginning, you will need a record of the heads of departments and managers of branch offices, similar to the list on Work Sheet 1. You may be able to obtain such a list from the mail clerks, from another secretary or stenographer, or from your chief. Refer to it for official titles, initials, the correct spellings of names, and addresses. You may wish to add to the list the residence address and telephone number of each executive.

Card Index. A card index should be kept of important callers whom your chief is always willing to see. This index should be

---

```
    Sawyer, Herbert M.
        (Sales representative, Scott & Weeks, Chicago)
    Suite 1417
    599 Fifth Avenue
    New York 17, N. Y.

    Ci 6-2781
```

A CARD FROM A SECRETARY'S "WHO'S WHO" FILE

The secretary's shorthand notations give her useful detailed information that she may need in making appointments for her employer—"Personal friend; vice-president Tennis Club; usually out of office on Mondays and Thursdays" kept where you can consult it immediately—perhaps in an upper drawer of your desk, if not on top. It should show names, business connections, and phone numbers.

Appointment Records. If your chief sees a great many people, you will probably make some of his appointments for him; and he will make still others. It is important that the appointment schedule be kept where both of you can consult it conveniently. Sometimes you may make an appointment for your superior at a certain time and he, unknown to you, may make another appointment for that same time. When such a thing happens, one of the persons must be reached and his appointment changed.

Look over the appointment sheet for the day the first thing in the morning, and give your chief a copy of it at once. You may also find it worth while to check over the appointment sheet at the end of the day, recording on it briefly the outcome of the various meetings scheduled there and filing it for future reference. Your

---

DAILY APPOINTMENT SCHEDULE

DATE *Monday, January 19, 19—*

TIME	APPOINTMENT WITH	PLACE	PURPOSE OF MEETING	REMARKS
9:00	H. W. Dickens	Smith's office	Warehouse contract	Take correspondence
9:30				
10:00	Board meeting	Board Room	Monthly meeting	
10:30				
11:00				
11:30				
12:00	Mr. Wallace	Pine Room	Luncheon	Cancelled
12:30				
1:00	Frank Boyd	Here	Personal	

AN APPOINTMENT SCHEDULE KEPT BY THE SECRETARY FOR HER EMPLOYER

file of appointment sheets will constitute a kind of diary of your chief's activities.

A secretary who really knows her chief's work can help him by arranging, before an appointment is kept, to have necessary papers taken from the files, and perhaps by having extra chairs brought in if a group is to meet.

Don't Be Too Helpful. You may have read stories about super-competent secretaries who are supposed to know more about the company's business than the company's executives themselves know about it. Do not take these stories too literally. A secretary can be exasperating by taking more responsibility than the chief wishes her to have, by implying curiosity about his personal affairs, and by seeming to order him around. Find out what kind of man you are working for; then see how you can help him. There is a difference between competence and officiousness.

Taking Messages. Callers often leave messages for your chief. Such messages are sometimes written on message blanks; sometimes on a simple memorandum pad. If you take the message in shorthand, you can get it faster and more fully than if you try to scribble in longhand. Immediately, write it legibly or type it, complete with all available details, to give to your employer at the earliest possible moment.

A good memory is a useful thing, but do not depend on it for relaying messages. Write them, and always date them. A slip of paper may come to light months or years afterward. If it carries no date, it may plunge you into complete bewilderment. (See page 71 for an illustration of a message.)

Insurance Records. If your chief expects you to take care of the details connected with his personal business affairs, you will no doubt keep his insurance records up to date.

He may carry many different kinds of policies. First classify them. You might, for example, group all life, accident, health, annuity, and personal property policies together. In another group you could include policies covering his automobile, as fire, theft, windstorm, collision, bodily-injury liability, and property-damage liability. Another group could cover policies on his private residence, including such other buildings as garages, barns, boathouses, and so on, with their furnishings. These policies may cover fire, windstorm, burglary, workmen's compensation, and employer liability.

Two forms of record may be kept to summarize the details on such a list of policies. One form is an insurance policy register, which may be purchased or obtained from insurance companies. Column heads should be provided for the following details:

Date issued	Face of policy
Number of policy	Time of policy
Name of company	Premium
Property covered	Expiration date

The other record form is a card file. The above information is listed on cards, each policy having a separate card.

Agenda. An agenda is an outline of the things to be done and the business to be transacted in a corporate meeting. An agenda should be prepared carefully, for it serves as a guide to the presiding officer in the orderly conduct of a meeting and eliminates the possibility of omissions that might occur through inadvertence or reliance on memory.

The bylaws of a corporation may set forth the procedure to be followed in meetings; but, where no such provision is made, a simple outline of the subject matter to be discussed should be made. An agenda may be typed in the form most convenient for the person who is to use it. A typical agenda is shown in your workbook.

Minutes of Meetings. Taking the minutes of a business meeting requires considerable special training, and many concerns call upon professional reporters to do this work. The secretary to an officer of a company, however, may be expected to write minutes of business meetings as well as of less formal meetings, as club meetings, employees' meetings, and so on.

The form and content of minutes of business meetings vary according to the group. The minutes of a meeting of a board of directors, of stockholders, and of a committee would present special problems. Standard forms for each type of meeting and practical suggestions for reporting the meetings appear in various reference books. Two books helpful to the secretary are *The Private Secre-*

tary's Manual, by Turner, and *Standard Handbook for Secretaries,* by Hutchinson.

Resolutions. Resolutions on such matters as condolences or felicitations are often passed at meetings. Resolutions are arranged according to a definite pattern. See Work Sheet 149 for a representative resolution.

HANDLING TRAVEL DETAILS

Note: In times of national emergency like a war, travel is one of the first things to be affected. Many services that are common in normal times are curtailed or discontinued.

The Executive Travels. Getting the chief off on a business trip is interesting in itself. His absence has at least two advantages for you: you will have more responsibility, and you will have extra time (you hope) in which you may catch up with many details of your routine. (You may not get all these things done, but it's pleasant to try.)

Some men prefer to make all preparations themselves, walk out with a brief case, and remark, "I'll be back from Detroit next Thursday." Secretaries who work for them have few travel problems, but the secretary whose employer wishes to rid himself of details will have many things to do.

Preparation for a Trip. If an employer mentions that he is planning a trip, find out as soon as possible which cities he will visit and for each one prepare a folder labeled "Mr. Blank's Trip to ...., Date ...." In these folders, put all correspondence and memoranda concerning the trip.

Your employer may tell you on what days he wants to be in certain cities, leaving you to make up his train schedule; or he may expect you to plan the whole trip on the basis of timetables and the contents of your file folders.

Timetables. Don't be one of those persons who say, "I can't make head or tail out of timetables," and never really try to understand them. Timetables are fascinating. They are distributed without charge, on request, by railroads, bus lines, and air lines. They are not all alike—that is what makes them so interesting. Most of them

PART OF A RAILWAY TIMETABLE

CHICAGO, TWIN CITIES AND PACIFIC NORTHWEST—Cont.							
Westbound—*Read Down*					Eastbound—*Read Up*		
Fast Mail 27 Daily AM	Empire Builder 1 Daily AM	Miles from St. Paul	TABLE 4 Mountain Time to Troy, Mont. Pacific Time west.		Miles from Seattle	Empire Builder 2 Daily PM	Fast Mail 28 Daily AM
e 3 30	a 8 10	905	Lv Havre† ......(Ft. Assinni- .... Ar		860	11 05	e 5 35
ef 3 38	a —	909	" Pacific June..boine 7 miles s.w.) Lv		856	b—	ef 5 27
ef 3 47	a —	913	" Burnham..................... "		850	b—	ef 5 19
ef 3 54	a —	919	" Fresno...................... "		846	b—	ef 5 07
ef 4 02	a —	924	" Kremlin..................... "		841	b—	ef 4 58
ef 4 12	a —	960	" Xenia....................... "		835	b—	ef 4 47
ef 4 19	a —	934	" Gildford.................... "		831	b—	ef 4 40
ef 4 29	a —	940	" Hingham.................... "		828	b—	ef 4 29
ef 4 39	a —	946	" Rudyard.................... "		819	b—	ef 4 16
ef 4 49	a —	952	" Inverness................... "		813	b—	ef 4 06
ef 4 55	a —	966	" Joplin...................... "		809	b—	ef 3 50
ef 4 59	a —	989	" Buelow..................... "		806	b—	ef 3 54
e 5 11	f 9 32	966	" Chester (County Seat)....... "		799	f 9 37	e 3 42
ef 5 20	a —	972	" Tiber....................... "		793	b—	ef 3 33
ef 5 32	a —	979	" Lothair (Sweet Grass Hills North) "		786	b—	ef 3 22
ef 5 42	a —	986	" Galata..................... "		780	b—	ef 3 11
ef 5 52	a —	991	" Devon (First view Rocky Mountain "		765	b—	ef 3 07
e 6 06	a —	1000	" Dunkirk.................... "		765	b—	ef 2 47
e 6 30	10 35	1000	Ar Shelby† 8, 59...(County Seat) Lv		756	8 30	e 2 33
6 30	10 39		" Shy..........(County Seat) Ar		756	8 30	2 33

Courtesy Great Northern Railway

have indexes. By consulting the index, you can learn whether that railroad or bus line goes through the city you wish to reach. Many timetables also have maps for your guidance in planning the trip.

In choosing a train, it is usually necessary to consider first what time the traveler should arrive at his destination; then locate the destination on the timetable and see what train reaches there before that time; then work backward to learn the leaving time of the train.

Trains are identified by numbers; sometimes also by names, such as the "Empire Builder" on the Great Northern Railway or the various "Streamliner" trains on the Union Pacific Railroad. A railroad timetable gives the number (and sometimes the name) of each train and the time when it arrives in and departs from each station. Light-face type is used to show forenoon time; bold-face type indicates time after noon.

A system of arbitrary symbols is often used to refer to exceptions, as "Stops on signal only"; and special accommodations offered, as dining-car equipment. These symbols are puzzling to the beginner; but they must not be overlooked, or your employer may find himself and his baggage waiting on a Sunday for a train that runs on weekdays only. A handy key to these symbols is included in each timetable.

Do not forget that the United States is divided into four time zones—Eastern, Central, Mountain, and Pacific. Timetables usually indicate the station where one's watch should be set ahead or back one hour. The time in any zone is one hour earlier than that in the zone immediately east of it. Time changes continue all around the world; and at the 180th meridian, in the Pacific Ocean, a whole day is lost or gained. When it is Saturday on the eastern side of this line, which is known as the International Date Line, it is Sunday on the western side.

Daylight-saving time is used in some localities during the summer months; this fact must be taken into account when planning itineraries and making appointments. Railroads usually operate on standard time even though daylight-saving time may be in effect.

Timetables for planes or busses give about the same kind of information as railroad timetables.

Do not depend on timetables several months old, because schedules often change. After planning the trip, check with the railroad, the bus line, or the air line in question to see that the schedule is still in force.

Up-to-Date Railroad Information. In place of a collection of timetables of uncertain ages, firms whose men do much traveling use the *Official Railway Guide*, published monthly. In one section, all the railroads of the United States, Canada, and Mexico are indexed. In another section, all the stations in these three countries are indexed, with the names of the railroads serving them. Information is given about each railroad, also.

The Monitor Guide supplies essentially the same information as the *Official Railway Guide*, but for the United States only. Weekly supplements are published.

Train Travel. There are two types of passenger service in the eastern part of the United States, and three types west of Chicago and St. Louis. In both the East and the West, the railroads offer day-coach service (in which one "travels coach") and standard Pullman service, consisting of various kinds of Pullman cars. The third type of travel accommodation, offered only by western roads, is second-class, or tourist.

Day Coach. The most economical way to travel is by day coach. The seats are comfortable; and, except on short lines and branch lines, most cars are air-conditioned. Day-coach passengers may buy meals in the dining car; but they are excluded from the standard Pullman-fare portions of the train, such as the observation car at the rear.

Standard Pullman. Sleeping and day parlor cars are called Pullmans since they are operated by the Pullman Company. "Sleepers" usually have lower and upper berths, which are made up at night by porters and fold away ingeniously during the day. More luxurious sleeping cars have private compartments and "roomettes," at a higher cost. Pullman accommodations may also be purchased for daytime travel. These accommodations consist of comfortable separate seats in parlor cars.

In traveling by Pullman, the passenger pays a higher mileage charge than for coach travel and also a charge for his berth or for his chair.

Tourist. On western railroads comfortable "tourist" sleeping car accommodations are available at much lower cost than standard Pullmans and at a slight advance over coach rates. Thus, coach travel is the cheapest, standard Pullman is most luxurious and expensive, and tourist is in between.

Extra-fare Trains. In addition to these three kinds of accommodations, especially luxurious accommodations and extra-fast schedules are maintained on some extra-fare trains. Businessmen whose time is limited often patronize such fast extra-fare trains as the Twentieth Century Limited, run by the New York Central system between New York and Chicago, and the Congressional Limited, run by the Pennsylvania Railroad between New York and Washington.

Buying Tickets. Interstate commerce regulations govern railroad passenger fares between states. The fare between two points served by two different railroads is the same on both roads. For a long trip, in the course of which the traveler will ride on several railroads, it is not necessary to purchase a separate ticket for each part of the trip. The whole ticket, and the reservations for sleeping accommodations, may be bought at one time and place from whatever railroad ticket agency is convenient. For example, a passenger going from New York to Portland, Oregon, and Seattle, Washington, and returning by way of Milwaukee, Wisconsin, may travel on the New York Central and the Union Pacific and may decide to return by three different roads—the Great Northern; the Chicago,

Northwestern, and St. Paul; and the Pennsylvania. He will, however, buy his ticket in New York for the entire journey for all the roads he uses, although he will usually buy it from the road on which he will start his trip, or from a travel agent.

A round-trip ticket, on which a certain time limit is set, is usually cheaper than two one-way tickets.

Baggage. The passenger carries whatever hand luggage he will need during his trip. Other hand luggage, and trunks weighing up to 150 pounds, may be checked and carried in the baggage car. This free baggage service is a great convenience to the traveler. Many travelers do not realize that they can check hand luggage and thus avoid the trouble of carrying heavy bags.

Plane Travel. Travel by plane is faster and more expensive than by other means, but it is not very much more expensive than Pullman travel when the meals and the tips on the Pullman are taken into consideration. Meals are complimentary on airplanes, and tipping is not permitted. A fast train between New York and Chicago makes the run in about 17½ hours; a nonstop plane covers the same distance in a little over 4 hours. Transcontinental planes and the transoceanic clippers provide sleeping accommodations.

There is usually an extra charge for transportation from the city to the airport.

A train passenger is allowed to check 150 pounds of baggage without extra charge, but a plane traveler is restricted to 40 pounds. If his baggage weighs more than 40 pounds, he pays an extra charge based on the excess weight and distance.

Plane reservations may be made through air-lines offices, hotel travel booths, and travel agencies. Telegraph offices will not only take the order over the telephone but will also procure the tickets, deliver them by messenger, and collect the money for them.

Air Travel Credit Card. Businessmen who travel by air often may make arrangements with the air lines to pay for the transportation on a monthly basis. When a business firm establishes a special credit account for air travel, authorized members of the organization receive air travel credit cards. A traveler presents his card to any one of several air lines and signs a ticket form on which an airline employee records the fare for the trip that is being arranged. The air line bills his company at the end of the month.

Bus Travel. A network of bus lines covers the United States. Bus travel is slower than train travel; but the cost is often less because busses use public highways and thus do not have the immense investment in equipment, right of way, and roadbed that railroads have. Some long-distance busses are air-conditioned, and some have sleeping accommodations. In congested areas, it is wise to telephone for bus reservations in advance.

Travel by Ship. Many details must be taken care of before a traveler boards a ship for a foreign country. Arrangements should be made through a travel agency or a steamship line, because passports and visas must be obtained in addition to steamship tickets.

Travel Reservations. Pullman accommodations, either standard or tourist, may be reserved in advance. Coach reservations, in general, are made only on de luxe all-coach trains.

Reservations may be made for plane or train travel either by telephone or in person. Tickets should be claimed and paid for without delay. Watch travel conditions and keep posted on how far in advance of the day of departure tickets should be obtained. Conditions vary greatly and frequently.

In telephoning about reservations and tickets, find out exactly what the cost will be—so much for fare, so much for Pullman space, and so forth. Your chief will probably wish to list these items separately on his expense report.

Itinerary. Type an itinerary as soon as all the details of the trip have been agreed to by your chief. Include reminders, with dates and times, about everything he is to do on the trip. He will refer to this itinerary constantly.

Accurate details are important. If a train, called the "Pathfinder," leaves Chicago on the Union Pacific from the Northwestern Station at 5:05, put all that information on the itinerary, not simply, "Leave Chicago 5 o'clock train." After you have made reservations, make a notation of the car number and the number of the chair or berth. If you learn that a sleeper leaving at 11 p.m. is ready for occupancy at 9 p.m., as is often true when the train is made up in the place of departure, indicate that fact also. If a round-trip

ticket must be validated (made effective by the railroad) some-
where along the route, include that information.

You may have to retype this itinerary several times before you
have it completed with all information, reservation details, and reminders. The Mailing Department, as well as each executive who
may have occasion to write your chief while he is away, should be
given a copy of the final schedule minus the details that are of interest only to the traveler and his secretary.

Itineraries should be filed and saved for several years, because
they sometimes provide a clue to the source of needed information.
Your chief may say, "Find me the letter I wrote So-and-So just before I went to San Francisco." If the San Francisco trip took place
two or three years ago, your correspondence is now in the transfer
files, and it may be hard to find. From the itinerary you have on
file concerning his trip to San Francisco, you can find out in which
year's transfer files you should search for the desired letter.

```
                            ITINERARY
                New York--Rochester--Buffalo--Detroit
                          July 7-12, 194-

Monday, July 7

  9:50 A.M. DST -- Leave Grand Central Station on Empire State Express.

  4:41 P.M. DST -- Arrive Rochester.  Meet Mr. March at the Central Hotel.
                   Be sure to bring up question of revises

Tuesday, July 8

  7:09 A.M. DST -- Leave for Buffalo.

  8:20 A.M. DST -- Arrive Buffalo.  Reservation at Hotel Chandler.

 10:00 A.M. DST -- Appointment with Mr. Reading at his office at
                   829 Fourth Street, telephone Main 2-9042.

 12:30 P.M. DST -- Give speech at luncheon of Businessmen's Association.

  6:00 P.M. DST -- Leave from Central Terminal for Detroit on Michigan
                   Central.
```

AN ITINERARY FOR A BUSINESSMAN

Even though you may not be required to prepare itineraries, you will find it useful to keep a record of your chief's trips.

Hotel Reservations. If you are to choose a hotel for your chief, consult the *Hotel Redbook* or similar travel guides. (See page 152.) Write a letter to each hotel at which he wishes to stay (and as long ahead as possible), specifying the kind of room desired (single, double, with bath, a suite, additional sample room, and so on), the approximate price he wishes to pay, the time of his arrival, and the time he will check out. Carbon copies of these letters, with the replies, should be placed in your employer's trip folders.

When speed is essential or there is a possibility that hotel rooms may be scarce, it may be necessary to telegraph or telephone for reservations at hotels. Hotels make no charge for reserving rooms in advance. If plans must be changed, notify the hotels at once. Hotels usually confirm reservations by letter or wire. These confirmations should be obtained and given your chief upon departure so as to make doubly sure his claim upon the space reserved for him.

Carrying Money. If your chief is going to cities where he or his company is not well enough known so that his checks may be cashed easily, you should arrange for traveler's checks covering the amount he may need in addition to the cash he will carry with him.

Traveler's Checks. Traveler's checks come in standard denomi-

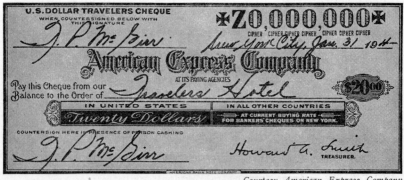

Courtesy American Express Company

A TRAVELER'S CHECK

The date and the name of the payee have been filled in, and the check has been countersigned

nations, the smallest of which is $10, and are fastened into easily carried wallet-sized books. For $100 worth, the purchaser pays $100.75. Your chief will have to obtain these himself, because he must sign each check in the presence of the person who sells them to him. At the time he cashes a traveler's check, he signs his name again. The duplication of his signature identifies him and enables him to cash these checks in places where he is not known.

Credit Cards. Large hotels often issue credit cards to travelers who patronize the hotel often. These cards permit the holders to cash checks and to pay their hotel bills on a monthly basis.

Expense Reports. If a business trip is to be short, a businessman sometimes draws from his company's cashier a lump sum of money for his expenses. For longer trips, he often makes arrangements to have additional remittances delivered en route. In some instances, he may spend his own money and then collect when he returns.

In any case, he is expected to account for all his company expenditures, usually once a week. A man's secretary often prepares the expense account from notes that he made. A typical expense report blank is shown on Work Sheet 140.

Forwarding Mail. One of the purposes of keeping your chief's itinerary is to enable you to forward his important mail as directed by him. You must plan ahead in doing this, just as the mail clerks do in using salesmen's route lists. (See Section 2.)

Personal mail is usually forwarded unopened.

Although first-class mail may be forwarded simply by writing the new address on the envelope, without using more postage, a much safer way of sending mail to a man who is making short stays in several cities is to put as much of each day's mail in one large envelope as the envelope will hold and affix the full amount of postage required by weight. If these enclosing envelopes are numbered in sequence, the traveler will know if he misses one.

Important correspondence that is opened should be copied and the original kept. With your copy or any other mail that you may read before forwarding, send additional data and notes if your judgment tells you they may be needed.

Reporting to the Chief. When your superior is away for several days, you will find it necessary to report to him on how things are going at the office, even though you may not have any questions you want answered for your own guidance.

A confidential report on daily happenings, from a secretary of long experience to an employer who trusts her judgment, might go as follows:

All of us here hope that you are enjoying your western trip in spite of your heavy schedule of appointments. Nothing very important is happening here, but I am forwarding some mail with this. Memoranda are attached to a few of the letters.

Dr. Marston inquired for you yesterday. He left no message. I did not tell him the exact date of your return.

Mr. Lampsoner telephoned to remind you that you want to discuss a renewal of the insurance coverage on the Redman Village warehouse. He is leaving for Washington soon. He will call on you the day you return.

Mill 2 had its first accident in two months this morning when the guard on a stamping machine broke. The operator was only slightly injured. Mr. Pulham is designing a new guard.

Rough proofs of the new catalogue pages arrived this morning. They are being proofread three times. Mr. Butler's page layouts are very attractive.

I deposited your salary check. Duplicate deposit slip is enclosed.

I took the liberty of contributing a dollar for you to the Flower Fund.

I am keeping Monday morning free of appointments so that you may dictate. You have a City Club luncheon at noon, and I am enclosing a notice of a meeting of the Charities Board at eight in the evening.

Such a report from a secretary less well acquainted with her chief's affairs would, of course, be more formally worded, but it should be equally informative.

ANSWERS TO "DO YOU KNOW?"

1. Procure traveler's checks, which may be cashed anywhere.

2. (a) Send the letter to the Shipping Department. (b) Refer this to the Personnel Department. (c) Send this to the Purchasing Department. (d) Hold for the sales manager's attention. (e) Refer to the Credit Department.

3. No. First learn from your chief whether he really expects him. The caller may be using a trick to gain admittance.

4. No. Give the expected hour of arrival, and, if possible, the duration of his stay.

5. Obtain from the files any material that may be required, see that there are chairs for the expected number of persons; see that there is a sufficient supply of memo pads, pencils, and other equipment convenient for the use of the conferees.

LETTER-WRITING SUGGESTIONS

Continued from page 197

Sales Letters. A sales letter is a specialized kind of persuasive letter. Here is a typical, but very simple, sales problem with the steps leading up to the writing of a persuasive letter.

You are selling electrical appliances in your home town during Christmas vacation. You are paid on a commission basis. Your sales manager is Alfred P. Tuttle, manager of the local power company. He gives you this information:

Mrs. Lindsay Harrison just telephoned. She thinks her sister, Mrs. William Rudyard, might be a prospect for an electric washing machine. Mrs. Rudyard lives on a farm and has just had electricity installed. She has an old Torrent gasoline-motor washer; it was a good machine in its day, but the manufacturer has gone out of business. Better write and ask whether she'd like a demonstration of our machine.

Mrs. Rudyard is "a cold prospect"—that is, she has not expressed interest in your product. In order to prepare your sales approach, you naturally find out all you can about Mrs. Rudyard's circumstances. There are seven persons in the Rudyard household, you learn: Mr. and Mrs. Rudyard, farmers; their three sons; a hired man; and Mr. Rudyard's aged father, whose health is poor.

On the basis of this information, you reason as follows: Mrs. Rudyard needs a new machine, because if her old one breaks down she cannot replace parts. She needs a good machine, because she washes for six men, and their work clothing is hard to wash. Being a farmer's wife, she works hard and should have efficient tools.

Since Mrs. Rudyard has just had the house wired, her interest in electrical appliances is probably keener than if she had been accustomed to the convenience of electric service.

The fact that her own sister made the suggestion will help you break the ice.

Although your goal is to sell a washing machine, you can reach it only by indirection. Your sales letter will not actually clinch the sale. The aim of your letter is to get Mrs. Rudyard to say, "Please bring out a washing machine for a demonstration. I want to see how it works."

You cannot come right out and make a comparison between the two machines. Never run down a competitor's product. You can always say, "Yes, that's a good feature, but did you notice how handy it is on the new machine?"

Your problem, even after you have a demonstration machine delivered to Mrs. Rudyard's home, is not so much to sell the machine as to sell what the machine will do for Mrs. Rudyard. A purchaser is interested in any article chiefly in relation to his own interests: he buys because he wants to use the purchase or show it off or make a profit on it. He is interested in what the article will do *for him*. A hungry man would rather have a 15-cent ham sandwich right now than ownership of a restaurant a thousand miles away.

Do you see now what the "you approach" is? We have considered it throughout this study of the washing-machine problem. It is simply the constant consideration of the interests of the purchaser. Mrs. Rudyard will buy a washing machine if she is convinced that she wants it; she will not buy it simply because you need the commission.

If she is interested in buying a new machine, some of these facts will appeal to her:

> The new machine is efficient, washes fast, and will save her time.
> The electric washer has a service guarantee; and if, after several years, a part should wear out, it can be replaced.
> The machine operates quietly, an advantage if Grandpa Rudyard is not well.
> The new washer is compact and designed to fit into a small space.
> It rolls easily; a woman can move it alone on washday.

Much of the strength of a sales letter is in the "clincher" at the end: the urge to action that makes the reader decide to do what the writer asks. Here is an effective "clincher" for the washing-machine letter:

Just give it a try; you don't have to buy. I shall be happy to come out to give you a free demonstration. Let me know when your next wash day will be, and I will bring out one of our machines and help you with your washing. There will be absolutely no obligation on your part. Here is a card, addressed to me. Just check the day and the time when you'd like to start washing, and I'll bring the machine out to help you.

Among words to be avoided in writing sales letters are *modern* and *quality*, two words that have been worn out. They do not carry much meaning any more, because they have been used too much.

This sales problem was chosen because the factors involved are familiar to you. A sales problem in a large business organization involves about the same steps of reasoning. For example, here are the same steps in a different setting.

1. A salesman of heavy machinery learns that a manufacturer is considering the replacement of some equipment. This is the salesman's "lead," just as Mrs. Rudyard's sister's suggestion provided a lead in the washing-machine deal.

2. He finds out all he can about the potential purchaser's needs and present equipment, just as you found out the number of persons in the Rudyard household and what kind of washing machine was being used.

3. He prepares a sales presentation that will show just what the new equipment will do for the prospective buyer. He speaks in terms of results, not of "high-quality machinery" or other vague terms. (This is the "you" attitude again.)

4. He is prepared to prove the excellence of his product—not by giving a free demonstration, but by presenting evidence provided by satisfied users. If the machinery has to be especially designed, he will call on experts in his organization to solve the particular problems that come up.

The product is different, the vocabulary is different, but the procedure leading to persuasion remains the same as in the simpler problem of selling a washing machine.

JOB AHEAD!
The secretary receives her first salary check

17

YOUR JOB-FINDING CAMPAIGN

You have now completed your fundamental training as a secretary. Your next step is to plan your job-finding campaign. Plan this campaign as carefully and as thoroughly as a salesman would plan his campaign to sell his biggest order of his firm's most valuable merchandise to his most difficult prospect. You are trying to find someone to buy your knowledge, your skill, your personality, your time, your loyalty. Just any kind of purchaser will not do.

You want your prospects to come from a carefully selected group of business firms that not only can use your services but that can, in return, give you an opportunity to advance and to carry out your plan for your business career. Your job-finding campaign must be a selling campaign.

PLANNING YOUR CAMPAIGN

Your Personal Work Sheet. A successful salesman must first know his merchandise thoroughly. You must, therefore, know yourself thoroughly. You must have at your finger tips a detailed and accurate knowledge of what you have to offer your prospective employer in return for a place on his pay roll. After you have obtained this information and have combined and arranged it in the most logical order, you must study various ways of presenting your qualifications. Select the most convincing way and practice it both before the mirror and before your instructor and other critics until you are sure you will do your very best when you meet your prospects face to face.

Remember always that you are not asking a favor or begging for a job. Employers are as eager to employ qualified personnel as you are to be employed.

The personal work sheet on page 297 will guide you in preparing your own.

The following headings will be useful in helping you to organize the material for your personal work sheet:

Vital Statistics	Special Interests
Education	References
Experience	

Your Educational Experience. List all your education beyond grammar school. Of course your grammar school education also should be included if the application form requests the information. Indicate the year you were graduated from high school, the name and location of the school, and the kind of diploma you received if the school gives more than one kind.

Write the name of the college you are attending, its location, the length of your course, with the degree or certificate you received or are going to receive, if any. State your major subject or special interest.

Mention additional educational preparation, such as extension or evening courses. The fact that you have taken such courses indicates that you are seriously interested in increasing your learning and your value to an employer.

Mention the number of times you were on the honor roll and any scholarships, honors, prizes, and certificates of excellence that you received, especially in business subjects. Mention the subjects in which you did especially good work.

In supplying all this information, avoid the negative approach; such as, "My typing was especially fast; but, to be frank, I never did very well in bookkeeping." That's not the way to sell yourself.

List your school experiences and capitalize on them. Mention offices you have held. Election to any office indicates that your personality and dependability impress your schoolmates.

Mention organizations to which you belonged in school. If the name of the organization does not indicate the nature of the group, supply the information. The Four C Club, for example, might be anything; so identify it.

If you were on the debate squad, you may have talent for selling, either in person or in the advertising field. If you never missed a rehearsal for a school play in which you took part, say so. Facts like these make you stand out in a crowd, and you will want to

DATA SHEET OF ELSIE SMITH

PERSONAL

Name: Elsie Smith
Address: 155 Franklin Avenue
         Yonkers, New York
Telephone No.: Yonkers 144-M
Age: 21
Religious Affiliation: Protestant
Type of Position Desired: Statistical typist, Research assistant,
                          Stenographer

My special interest is mathematics. In high school I studied
all the courses that were offered in this field, and in college I
majored in mathematics as well as in commerce. I believe I am
exceptionally well qualified to do statistical typing and to assist
in compiling research reports.

EDUCATION

High School: Yonkers High School, 1936-1940
             College Entrance Diploma
             Mathematics - 4 years

College: New York State Teachers College, 1940-1944
         A.B. Degree
         Major - Commerce and Mathematics
             Shorthand, Typewriting, Business Correspondence,
             Organization and Management of Business, Business
             Law, Business Arithmetic, Economics, Finance,
             Statistics, Calculus, Analytical and Synthetic
             Geometry, Differential Equations

Business School: Parkman Commercial School, Sept., 1944-Dec., 1944
                 Intensive Secretarial Diploma
                     Typewriting - speed of 50 words a minute
                     Shorthand - speed of 120 words a minute
                     Transcription - speed of 25 words a minute
                     Business Correspondence, Filing,
                     Office Machines (Burroughs Calculator,
                     Comptometer, Monroe, Marchant)

EXPERIENCE

General office work (filing, typing, transcribing, dictation,
mimeographing) in the Boy Scout Council Office. Feb., 1944-May,
1944 (three afternoons a week and Saturdays)--experience only

Manuscript typing, Oct., 1943-Dec., 1943--10 cents a page

Treasurer of local chapter of Kappa Delta Sorority, 1938-1939

MISCELLANEOUS

High School: Member of the Alpha Society, honor society for
             scholastic achievement
             Service Award for participation in extracurricular activities

College: Class representative to Women's Athletic Council - one year
         Cocaptain of swimming team - one year
         Member of Kappa Delta Sorority, a social sorority - officer for
         three years

REFERENCES

Mr. Xxxx X. Xxxx, Scout Executive   Miss Xxxx X. Xxxxx, Instructor
Boy Scout Office   Parkman Commercial School
Albany, New York   New York, New York

A PERSONAL DATA SHEET

stand out from the crowd of job seekers. This suggestion applies also to athletics and to most other extracurricular activities.

If you played in the orchestra, indicate that fact. (You may not mention all these facts in your applications; but if you don't write them beforehand, you may forget something important.) If you taught or are teaching a Sunday School class or are engaged in other church work or in civic activities, enter the information.

From all this, you, as well as your future employer, will learn something about your personal characteristics.

Job Experience. If you have ever worked, whether for wages or not, you have had job experience; and the fact should be mentioned. Even if you did nothing more to earn money than to mow lawns or take care of the neighbors' children, this is experience of a kind. Do not apologize for it. The fact that you worked indicates that you were alert to grasp opportunities.

Remember, you are selling something—your own services. Telling in what way your services have been valuable to other employers is simply a way of pushing your sale.

Now, what about the jobs for which you were not paid? List them, too. Such jobs are of two kinds: those supervised by the school, and those that consist entirely of volunteer work. School-supervised work is often called "co-operative secretarial training." Sometimes a small sum is paid for the work done, but often the student works without remuneration in order to gain experience.

The office work you have done voluntarily for church, civic clubs, and welfare organizations is well worth mentioning. The prospective employer will notice that you were an alert citizen who gave up time to help a worthy cause.

In describing volunteer work, enumerate as many details as you can—typing; filing; alphabetizing; addressing envelopes; dictation from John Smith, president of the Civic Club; and so on. If you did a mixture of small, separate jobs and do not know how to describe them, say "general clerical work."

References. If you have had experience, the names of your previous employers are more important than any other reference you can give. If you have had no experience, you can give the names of teachers who know of your work. Be sure to find out the full, correct name and use the correct prefix: *Mr.*, *Miss*, or *Mrs.* Find out and state the address at which the teacher may be reached. This information is especially important during the summer vacation months.

Obtain this information before you have to fill out any application blanks, and carry it with you.

Sometimes you will be asked to give character references—names of persons who know you personally—friends of your family; your clergyman; the family doctor. Give the full and correct name, the business position, the address, and the telephone number if possible in each case.

Letters from friends who are not accustomed to writing letters will not help you very much. An unbusinesslike letter is not likely to recommend you very highly to a prospective business employer.

On the list of references that you will carry with you, be sure to have many more names than you will need to use on any one application, and be sure they are all spelled right! If possible, give as character references the names of persons who are in businesses related to that in which you are seeking employment.

Be sure to obtain permission from a person before giving his name as a reference. When you learn that someone has recommended you for a position, express your gratitude in person or in a courteous note of thanks.

Have You Ever Been Discharged? Many application forms ask whether you have ever been discharged from a job. If you have, this question may be embarrassing.

If you were discharged for something really serious, you might ask a businessman of your acquaintance how you should answer this question—and make sure you have completely cured the fault that resulted in that unfortunate discharge! If you have to fill out an application form that asks for all your previous experience in detail, the prospective employer will probably write to your previous employers; so do not try to conceal your shortcomings. But even an employer who has discharged you will usually write a fairly favorable answer to such an inquiry, although he may qualify it by saying you were not entirely suited to the particular work you were doing for him.

Application Blanks. You will probably be required to fill out an application blank before you are granted an interview for a position. You must, therefore, have some experience in filling out typical blanks beforehand. Your personal work sheet will contain all the necessary information to enable you to fill out the blank accurately and quickly. Legibility is essential. Keep in mind, then, when asked to fill out an application blank, that you will be graded on three things—each of which is important—speed, accuracy, and legibility. Assignments to help you acquire facility in filling out application blanks appear in your workbook.

Have You an Employable Personality? After you have prepared your personal work sheet and become familiar with application blanks, you must check up on each quality that makes up an employable personality. These qualities, as you know, are:

Dependability	Mental alertness
Cultural refinement	Thoroughness
Leadership	Personal grooming and appearance
Industriousness	Ability to get along with others

At the beginning of your course and at various stages of your training you have rated yourself, and your instructors have rated you, on a personality rating scale containing these eight qualities. Various personality rating scales are in use. The one illustrated in your workbook is excellent. As you have already used it in this course, no further explanation is necessary. You will be given the opportunity for a final checkup before the course is completed. Be as severe a critic of yourself as it is humanly possible to be. It is better to discover all your weaknesses before an employer finds it necessary to call them forcibly to your attention.

GETTING YOUR JOB

Start Early. Even before your formal business training is completed, begin to watch for job leads. Cultivate a "nose for news," so that, when you are ready to look for your job, you will know how to find it. Ask employed friends what business firms there are in your or in neighboring communities, what kinds of office work they offer, and the names of department heads.

A Personality Profile Check List

Hat smart—rakish but not garish.

Make-up conservative —daytime, not evening.

Eyebrows natural or following a natural line.

Natural eyelashes; mascara and eye shadow taboo when job seeking.

Eyes clear; gaze straight-forward.

Rouge well applied; a harmonizing powder base.

Conservative lipstick deftly applied to match make-up and personality.

Garish and expensive jewelry to be avoided.

Underwear straps not showing.

Business dress without frills.

Tailored suits in season always in good taste.

Hands well cared for and well manicured.

Nails not too long.

Polish not too bright. (Red disliked by many.)

Stockings and garters to be worn.

Clothing to be adjusted if legs are crossed.

Shoes conservative.

Extremely high heels undesirable. (Accident hazards.)

Hair properly coiffed.

Scalp and hair clean.

Be prepared to remove hat, as in an office.

Ears clean.

Teeth carefully attended to.

Mouth free from odors.

Gum chewing to be avoided.

Neck clean (especial care if wearing a fur collar).

Elaborate fur neckpiece a nuisance.

Conservative dress neckline.

No body odor.

Daily bath, preferably a warm tub at night and a shower in morning.

Dark cloth or simple fur coat.

Dress properly closed.

Slip not showing.

Properly fitting abdominal and bust foundation garments.

Blouse and skirt meeting.

Blouse tailored and clean.

Perfume, if any, appropriate.

No runs in stockings or holes in heels.

Heels not run down.

From Seven Keys to Getting and Holding a Job

There are several sources for job leads:

1. *Friends in Business*. Do not hesitate to ask friends whether they know of openings.

2. *Employment Agencies*. Your own school may have a placement bureau. Commercial employment agencies will make a charge for finding you a job. No bureau or agency can find you a tailor-made job and put you into it; but they can give you suggestions about places to apply. The United States Employment Service (USES) is a free employment service maintained by the United States Government, with offices in all cities and most towns.

3. *Help-Wanted Advertisements*. There are two kinds of help-wanted ads: identified and blind. Identified ads give the name of the advertiser; blind ads give a box number to which the applicant must write a letter of application. The advertiser who uses blind ads can avoid an influx of eager applicants and can read their applications at his leisure.

If any special requirements are stated in an ad, your application letter and your interview should be pointed toward those requirements. The intelligent applicant will not waste her time by applying for a specialized job to which her talents are obviously not fitted. Ads are paid for by the word, and therefore the advertiser means just what he says. If the advertiser gives some hint as to the qualities he wants, and the applicant has them, the applicant has a good selling point and should use it. For example, if a rapid typist is answering an ad for a rapid typist, she should say how fast she can write and what proofs she has of her speed.

4. *Employment-Wanted Advertisements*. You, too, can use advertising in your job hunt; but unless you have something unusual to offer, such advertising may not be effective. All that such an ad is likely to bring you is an invitation to come in and be interviewed. That is your goal in any job-getting campaign.

5. *Cold Prospects*. Always ask whether a company in which you are interested has a central Personnel Department, and try to obtain the correct name of the manager. Consult your city directory, if there is one, or ask for the information by telephone. Names of department heads are usually no secret. Ask for this information in a pleasant, businesslike way, without embarrassment. It is no disgrace to be looking for a job.

You might approach a large concern in this way. When someone answers the telephone, say: "I'd like some information about employment possibilities with your company. Do you have a personnel department?"

If the answer is "Yes," ask: "Will you give me the name of the personnel director, please? I'll take it down. . . . I'll read it back—is this spelling correct? . . . Thank you *very* much."

If there is no personnel director, ask: "Whom would you recommend that I see about employment as a stenographer? . . . Perhaps you could give me the names of several department heads. . . . Thank you so much—that's really a big help."

In applying to a small office, make your initial approach by telephone or by letter, depending on which method will enable you to make the best impression. Remember that your chief and only purpose at this stage is to obtain an appointment for an interview. It is not advisable to wander into an office unexpectedly without an appointment to ask for a job. Even if the person in charge of employment is not especially busy, it is subtly flattering to him if you assume that he is and ask him in advance for an appointment.

6. *Civil Service.* Information regarding United States Civil Service positions may be obtained from your local post office. Civil service examinations are also required for employment in many state and city governments. Information regarding such positions may be obtained from the state capitals and city halls involved.

THE APPLICATION LETTER

When to Write an Application Letter. Sometimes the only way you can arrange for an employment interview is through a persuasive application letter. Some employers require application letters even from persons whom they have every intention of interviewing. Therefore, even though you may live in a city where there are many employment opportunities and where you can easily call at business offices, you must know how to write an effective sales letter about the skills, abilities, and personal traits you have to offer.

Letters That Did Not Win an Interview. The following letters are worthy of study. Letter 1, on page 304, is an actual application. It was written on a penny postal card, addressed to a business firm. There are at least five reasons why its writer has no chance of obtaining a job with the company to which he wrote. List as many of them as you can, after careful study.

Now read Letter 2. It is not an actual letter, but it is typical of dozens that every employing executive receives.

Letter 1   *Letter 2*

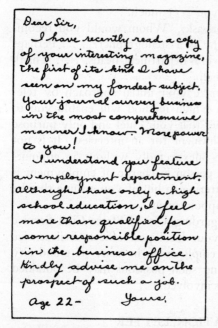

Dear Sir,

I have recently read a copy of your interesting magazine, the first of its kind I have seen on my fondest subject. Your journal survey business in the most comprehensive manner I know. More power to you!

I understand you feature an employment department. Although I have only a high school education, I feel more than qualified for some responsible position in the business office. Kindly advise me on the prospect of such a job.

Age 22—   Yours,

Gentlemen: Please consider my application for any office position you may have open in the near future. I am eighteen years old, a graduate of East High School, and live at home. I will do any kind of work. I will be glad to call at your office at your convenience. Please put my application on file.

See how many things you can find wrong with both letters and then check with the following:

Some Faults of Letter No. 1:

1. It is bad taste to write an application on a postal card.
2. The message is addressed to the firm, but the salutation is "Dear Sir."
3. The flattery in the first paragraph sounds insincere.
4. There is an error in grammar.
5. The applicant defeats his own purpose by using the word "only" in mentioning his education.
6. He sounds conceited. Why should he feel "more than qualified for some responsible position"?
7. He does not give a single reason why he should be hired; he does not mention any training, experience, or ability.
8. "Kindly advise me" is peremptory and out of place. It should be avoided in any letter.

Some Faults of Letter No. 2:

1. "Any office position" includes many for which the applicant doubtless has no training. The writer means "any position for which my training qualifies me."
2. "Put my application on file" is not what the applicant means at all. He wishes

to be called right in for an interview, and he should say so tactfully. With applications, to file is often to forget.

3. The writer fails to mention his training or any other special qualification. He sounds willing, but that is not enough.

4. There is no request for action in this letter—that is, the applicant does not ask the employer to arrange an interview.

5. The letter is colorless, uninformative, and without interest or personality.

Employers Wish to Know. Here are the facts that an employer wishes to know about a candidate for a secretarial position:

1. What is your stenographic skill? (It is not necessary to give the number of words a minute unless this information is specifically requested, but do state whether your speed is average or better.)

2. What machines can you operate? (Whether your prospective employer has all the machines you list is not important.)

3. Have you studied bookkeeping, and for how long? (If you have not studied it, do not mention it at all.)

4. What miscellaneous business training, study, and practice have you had? List all the business courses you have taken.

5. What business experience have you had? Mention all of it, no matter how meager it is. If you have never had any, mention, instead, any ways in which you have ever earned money. Earning and sensibly spending money involve business transactions.

6. How old are you?

7. Do you learn new things easily? Employers prefer adaptable people.

8. Do you get along well with other people?

What Not to Say. The beginning of your letter is important. Many young applicants begin, "Do you want a capable secretary?" Obviously, if a man wants any secretary at all, he wants a capable one. Avoid so obvious an opening.

"Here is Opportunity knocking at your door!" others announce. This opening sounds condescending and egotistical.

Virtually all the old adages—"a stitch in time," "spilt milk," "the rolling stone," and the rest of them—have been overworked in letters. Do not use an old adage to begin your letter unless you can find an unusual one, very much to the point.

Some applicants (and many writers of sales letters) begin with a little anecdote. This method is suitable only if the story has some connection with the rest of the letter. A good, brief, pointed little story that you can tie up with your application and with yourself will attract the employer's attention to your letter.

"Please consider my application" has nothing seriously wrong with it as an opener except that too many applicants use it.

Sometimes the best way to begin a letter is to omit the beginning and plunge into what you assumed was to be the middle of the letter.

Do not let your letter make you sound pathetic. You are not a humble petitioner; you are a qualified applicant for a respectable job. Avoid such statements as "I will take any kind of job if you will just give me a chance." An employer does not wish to feel that he is taking a chance in hiring you. He prefers to choose from application letters those that convince him he is employing some-one really qualified.

Do not underestimate your own skill and experience. Avoid this kind of negative suggestion: "I have had no experience except in school." The same thing may be said effectively thus: "In addition to classroom training, I have had actual experience in school, work-ing for various teachers."

Another kind of negative suggestion to be avoided is: "If you are interested, I can call to see you."

Never, never use words incorrectly. More than one employer has frowned and discarded a letter in which the applicant inno-cently but incorrectly wrote, "I shall be glad to interview you at your convenience." The employer, remember, does the inter-viewing.

Write and then rewrite. Your application letter is important to you; it deserves all your skill and much of your time. The employer will judge you by its appearance and its content.

Your letter may be a sales letter, pure and simple, with your per-sonal data very neatly typed on an attached sheet, or you may wish to weave some of the personal details right into the letter.

Postal Card Enclosed. Your chances of receiving a reply to your application letter may be improved if you enclose a postal card (stamped), addressed to yourself, on which you have typed a form like that shown on page 307, to be filled in by the prospective employer:

Please call at_____a.m. on_____
p.m.

for an interview. Ask for Mr._____

Firm_____

Address_____

Remember: You are not asking for a job. You are asking for an interview.

THE INTERVIEW

The interview is your big opportunity; it is toward the interview that you have been working all this time. Not one person in a hundred is employed without an interview, no matter how satisfactory an application he may write.

If you happen to apply to a man who is not experienced in interviewing, he will be almost as uncomfortable as you yourself. If he is experienced in interviewing applicants, remember that he has seen many who made a much worse impression than you will.

You have an obligation: to help him along if possible. If he has a job opening, he wants to fill it. He cannot decide that you are the right person for it unless you tell him what he must know. Therefore, answer his questions rather fully, avoiding simple "Yes" and "No" answers. This does not mean, of course, that you should talk constantly.

You are temporarily in partnership with the interviewer in trying to help him decide whether you are the person for the job he wishes to fill. You must not expect him to pry information from you; he will give you leads, and you can tell him what he wishes to know.

Approach the interview with a businesslike attitude. It is not at all likely that the employer will engage a person and then look around for a job that fits him. If a job is open, a person who has certain required qualifications will be employed to fill it.

Job Hunting in Feast and Famine. When jobs are scarce, prepare for disappointments, but never stop trying. Make job hunting your business, and work all day at it, not simply a few hours when you happen to feel like it.

When work is plentiful and employers are bidding for office workers, you may be able to choose your own job. Do this intelligently, with an eye on the stability of the job in the future. Base your decision on several factors, in addition to the size of the salary. Sometimes it pays to take a job that offers interesting work and congenial surroundings in preference to one with higher salary but less peace of mind.

When jobs are plentiful, superior ability sometimes enables one to obtain a superior job. When work is scarce, superior ability sometimes means the difference between a very ordinary job and none at all. In times of depression, very capable people often work at nondescript jobs for very little money. Those who do their work with dignity and without giving the impression, "I'm too good for this work; I've seen better days," are usually happier and more highly valued. Nobody likes condescension.

As you go up the ladder in business to jobs that require more ability and give you more responsibility and a higher salary, you will become a specialist and will, as a consequence, find fewer job openings that call for your particular talents. For example, there may be a hundred stenographers in an office but only four or five secretarial positions. While a specialist finds fewer job opportunities than a jack-of-all-trades, she also has less competition in her specialty, and she is not bound to remain within it. In an emergency, she can always go back to compete with the jacks-of-all-trades.

GOOD LUCK TO YOU!

Assume, now, that your job-finding campaign has been successful and that you have been employed. A wonderful opportunity is yours. You and you alone will determine whether you will progress steadily forward and upward in your career. Good luck to you!

INDEX